INTERVENTION RESOURCE GUIDE

INTERVENTION RESOURCE GUIDE

50 Performance Improvement Tools

Danny G. Langdon
Kathleen S. Whiteside
Monica M. McKenna
Editors

San Francisco

Copyright © 1999 by Jossey-Bass/Pfeiffer

ISBN: 0-7879-4401-7

Library of Congress Cataloging-in-Publication Data

Intervention resource guide : 50 performance technology tools / Danny
    G. Langdon, Kathleen S. Whiteside, Monica M. McKenna, editors.
        p.   cm.
    ISBN 0–7879–4401-7
    1. Performance technology   2. Performance standards.
    3. Employees—Training of.   I. Langdon, Danny G.   II. Whiteside,
    Kathleen S.   III. McKenna, Monica M.
    HF5549.5.P37I57   1999
    658.3'045—dc21   98-39590

Printed in the United States of America

Published by
Jossey-Bass
Pfeiffer

350 Sansome Street, 5th Floor
San Francisco, California 94104-1342
(415) 433-1740; Fax (415) 433-0499
(800) 274-4434; Fax (800) 569-0443

Visit our website at: www.pfeiffer.com

Acquiring Editor: Matthew Holt
Director of Development: Kathleen Dolan Davies
Developmental Editor: Susan Rachmeler
Copyeditor: Carol Nolde
Senior Production Editor: Dawn Kilgore
Manufacturing Supervisor: Becky Carreño
Cover Design: Paula Schlosser Design

Printing 10   9   8   7   6   5   4   3   2   1

CONTENTS

PREFACE

The evolution of performance technology probably began with Mager and Pipe (1970) describing when training should or should not be used to address performance problems. In their book titled *Analyzing Performance Problems or You Really Oughta Wanna,* they suggest that training should be used only when the performer could not perform as desired even if a gun were put to his or her head. They further suggest that if the performer could complete the task as desired but is not doing so, the correct approach to improving performance is to provide feedback, incentives, and performance standards, or to reengineer the job.

The alternatives to training proposed by Mager and Pipe eventually became classes of interventions designed to improve performance. Some interventions provided feedback; some motivated employees through a variety of incentives; others provided performance standards; and still others concentrated on redesigning the job. The process of analyzing performance, identifying the gaps between desired and actual performance, and selecting interventions to close those gaps became known as *performance technology.*

In 1990 Stein and Hutchison published a landmark article titled "A Process Model for Performance Technology"—an exciting breakthrough in that it offered a list of approximately one hundred interventions for improving performance. Yet many trainers still found it difficult to use different interventions in their practice, perhaps because there was no clear road map.

Then in 1992 we, as Performance International, began offering a workshop titled "How to Become a Performance Technologist," which addressed the development of the necessary skills. During the course of the workshop, participants received a glossary of terms representing 101 interventions. The overwhelmingly positive response to this glossary indicated a real need for knowledge on the part of performance technologists.

The recognition of this need led us to the idea of developing a reference guide on interventions for improving performance. This book is the result; it was conceived as a way for practitioners to teach other practitioners about the interventions that they have developed, expanded, or refined. We designed it to provide the road map that had been missing.

In preparing this book we decided to narrow the original 101-term glossary and to concentrate on fifty interventions. To identify experts on various interventions, we not only drew on our own networks but also conducted literature searches. Consequently, some of the experts represented in this book are our friends and colleagues, and some were discovered through our research. We eventually found what we believed to be the right person to provide information on each of fifty specific interventions. Of course, these fifty do not represent the entire universe of possibilities, but we believe they constitute a good initial road map that may be expanded in the future.

Acknowledgments

As a result of this undertaking we have learned so much—not only about professional practices in performance consulting but also about the generosity, flexibility, and dedication of our contributors and the people who support them. We thank each author and his or her support staff for their contributions to this book. Their patience, their tenacity, and their willingness to attend to details resulted in the excellent resource that we believe this book to be.

We have also learned a lot about technology and the possibilities and pitfalls of writing a book in an electronic environment. Only the cheerful hand-holding of Jordan Young, Karen Danyow, and Catherine Scholl allowed us to overcome our frustration with this new and demanding technology. We also appreciate the patience shown by Monica's husband, Jim Arnold, as he offered his support during this effort.

We thank Matt Holt of Jossey-Bass/Pfeiffer for supporting us after we sketched the idea for this book on a napkin in a restaurant. (Yes, it truly happened that way.) He carried the idea forward and obtained approval from Jossey-Bass management so that we could go from mere idea to printed page. We also thank Kathleen Dolan Davies and Susan Rachmeler for the editing roles they played.

In addition, we thank our clients, internal and external, who have given us the opportunity to practice and improve in our craft over the years. And we thank all of our colleagues who have made presentations at conferences, attended our own sessions, challenged our thinking, given us feedback, and helped us to become the professionals we are today.

January 1999

Danny G. Langdon
Kathleen S. Whiteside
Monica M. McKenna

Resources and References

Mager, R. F., & Pipe, P. (1970). *Analyzing performance problems or you really oughta wanna* (3rd ed., 1997, currently available from the Center for Effective Performance, Atlanta, GA, phone: 800-559-4237).

Stein, F., & Hutchison, C. (1990). A process model for performance technology. *Performance and Instruction Journal, 29*(3), 25–32.

INTERVENTIONS

Their Place and Use in Human Performance Technology

This book is designed to help human resource development (HRD) practitioners and trainers to develop their skills as performance technologists. This introductory material offers some basic information that will prove helpful to you: definitions of the major terms used in this book, the evolution of human performance technology, how performance technology can enhance your value to your organization or your clients, and how the book is organized.

Definitions of Terms

The following major terms are used in this book:

- *Human performance technology (HPT):* A systematized process for solving problems or realizing opportunities related to people's performance (International Society for Performance Improvement, 1997)
- *Human performance technologist:* "[A person who uses a systematic process to identify] need . . . to establish, maintain, extinguish, and/or improve performance in an individual and/or organization; defines the need; identifies, implements and networks appropriate interventions; and validates that the results are true improvements" (Langdon, 1991, p. 1)

interventions in your repertoire. If your organization's or your client's management is not familiar with the concept of performance technology, we do not advise you to try to "sell" the concept; instead, let management know that you have been introduced to some performance improvement interventions that are new to you but have proved successful for others. However, if management has already accepted the concept of performance technology as viable, simply state that you are building a repertoire in performance technology and that you are prepared to consult with managers on a number of useful interventions.

How This Book Is Organized

The editors' intent in selecting and arranging the contents of this book has been to create a practical, hands-on resource. This section describes how the book is organized.

Part One, written by the editors, consists of four chapters: the Introduction, "How to Use This Resource," "Selecting Interventions," and "Implementing Interventions." The chapters on selection and implementation are based on the experiences of editors Langdon and Whiteside in organizations across the United States. We recommend that you read all of the Introduction and "How to Use This Resource" before you read the individual interventions, but you might want to wait until you have reviewed some of the interventions to read the other two chapters.

Part Two consists of fifty chapters, each describing an intervention currently used by practicing performance technologists. These chapters are presented in alphabetical order by topic. In addition, each intervention is categorized in two ways:

- According to whether it is used *for establishing, improving, maintaining, or extinguishing performance*
- According to whether it is used *for facilitating change in the performance of an individual, a work group, a process, or the entire organizational unit*

Part Two opens with an intervention matrix, which lists and classifies all fifty interventions. (See the chapter "How to Use This Resource" for a full explanation of the classification system.)

Conclusion

The field of HPT is still evolving. The profession has developed thus far through the work of practitioners and theorists alike. As editors, we are excited to have compiled this resource for you. Use it, share it, and discuss it with your colleagues. We encourage you to help shape the next stage of HPT evolution.

Resources and References

International Society for Performance Improvement (ISPI). (1997). *1997–1998 performance improvement resources and membership directory.* Washington, DC: Author.

Langdon, D. G. (1991, August). Performance in three paradigms. *Performance Improvement Journal,* pp. 1–7.

Langdon, D. G., & Whiteside, K. S. (1990). *How to become a performance technologist.* Workshop presented by Performance International, Santa Monica, CA, various dates from January 1990 to the present.

HOW TO USE THIS RESOURCE

We have designed this book to be useful in a variety of situations. You will find it helpful in enhancing your professional repertoire, regardless of whether you are a beginning or veteran performance technologist and regardless of whether you work in a small nonprofit agency, a consulting firm, or a multi-national corporation.

The intervention designs that we have included are not intended to be exhaustive resources. We have not represented all possible interventions in the field of human performance technology. We also do not intend to suggest, as a result of our choices, that these particular interventions are more useful than others in terms of improving performance. Instead, we have set out to offer you a variety of interventions and to provide enough information on each so that you know that the intervention exists, what its most salient characteristics are, how it is used to effect change, and where additional information can be found.

As you read some of these interventions, you will find that you are confirming what you already know or believe. As you read others, you will discover approaches that are new to you. In still other cases, you will find information that helps you to fill in the blanks on topics that were previously only partially familiar to you. We believe, though, that in every case you will find something that assists you in offering solid performance interventions as alternatives to training.

We do not recommend reading this book from cover to cover. Instead, we suggest that you select a single intervention to read. Think about its uses and implications for your internal or external clients; study it in greater detail, if appropriate, by pursuing sources listed in the "Resources and References" section. Then proceed to another intervention.

You can determine the order in which to address the interventions in several ways. One approach is to read the table of contents and prioritize the interventions that you would like to read and research. Another approach is to use the intervention matrix to identify all the interventions that are appropriate for use with the level of audience with which you typically work. For example, if most of your work is done with *individuals,* then you would find all the interventions that are likely to change the performance of individuals. If you tend to work at the work group or departmental level, then you would locate all interventions that target *work groups.* And, if you tend to work primarily at the *process* level or with entire *business units* or organizations, you would concentrate on the interventions that deal with those audiences. Another approach is to start with a particular goal in addressing performance on a specific occasion and to choose interventions that meet that goal: *establishing, improving, maintaining,* or *extinguishing* performance. (See also the sections in this chapter titled "Performance Change/Level Grid" and "How to Read the Matrix of Interventions.")

Intervention Design

Each intervention follows a standard design format consisting of the following elements. (If an element is missing from an intervention, you can assume that it is not relevant to that intervention.)

Performance Change/Level Grid

The first component of each intervention is what we call the *performance change/level grid.* The grid classifies an intervention according to its most likely use in two dimensions: the *kind of performance change* the intervention seeks to make and the *level of audience* at which that change is targeted. (See the Matrix of Interventions, pp. 36–37, for a complete listing of all fifty of the interventions discussed in this book and their most likely uses.)

An intervention can be aimed at any of the following four kinds of performance change:

- *Establishing performance:* Creating performance where none currently exists
- *Improving performance:* Improving existing performance that does not meet goals or expectations

- *Maintaining performance:* Ensuring that existing performance remains as effective as it currently is
- *Extinguishing performance:* Eliminating existing performance

An intervention also can be aimed at one or more of the following four audience levels:

- *Individuals:* The executives, managers, and nonmanagerial employees who do the work through work groups, using processes, and for the benefit of the business unit(s) or organization(s)
- *Work group:* The organizational groups established to facilitate process completion and individual work
- *Process:* The methods and/or steps used to produce and support the production of outputs to customers
- *Business unit:* The level of organization that exists to meet external customer needs

Alternative Names

Any other names by which the intervention is known are listed in this section.

Definition

This section presents a definition of the intervention, including a brief statement about the nature and scope of the intervention.

Description

This section describes the fundamental composition of the intervention as well as its origin and use.

When to Use

This section describes when it is appropriate to use the intervention. (Some interventions also include a section titled "When Not to Use.")

Case Study

Each case study is an application of the intervention in a real-world environment. It is included not only to provide additional clarity but also to demonstrate the use of the intervention at a particular level within an organization.

Where possible, we have included a sample of the intervention or a portion of one. In the case of the job aid intervention, for example, a complete sample has been included. In the case of the learner-controlled instruction intervention, however, it has been possible to provide only a representative piece of the intervention; nevertheless, we believe that this sample does help to clarify the intervention.

Resources and References

The "Resources and References" section offers, as appropriate, on-line resources, associations, and groups that can provide you with additional information about the intervention. It also includes bibliographic information for sources cited in the discussion. We chose not to develop an extensive bibliography because so many new resources are becoming available daily. Instead, each list of resources and references is intended to be a starting point: as you investigate these materials, you will find others, and you will develop your own database of resources on each intervention that interests you.

Intervention Author(s)

This section includes the name, title, organization or affiliation, address, telephone number, fax number, e-mail address, and Web site of the author(s) who wrote the intervention. We encourage you to contact any author for additional information.

Case Study Author

If someone other than the intervention author provided the case study, that person's name, address, phone number, and so on are provided.

How to Read the Matrix of Interventions

As mentioned previously, the discussion of each intervention begins with a grid that classifies the intervention's use. We have also provided the intervention matrix that contains all the classification information on all fifty interventions (pp. 36–37). This matrix can be used to help determine the range of possible interventions that will meet a specific need. The vertical axis lists the fifty interventions in alphabetical order (as they are presented in this book). The horizontal axis lists the four kinds of performance change and the four levels of audience for each kind of change. Each "X" represents the likelihood that the intervention in the left-hand column could be used to change the performance at the audience level indicated. Thus, if you refer to the matrix, you will see that accelerated learning, the second intervention discussed in this book, is an appropriate intervention for *establishing* and *improving* performance in *individuals.*

This matrix offers a systematic means of selecting interventions. If your analysis of the performance gap in a particular situation has determined the kind of performance change needed (establishing, improving, maintaining, or extinguishing performance), you can use the matrix to identify all of the potential interventions that will achieve that kind of change. If your analysis also includes the level of the organization that will be targeted, you can then identify all of the interventions that can effect the desired change. You can then read about each potential intervention; based on your own criteria for such issues as organizational readiness, budgetary considerations, and urgency, you can select the ones that might be appropriate for your situation.

How to Build Your Repertoire of Interventions

There are a number of ways to build expertise in an intervention. Contact the author directly if you have questions. Read all of the books and articles listed and find additional ones. Attend presentations on the subject at local and national meetings. Find experts on the Internet and begin to participate in chats and discussions. You can even initiate the founding of a local chapter of a professional society devoted to the development and exploration of a particular intervention or cluster of interventions. Identify a project that can use a given intervention, then hire an expert consultant to lead the project and teach you. By aggressively building your knowledge, you and your peers will develop the expertise needed to employ a broad range of interventions. You will find opportunities to expand your repertoire and increase your own career resiliency.

In addition to reading about the interventions, you might want to try different ones in volunteer settings. Local professional societies can be excellent laboratories for experimentation. If you work with a large group of performance technologists, you might consider asking each member to try a different intervention, then your regular group meetings would include reports and descriptions of your coworkers' experiences with the interventions as well as any recommendations they might have. Identify the interventions that are most likely to fit your organization's needs and environment, then you can create a plan for developing expertise in conducting particular interventions.

Call for Additional Interventions

We are continuing our search for new or improved interventions. If you care to share any particularly useful ideas, resources, or interventions with the editors, please submit a brief description and sample for each. It would be helpful if you followed the format provided in this book, describing the intervention in no more than twelve double-spaced, typed pages.

   Send your submissions to:

Danny G. Langdon and Kathleen S. Whiteside
Performance International
1330 Stanford Street, Suite D
Santa Monica, CA 90404
E-mail: PerformI@aol.com

PART ONE

INTRODUCTION TO INTERVENTION SELECTION AND IMPLEMENTATION

CHAPTER ONE

SELECTING INTERVENTIONS

Danny G. Langdon

For decades performance technologists (PTs) have been searching for a systematic process that can be used to select interventions as part of a performance improvement effort. Although those of us who practice performance technology have no doubt developed our own personal approaches to selecting interventions, until now there has been no single, commonly accepted, systematic way to accomplish selection. The limited application of scientific methodology to selection has been a hindrance in performance technologists' work, and as a result I have developed a method that we find reliable.

The Beginning: Analyzing Performance

Good intervention selection begins with good performance analysis. If you do not accurately and completely define the performance gap, you cannot hope to select all the needed interventions. Also, if you are not accurate in the performance definition, you might not select appropriate interventions and might actually choose ones that interfere with your objectives. *Performance Improvement Pathfinders: Models for Organizational Learning Systems* (Dean & Ripley, 1997) is an excellent resource for learning more about performance analysis.

The kind of analysis you conduct must meet two fundamental requirements. First, the analysis must be complete, which means it must reflect all the changes in performance that are needed. Second, the analysis must be accurate, which means it must reflect the reality of the situation.

Stated in other terms, the paradigm you use for analysis must be a good one. If, for example, you use a general content analysis methodology based solely on your intuition and common sense—both of which are important, but not the key to good analysis—then you might be only partially accurate. Even if you conduct a variety of interviews and focus groups, collecting masses of data, unless the paradigm for analysis is solid for use in performance analysis, your analysis will not be accurate or complete. So until you have completely developed your own model, it is better to use one of the existing models referenced in the Dean and Ripley book.

The history of instructional designers in using a single intervention to meet most needs may well have misled them into believing that the intervention positively affects all of the performance needs or gaps that have been identified. For example, training can adequately meet everything that has been identified as a *learning gap*. But training is not a single intervention; rather it is composed of several different interventions, each used for a different purpose: words and pictures, questioning, feedback, motivation, and so forth. Using the various interventions associated with training correctly is critical. One should probably not, for example, use questioning as the intervention to introduce new content, as certain information and media sources are more appropriate. Choosing to use the correct intervention from those described in this resource guide is just as critical as training decisions are.

Selecting Interventions

Assuming you have done a complete and accurate performance analysis and are ready to select interventions to meet the defined need, you now need to answer two questions:

- Where are the gaps in performance between existing and desired performance?
- What kinds of performance changes are indicated by the gaps?

Defining Gaps

Performance change cannot be seen as one massive piece of change. To do so fails to consider the complexity of the issue and guarantees that the change to the desired state will not occur. To illustrate the complexity of the selection of interventions and the number of interventions that might be interwoven to achieve the necessary performance change, we will use an example from a typical business environment.

While working for a large construction-engineering company, I was asked to help change the performance of engineers and construction professionals who were occasionally required to give oral presentations together in front of a potential new client. When a potential client wanted a new office building built or a dam constructed, he or she approached several companies with a request for proposal (RFP). The RFP asked several companies to write a proposal plan, bid a price, and, through a project team, give an oral presentation to a review board so that the client could meet the team, ask questions, and make a final selection. Clients generally chose this process when the project was very large, usually in excess of $50 million; when there was technical information that needed clarification; and when they wanted to judge the potential project team. Otherwise, engineers and construction personnel typically had little opportunity to give good oral presentations. So in this case the vice president of marketing asked the training department to solve this "communication problem."

Looking at oral presentation as a performance problem might cause you to draw the conclusion that some training in organizing information, some practice, and some feedback might well take care of the performance need. Indeed many instructional and training programs have been devised to do just that. Unfortunately, although these programs accomplish some goals, they do not necessarily address all of the changes needed. To provide only training in this circumstance would be the result of either an incomplete performance analysis or limited experience in the power and efficacy of other interventions. In this instance, training was neither needed nor practical; for geographical and other reasons the audience was not available to receive training.

The first step in performance analysis was to determine all the performance gaps that needed to be filled. Thus, using the Language of Work paradigm for doing performance analysis, developed by the author, the performance technologist first set about to identify the changes in inputs, conditions, process, outputs, consequences, and feedback. (You may use any performance paradigm that works for you, keeping in mind the need for completeness and accuracy.) Rather than listing all the changes that were actually identified in this performance analysis, I will offer some examples of the range of changes required to change oral presentation performance. This will show how interventions can be selected systematically.

As summarized in Figure 1, the performance technologist analyzed performance by setting up a matrix that listed on the horizontal axis the six elements

FIGURE 1. ORAL PRESENTATION IMPROVEMENT PROJECT PERFORMANCE ANALYSIS AND INTERVENTION SELECTION WORKSHEET.

	Input	Conditions	Process	Outputs	Consequences	Feedback
Process (What Exists)	1. Marketing 2. Request for proposal 3. Letter requesting presentation 4. Team	1. Accepted written proposal 2. AV services/ capabilities 3. Company policies 4. Government rules	MARKETING VP 1. Analyze RFP 2. Analyze audience 3. Define content 4. Organize presentations TEAM 5. Define visuals 6. Practice 7. Deliver No guidelines	1. Oral presentation materials and audio-visual support 2. Project knowledge 3. Q and A 4. Project organization 5. Technical information	1. Increased likelihood of winning new work based on presentation 2. A "team" 3. Skilled and non-skilled presenters 4. Information presentation	1. Postpresentation review by customer 2. Sometimes Red-Team review during process of development
Process (What Should Exist)	1. Marketing 2. Request for proposal 3. Letter requesting presentation 4. Team 5. Customer 6. Project manager 7. Project files	1. Accepted, with addendum, written proposal 2. AV services/ capabilities 3. Company policies 4. Government rules 5. Presentation environment	1. Analyze RFP 2. Analyze audience 3. Define content 4. Define visuals 5. Organize presentation 6. Practice 7. Deliver	1. Oral oresentation materials and audio-visual support 2. Demonstrated project management leadership 3. Project knowledge 4. Q and A 5. Presentation and project organization 6. Technical information 7. Benefits (selling points)	1. Increased percentage of winning new work based on presentation 2. A "team" 3. Skilled presenters 4. Process for next presentation	1. Postpresentation review by customer 2. Postpresentation review by presentation team 3. Red-Team review 4. Proposal-writing team review
Interventions	• "Presentation Preparation Checklist and Resources Guide"	• Company • Presentation Standards • Book • RFP	• Coaching • "Project Team Presentation Package" • Team building	• Model presentations	• Group dynamics • Team building	• Evaluation checklist • Videotaping • Client evaluation • Verbal feedback

O Business Unit   O Work Group

O Process   O Individual

of the performance to be analyzed: inputs, conditions, process, outputs, consequences, and feedback. On the vertical axis, the technologist put "What Exists" and "What Should Exist." In this matrix, the technologist then completed the various boxes with performance information identified through observations, measurement, interviews, and other data collection means.

Figure 1 offers a summary of the performance technologist's conclusions. You can see that there are several changes needed in each of the six elements of the performance definition, called a *proforma* (Langdon, 1997). For example, in the proforma, you see in "What Exists" that four sources of input are indicated. In the "What Should Exist" area, the analysis showed the need for seven kinds of input—four from the "What Exists" and three new ones. Similar numbers of changes are indicated for conditions, process, outputs, consequences, and feedback. The following paragraphs explain two of the indicated changes.

The marketing manager played a key role in the "What Exists" state. He determined how the presentation was structured, its content, and the visuals. Often the dominating personality of the marketing manager was overwhelming for project personnel, who saw him or her as a corporate authority figure. The process change needed was to move the marketing manager from playing the key role and to have the project manager lead the development. The project manager needed to develop the presentation to establish himself as the *team leader* during the actual presentation. He also needed to ensure that other team members made significant contributions of content and visualization. This was a change in the *process* element of this performance example.

Another example of change is in the *feedback* element of performance. Note the new role of the proposal-writing team in giving feedback to the oral presentation team on its presentation. The proposal-writing team represents those people in the company who originally responded to the RFP and wrote the proposal; they possessed a vast array of knowledge about the client, the client's needs, and the project. However, the proposal-writing team was not included in the feedback loop of "What Exists" for evaluating the oral presentation before it was delivered to the client. Including this team in the "What Should Exist" feedback loop ensured a link between the written proposal and the oral presentation. This solved the performance problem of the oral presentation team's structuring the presentation with little regard for what was in the written proposal.

In summary, it is critical in intervention selection that you first determine, as part of the performance analysis, what the various changes in performance will be. When the analysis is structured to reveal the various elements of the performance, greater accuracy in the selection of interventions will be ensured for each performance change.

Change of State Analysis

There are four possible kinds of performance changes:

- *Establishing performance:* Used when performance does not currently exist in the individual, work group, business unit, or process and must be put in place
- *Improving performance:* Used when the performance currently exists in the individual, work group, business unit, or process, but must be made better in terms of quality, quantity, timeliness, or cost
- *Maintaining performance:* Used when the performance currently exists in the individual, work group, business unit, or process and must be kept as is
- *Extinguishing performance:* Used when the performance currently exists in the individual, work group, business unit, or process, but must be eliminated entirely

The kind of performance change needed must be identified for each performance gap. An example of each of the four kinds of performance change is offered in Figure 2.

Example 1: Establishing Performance. In the process element of the oral presentation proforma, there was a need to provide the presentation team with a way to structure the presentation so that it "sold" rather than merely informed. This was a new skill for project managers and engineers. To *establish* this performance, a job aid intervention was developed to show the steps to follow in structuring a selling presentation; it included samples of good presentations. Thus the team members, led by their project manager, developed their presentation according to a defined order and structure. Their work together resulted in team building

FIGURE 2. SAMPLES OF THE FOUR KINDS OF PERFORMANCE CHANGE.

IF performance state of change is . . .	Establish	Improve	Maintain	Extinguish
Sample intervention	Project team presentation package	Videotaping	Company presentation standards book	Role of marketing manager reduced
Intervention class	**Job aid**	**Feedback**	**Performance standards**	**Withhold information**

and a great familiarity with project content and approach. Thus the new desired performance was established.

Example 2: Improving Performance. The team members already knew how to speak and could give presentations. They were not professional speakers, but they had made a number of presentations; their work required them to speak to clients frequently in group settings. Consequently, performance had already been established, but the quality of that performance needed to be improved. The performance technologist selected a videotaping intervention in an effort to *improve* performance through feedback.

Improving performance is fundamentally different from establishing it. Different interventions are generally—although not always—selected. As shown in the grid included with each intervention in this book, only a few are useful for both improving and establishing performance.

Example 3: Maintaining Performance. A third kind of performance change is to maintain performance. In the oral presentation, one of the condition elements was maintaining the visual quality and the format of the oral presentation. In order to *maintain* this performance, standards and guidelines were developed and used by the team. As minimal a level of performance as it may seem, this helped to ensure use of the company logo on all visuals, to ensure a font size large enough for readability, and so forth.

Example 4: Extinguishing Performance. Finally, in this example there was a need to *extinguish* performance at the input and process level. The marketing manager was giving too much input to the team and guiding too much of the development. Extinguishing his performance was accomplished by naming the marketing manager only one of several resources of information that the team could call on when necessary. In fact, unless he was asked, the marketing manager could not be in the room with the team during the development and practice of the presentation. By removing his presence, his dominating behavior was extinguished (as far as his influence on the team was concerned).

Interventions can be selected to match the kind of performance change desired. A job aid listing a few appropriate interventions to use to achieve various changes of state is shown in Figure 3. Additional interventions that you use in your own organization may be added to this list.

As a further aid to intervention selection, in the discussion of the various interventions throughout this book we have indicated the changes of performance

FIGURE 3. JOB AID: SAMPLE INTERVENTIONS BY CHANGE OF STATE.

Improve Performance	**Establish Performance**
Action research	Employee selection
Business planning	Job aids
Coaching	Mentoring
Feedback	Modeling
Training	Training
Maintain Performance	**Extinguish Performance**
Compensation	Outplacement
Feedback	Upward evaluations
Performance standards	Withholding information
Work schedules	Withholding rewards

state with regard to the level (business unit, process, work group, individual) of performance that the intervention is typically used to address. Figure 4 is a sample matrix that illustrates this classification.

FIGURE 4. SAMPLE GRID.

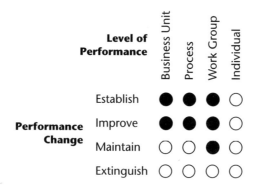

Other Intervention Selection Issues

Two other issues are important in selecting interventions, intervention interference and networking with other performance technologists.

Intervention Interference

One of the things you want to be aware of is that sometimes one selected intervention can have an adverse effect on other interventions that you plan to use. In the oral presentation example, the performance technologist wanted to retain the role of the marketing manager as an information source but decrease his role in the development of the presentation. The project manager needed to assume this lead role, but the marketing manager was quite used to dominating in this arena. Just by being present, he would interfere with the job aid intervention that had been constructed to guide the development effort. Therefore, to prevent intervention interference, the marketing manager had to be located in an area that precluded his interference with other interventions. His new role was an intervention itself (to serve as a resource person), but he could not be allowed to interfere with other interventions, such as giving feedback to the team during practice, and so on.

In another performance improvement instance, service representatives repairing equipment in the field were asked to collect client data (through a questionnaire intervention) that did not directly relate to the repair. This interfered with both the quantity and quality of their performance. An alternative intervention—using a follow-up call made by others—collected the needed data without interfering with the performance of the service representatives. You need to be alert for such intervention interference, which often comes in very subtle ways.

Networking with Others Who Conduct Interventions

Involving others who are responsible in your organization for various interventions will help in intervention selection. This is as much a politically savvy move as a useful aid to intervention selection, use, and maintenance. The project steps used by a performance technologist—analysis, selection, implementation, and evaluation—are all interrelated. It is advisable to involve others in the organization who may "own" certain interventions, whether they consider themselves this way or not.

As illustrated in Figure 5, for instance, the oral presentation example involved the marketing manager, experts from graphics, legal (for contract management), and so on. By involving everyone who might be a part of the solution in the initial analysis and development of the performance solution, you develop ownership of the solution and its maintenance. These people will be more willing to contribute to the future use of the solution in other settings. Your success will not depend on your ability to sell them on the situation and interventions after the fact. They typically have resources at their disposal that will be useful with other

FIGURE 5. SAMPLE PERFORMANCE IMPROVEMENT NETWORK (PIN).

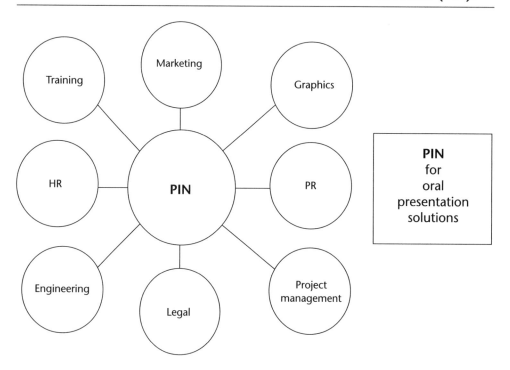

interventions. For example, the marketing manager knew how to get specific information about the clients that no one else knew existed. Incorporating other people at the performance analysis stage can be critical to your own success as a performance technologist.

Conclusion

Intervention selection is no easy matter. At its worst, it means selecting and using only those interventions known to the performance technologist, which might lead to an improvement project that misses the mark. At its best, intervention selection involves conducting an accurate and complete performance analysis, identifying what change is needed, determining the exact kind of change that is needed and at what level, knowing about and selecting the best of available interventions, and implementing the change by working with others who also conduct interventions. The results, assuming implementation is superb, will be improved performance for the audience targeted and learning for all those participating in the project.

Resources and References

Dean, P. J., & Ripley, D. E. (1997). *Performance improvement pathfinders.* Washington, DC: International Society for Performance Improvement.

Langdon, D. G. (1995). *The new language of work.* Amherst, MA: HRD Press (currently out of print; a new version is being planned by Jossey-Bass).

Langdon, D. G. (1997, October). Are objectives passé? *Performance and Instruction Journal.*

Stolovitch, H. D., & Keeps, E. J. (Eds.) (1992). *Handbook of human performance technology: A comprehensive guide for analyzing and solving performance problems in organizations.* San Francisco: Jossey-Bass (revised edition due to be published in 1999). See especially chapter seven, "The New Language of Work."

CHAPTER TWO

IMPLEMENTING INTERVENTIONS

Kathleen S. Whiteside

In many ways implementing an intervention is like launching a product. New cars, new software, and new fashions are launched amid a well-orchestrated array of events, activities, and media buzz known as communication. In the same way, performance technologists need to plan and arrange a launch for any new intervention. But performance technologists, unlike marketers, are also often responsible for the development of the intervention. The following paragraphs highlight some of what must be done in order to have a successful implementation. It answers questions such as the following:

- What plans are needed?
- What is different about implementing a single intervention as opposed to several at once?
- What can help to ensure success?

Master Project Plan

On the one hand, intervention implementation is no different from any other project management activity. On the other hand, implementation must be handled carefully because the intervention is almost always a source of change in an already complex setting and because it involves performance and behavior and other sensitive issues.

Implementation requires a *master project plan*, which consists of six elements: (1) a plan for developing the intervention itself, (2) a strategy for ensuring communication throughout the intervention, (3) an analysis of the target population, (4) a plan for assessing the political bases that must be covered, (5) an analysis of the intervention sequencing and a review for intervention interference, and (6) a project plan for the rollout. These elements are described in the following paragraphs.

Plan for Developing the Intervention

This plan includes the internal and external resources needed to complete the development, all the artifacts for the intervention, and the timelines needed. Budgets and other resources may be included. If experts are to be used, they must be identified and obtained. Rollout dates and milestones need to be identified.

Strategy for Ensuring Communication

A strategy must be established for ensuring communication throughout the intervention. Questions such as these must be answered:

- What are the messages about the intervention that need to be developed?
- Who must be told what?
- What media will be used?
- What preparation or lead time is necessary in order to ensure that the communication is prepared well and on time?

In conjunction with the political analysis, certain presentations may need to be planned for and scheduled. Celebrations can be an important vehicle for communications and politics, so they will need to be scheduled and budgeted as well.

Analysis of Target Population

Just as a target-population analysis is needed for a successful training program, so too should one be developed for an intervention. It does not have to be long or elaborate; but it does need to reflect an understanding of the implications of the target population's age, computer comfort (if applicable), typical reactions to and acceptance of change, learning styles, language, and other attributes that can affect success.

Plan for Assessing Political Bases

An assessment of the political bases is critical to the success of most interventions. For example, if an intervention on performance appraisals or leveraging diversity is to be launched, the political impact must be weighed and planned for. Key sponsors need to be identified and informal leaders included. Not all political bases have to be at the very highest reaches of the organization. Sometimes a supervisor, manager, or informal opinion leader needs to be informed in order for a successful implementation to occur. Attention paid early and often to innovators in, sponsors of, and resisters to the intervention can reap enormous benefits throughout the project.

Analysis of Intervention Sequencing and Review for Intervention Interference

When several people are implementing interventions in a large organization, it is easy for multiple interventions to be planned to occur at the same time. For example, new software may be scheduled for installation at the same time that reengineering has changed jobs significantly. Training some employees and changing their compensation while transferring others are three interventions that need to be orchestrated carefully to avoid undue confusion. The performance technologist needs to ensure that all parties are communicating with one another. Ensuring that all interventions are sequenced correctly, do not contradict one another, and will not confuse the target populations is a critical step for success. This work cannot be done in a vacuum; it requires the collaboration of internal and external consultants, line managers, and informal leaders.

Project Plan for Rollout

The rollout itself needs a plan, which is a subset of the master plan. Once all the political bases have been attended to, the intervention has been developed, the audience has been analyzed, and the message has been communicated, the actual rollout of the intervention can occur. The more planning the better on the many decisions that need to be made: deciding who will be where and when, what the change artifacts will be, and who will receive what in what kind of packaging. Recognize this important rule: the larger the group receiving the intervention, the more planning that is required.

Number of Interventions

Once the analysis has been completed, you may find that a single intervention is needed, that several are to be implemented at the same time, or that several need to be implemented singly or in pairs. The implementation of each alternative is quite different.

One Intervention

Although it is rare, it is possible to find that a single intervention is all that is needed to solve a performance problem. The intervention might be team building, a job aid, or work group alignment. Generally the target of the intervention has been involved in the identification of the performance problem and the development of the solution. Therefore, the implementation planning process is fairly straightforward.

For example, an analysis of a client request demonstrated that team building was needed. The team consisted of a small group of unrelated employees who had to work together for three days before presenting a proposal to a potential client. There was no time for training; the parties might never work together again. They needed an intervention that would help them forge themselves into a short-term team. The implementation was an invitation to all appropriate parties to an event that had been planned for them.

A large corporation founded in 1993, blending several companies into one wholesaler, provides another example. The treasurer had identified a need to establish policies and procedures in order to meet investor needs. Performance would be enhanced by having the relevant statements accessible and in writing. After the policies were written and approved, implementation included sending a cover letter to each manager with one policy manual per employee. A system was established to ensure policy updates and to provide policy manuals to new employees.

Many Interventions, Implemented One at a Time

In a small consulting firm, many interventions were identified during the initial analysis. However, given the lack of sophistication of the organization, readiness was established for only one intervention: improved communication. The intervention selected was facilitated monthly management meetings. Over time, the need grew for the other interventions that had been identified in the initial needs assessment. Gradually, mission and vision statements, organizational hierarchy, job descriptions, policies and procedures, employee handbook, job methods, and job aids were developed and introduced to the company.

Another organization identified work group alignment as the intervention it needed to improve its performance. Once the alignment intervention had been completed, the organization was ready to engage in reengineering, the development of policies and procedures, the creation of job descriptions, and the development of job aids. Implementation was organized as a series of projects, each of which required a stage of design and development followed by an extensive implementation plan that included communication planning, publication, distribution, and change management.

Many Interventions, Several Implemented Simultaneously

There are often cases in which multiple interventions are needed simultaneously. These are generally large-scale, organization-wide situations that involve teams of consultants or even a network of people to implement interventions. Mergers and acquisitions are often the source of such large-scale interventions; others are changes in the strategic plan, a move from a regulated to a deregulated business, or the hiring of a new president.

In one example, two organizations that had been rivals for a more than a century were forced by economic necessity to merge. The human resource team was assembled to develop and implement many interventions: policies and procedures, compensation system, new job descriptions, new organizational structures, orientation, team-building activities, new-employee handbook, and so on.

In this case, implementation required a prioritization process that rested with the vice president of human resources. After his assessment of a complex array of factors—including readiness, resources, impact on the organization, political feasibility, and organizational support—he identified the order for intervention implementation and included it in his annual business plan. Each year for five years, a number of interventions were identified, selected, designed, developed, and implemented. The improvement in the organization as a result of these interventions was measured annually, and those data were used to plan the following year's activities.

In another example, a new manager assumed responsibility for a department that needed multiple interventions to improve performance. Clients complained that they were not receiving good service, which was at least partially true. There were employee complaints about the workload, and the manager found the practices in the inherited department bordered on the unethical. Given this disarray, a first tier of interventions was selected; once these interventions had been implemented, a second tier of performance improvement interventions was selected, designed, developed, and implemented. Implementation at every tier varied from a simple explanation and introduction at an all-personnel meeting to elaborate affairs that included an off-site meeting; training; communication; and even mugs, posters, and balloons. Each tier or group of interventions was written in a proposal format, with implementation factors identified. The complexity of the intervention, the amount of change required, and the projected resistance to the intervention were all assessed; based on these factors, the implementation strategy was planned to meet the objectives of the intervention.

Strategies That Work

Here are three strategies for making a positive difference in an organization through interventions.

Build Credibility with One Intervention

Building credibility with one intervention can earn you the right to plan and develop others. Sometimes internal or external consultants have not yet earned the right to implement interventions based on an analysis or on indications that further analysis is needed. Consequently, credibility in the consultant's ability to produce the needed performance change is doubted. One simple case involved a conflict between two executives. The president called in an external consultant for a conflict resolution intervention. When asked what he expected as a result of the intervention, the president replied, "Oh, that everything will be worse!" Because he had not seen a conflict resolved through a third-party facilitator and had failed to resolve the conflict himself, he was sure that it could not be done. Imagine his surprise and delight when the two parties left the meeting agreeing to consult each other before the development of future problems. This consultant earned her stripes and subsequently was asked to solve many other problems as well.

In a high-tech organization, human performance consultants had improved the percentage of on-time repair orders that were processed by 50 percent by using a simple feedback intervention. This allowed the client to see that the skills and abilities needed to improve the performance of his organization resided in the staff department. Based on this success, the consultants were then able to obtain permission, resources, and data to examine other interventions that could be used to increase the accuracy of the repair orders. As this was a long-standing and expensive performance problem to solve, the credibility in the first intervention opened doors to the second, and even more powerful, analysis and intervention proposal.

Use an Initial Intervention to Collect Data for the Next Intervention

One client knew his work groups were not aligned, so he contracted for a work group alignment intervention. Doing the alignment work revealed the need for a new organizational structure, a new compensation system, new job descriptions, and a new governing structure. The quality and cost of the work on the first intervention satisfied the client's need; he was therefore open to proposals to continue the improvement work.

A second client was flabbergasted to see how expensive it would be to meet his need for job descriptions, policies, and procedures. He opted to introduce the intervention, the consultants, and the process to his group by beginning with just thirty policies and ten job descriptions. This allowed the consultants to enter the organization, see firsthand how the department was organized, how the players cooperated, and how complex the intervention design would be. By doing the initial work, they had enough information about the organization to project hours accurately, contain costs, and keep the price down. Both parties won in this situation.

Amaze the Client with Your Savvy and Ability

Sometimes it is mere timidity that prevents performance technologists from recognizing the opportunity to make a significant difference in an organization. Some clients are not familiar with the power and analytical tools of performance technology and need to be *amazed*. One client began the performance improvement process with a team-building request. Once the analysis had been completed, it was obvious that multiple interventions were needed: conflict resolution, relationship building, career development, and a decision-making process. Providing a structure that allowed all those interventions to be prioritized, planned, and scheduled almost simultaneously allowed the group to experience performance improvement, use data collected from the field, plan multiple interventions, and develop measurement criteria in a very short period of time. Knowledge and ability in multiple interventions and an analytical tool that could organize data sold the client on the whole project. Success breeds success.

Final Words of Wisdom from the Field

There are numerous ways in which a project can go awry. Faulty analysis is a major culprit. However, all you need to do to make implementation fail is to ignore it. All the implementation questions can be answered with the famous five W's that journalists use:

- Who
- What
- When

- Where
- Why

By answering these questions, you can help ensure successful implementation. There are numerous strategies that can be employed in order to ensure steady work as a performance technologist, but the strategies are useless if competent project planning and management do not take place. If you lack skills in project planning and management, use an analytical process on your own performance, identify the gaps, make a plan to close those gaps, and implement it.

MATRIX OF INTERVENTIONS.

	ESTABLISH				IMPROVE				MAINTAIN				EXTINGUISH			
	Business Unit	Process	Work Group	Individual	Business Unit	Process	Work Group	Individual	Business Unit	Process	Work Group	Individual	Business Unit	Process	Work Group	Individual
360-degree feedback				●				●				●				●
Accelerated learning				●				●								
Action learning	●	●	●	●	●	●	●	●								
Assessment centers			●					●				●				●
Automated resume tracking system	●		●		●		●		●		●					
Challenge education		●	●	●		●	●	●		●	●	●		●	●	●
Change style preference models			●					●			●					●
Cognitive ergonomics	●	●	●	●	●	●	●	●	●	●	●	●	●	●	●	●
Communication					●		●	●	●		●	●	●		●	●
Compensation systems							●	●			●	●				
Competency modeling			●	●			●	●			●	●			●	●
Conflict management			●	●			●	●							●	●
Critical thinking systems		●	●	●		●	●	●								
Cultural change	●		●	●	●		●	●					●		●	●
Customer feedback	●	●	●	●	●	●	●	●	●	●	●	●	●	●	●	●
Electronic performance support system		●	●	●		●	●	●								
Employee orientation			●					●								
Expert systems	●	●	●		●	●	●									
Flowcharts	●		●			●		●		●	●			●		●
Fluency development			●					●								
Human resource information systems	●		●		●		●		●		●		●		●	
Job aids		●	●	●		●	●	●		●	●	●		●	●	●
Leadership development programs			●					●								●
Learner-controlled instruction			●					●								●
Leveraging diversity	●		●	●	●		●	●					●		●	●

MATRIX OF INTERVENTIONS *(CONTINUED)*.

	ESTABLISH				IMPROVE				MAINTAIN				EXTINGUISH			
	Business Unit	Process	Work Group	Individual	Business Unit	Process	Work Group	Individual	Business Unit	Process	Work Group	Individual	Business Unit	Process	Work Group	Individual
Mentoring/coaching				•				•				•				•
Motivation systems			•	•			•	•			•	•			•	•
Needs assessment							•	•			•	•			•	•
On-the-job training				•				•				•				•
Organizational development	•	•	•		•	•	•		•							
Organizational scan	•				•											
Outplacement																•
Partnering agreements			•	•			•	•			•	•			•	•
Performance analysis	•	•	•	•	•	•	•	•	•	•	•	•	•	•	•	•
Performance appraisal				•				•				•				•
Performance management			•	•			•	•								
Policies and procedures				•	•	•		•	•	•		•				•
Process mapping		•					•		•				•			
Recognition programs			•	•			•	•			•	•			•	•
Reengineering	•	•	•	•	•	•	•	•					•	•	•	•
Results-based management	•	•	•	•	•	•	•	•	•	•	•	•	•	•	•	•
Safety management								•				•				•
Simulation			•	•			•	•			•	•			•	•
Strategic planning and visioning	•		•		•		•		•		•		•		•	
Structured writing		•	•	•		•	•	•		•	•	•		•	•	•
Team performance			•	•			•	•			•	•			•	•
Teaming	•	•	•	•	•	•	•	•					•	•	•	•
Training			•	•			•	•								
Usability assessments		•	•	•		•	•	•			•	•		•	•	
Work group alignment			•				•				•				•	

Source: 1998 Performance International workshop, *How to Become a Performance Technologist.*

▪ ▪ ▪ ▪ ▪ ▪ ▪ 360-DEGREE FEEDBACK

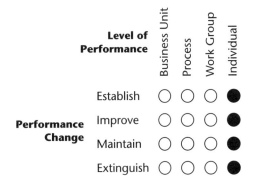

		Level of Performance	Business Unit	Process	Work Group	Individual
		Establish	○	○	○	●
Performance		Improve	○	○	○	●
Change		Maintain	○	○	○	●
		Extinguish	○	○	○	●

Alternative Name

Multirater feedback

Definition

The *360-degree-feedback* intervention is a process in which subordinates, superiors, peers, and customers provide feedback to employees.

Description

The intervention of 360-degree, or multirater, feedback has its roots in the fields of social psychology and organizational development (OD). The OD building blocks of research and survey feedback provide the historical foundations for all 360-degree-feedback interventions used in organizations today. Typical 360-degree-feedback interventions include a number of elements that can be traced to fundamental research and survey feedback tools: the inclusion of multiple perspectives, a focus on specific behavioral change efforts, an emphasis on addressing business needs, and reliance on continually measured improvement.

The major goal of a 360-degree-feedback intervention is to facilitate purposeful change in individual or team behavior. Successful behavioral change at the individual or team level depends on the existence of *self-awareness/insight, motivation/self-efficacy,* and *ability.* When properly designed and implemented, a 360-degree-feedback intervention provides specific feedback that enhances the insight and self-awareness that the recipient needs in order to embark on a behavioral change effort.

However, if people engage in such efforts without sufficient motivation, their efforts are generally unsuccessful. Effective 360-degree-feedback interventions enhance motivation on the part of individuals and teams to make constructive behavioral changes in order to meet the needs of both internal and external stakeholders (customers, direct reports, team members, and so on).

A 360-degree-feedback intervention involves the systematic collection of specific information from multiple sources to enhance the self-awareness of individuals and teams. Focus groups, interviews, or paper-and-pencil instruments are used to obtain data from multiple sources that have a relevant perspective to share. These data are summarized quantitatively or qualitatively and are then shared orally or in writing with one or more members of the organization.

Today the most common form of 360-degree-feedback interventions typically uses an off-the-shelf or in-house-designed instrument that measures critical competencies required for competitive performance. Most feedback from these interventions is collected from multiple perspectives (for example, an individual's supervisor, direct reports, peers, and team members) and is summarized in the form of a written or computerized report (often including graphic comparisons of the perceptions of the individual and others, written comments, and narrative information).

The interventions based on 360-degree feedback that are most commonly used are

- Executive and management coaching
- Training and development
- Career counseling
- Succession planning and development
- Training needs assessment
- Training evaluation
- Performance appraisal and evaluation

Before using 360-degree feedback, the practitioner needs to address the following issues.

What Competencies Should Be Assessed?

A 360-degree-feedback intervention should concentrate on specific competencies related to core business needs or job-specific skills, knowledge, and abilities. To be effective, the intervention must assess measurable, observable, and specific behaviors. Practitioners who are considering the use of 360-degree feedback must decide whether it is better to design or customize the competencies to meet the unique needs of a client or to use off-the-shelf tools that have been well established and validated.

How Many Individuals Should Provide Feedback?

Multirater interventions are based on the tenet that an adequate sampling of those who can provide information and feedback will result in a reliable (consistent) and valid (accurate) picture of a person's job performance. Current research suggests that maximum utility for a reliable and valid measure of performance is obtained when feedback is collected from approximately nine to twelve observers of the person's performance. Depending on the situation, it might be politically advisable to obtain feedback from additional observers, but a greater number of observers is unlikely to enhance the accuracy of the feedback.

Who Should Provide Feedback?

The determination of who should provide feedback depends on the purpose of the intervention. Feedback is typically sought from a person's supervisor(s), direct reports, peers, and customers. Current research suggests that at best modest intercorrelations will exist between these groups of individuals providing feedback. In general, supervisors tend to focus on bottom-line performance and competence; direct reports tend to focus on interpersonal and communication factors (*emotional intelligence*); and peers tend to focus on leadership potential.

How Should Individuals Providing Feedback Be Identified?

Research shows that when an individual rater can be identified, ratings in a 360-degree-feedback intervention tend to be inflated (for example, when used in performance evaluation). However, it might be helpful to the feedback recipient to know which feedback came from his or her supervisor.

In general, practitioners who use 360-degree-feedback interventions must determine in advance whether the feedback will be completely anonymous or merely confidential. This decision is critical in determining the best way to present and deliver feedback. If the feedback is not presented (qualitatively or quantitatively) in a manner that enhances receptivity and minimizes defensiveness, the entire intervention can be jeopardized. Consequently, care should be taken to contract with those providing feedback about the level of anonymity and confidentiality of the information being collected.

It is important to understand that confidential feedback may not be anonymous. For example, an employee might receive feedback whose origin can be identified (so that it is not anonymous), but that feedback might be delivered only to the employee and not to his or her supervisor (so that it remains confidential). Furthermore, how the feedback is summarized (pooled across all raters, for example, or broken down by rating category) can greatly enhance or diminish the recipient's acceptance of the data.

When to Use

The use of 360-degree feedback is appropriate in the following circumstances (Nowack, 1993).

When Individual or Team Behavioral Change Is Required

A 360-degree-feedback intervention is useful in providing individuals and team members with specific information from multiple perspectives about strengths and areas for development. This information increases self-insight and self-awareness and becomes a catalyst for behavioral change efforts. In this way a 360-degree-feedback intervention serves as a powerful tool for both individuals and teams in measuring and improving performance.

When Insight or Self-Awareness Appears Lacking

It is not uncommon for an individual to lack insight about the impact that he or she has on others or about the way he or she is perceived by others. In such circumstances a 360-degree-feedback intervention helps individual team members to compare their perceptions of themselves to those of others (fellow team members, customers, direct reports, supervisors, and so on). Multirater feedback has been shown to increase self-awareness and insight for both individuals and teams, often resulting in successful behavioral change efforts.

When Multiple Perspectives Will Provide a Holistic Picture

An intervention involving 360-degree, or multirater, feedback is most appropriate when multiple perspectives about individual or team behavior are required. Although research suggests that agreement among raters may be at best modest, different perspectives (such as those of the supervisor and several peers) provide the respondent with information about how he or she is perceived and the impact that he or she has on various internal and external stakeholders.

When Not to Use

The circumstances under which 360-degree performance feedback may *not* be appropriate are these:

- When a high level of defensiveness exists on the part of the feedback recipient
- When individual raters other than the feedback recipient's supervisor can be identified (when anonymity cannot be maintained)
- When the feedback results will be used in a manner other than initially contracted and intended
- When the intervention would be used by practitioners with limited or no training in handling 360-degree feedback
- In organizational cultures that do not support, reinforce, and encourage open and honest two-way feedback

Case Study

Sam is a manager of a technical department that has recently been restructured to reenergize autonomous work teams. Although Sam is technically competent and experienced, many people find him difficult to work with because of his lack of interpersonal skills and his controlling leadership style. Sam struggled with the implementation of the *team concept* in his department and spoke to his boss about what training programs he might attend to become more effective as a manager in this new environment.

Sam's boss suggested that he consider a recent program offered by the company's human resource department. This program was based on a 360-degree-feedback instrument that targeted the critical competencies required of technical managers working with teams. His boss told him that she had just completed the program and found it to be very helpful in identifying her managerial strengths and areas for development.

Sam was interested in hearing more about the program. His boss explained that she, Sam, and the members of his team would provide him with feedback about their observations of his interpersonal, communication, leadership, problem-solving, and task-management behaviors. The instrument would offer Sam a chance to compare his own perceptions of his behavior with the perceptions of others who completed the same instrument.

Sam was curious about a few things. He wanted to know how many team members should complete the instrument and whether their input would be anonymous. Sam's boss suggested that he decide how many team members he wanted feedback from and assured him that their perceptions and comments would be completely anonymous. She clarified that the only feedback that would not be anonymous would be from her.

Sam also was curious about what kind of feedback report would be prepared by the human resource department. His boss explained that the feedback consisted of a written report that would be delivered and discussed in a one-to-one meeting with a performance consultant from the human resource department. She also assured him that she would not see the final results and would only be informed about the professional development plan that Sam would design with the help of the performance consultant. Sam again stated his interest in the program and said that he would call the human resource department about it.

Soon after he called, a performance consultant contacted Sam and described the program in more detail. The consultant showed Sam the 360-degree-feedback instrument, which had been designed in-house to assess critical team and managerial competencies. Sam was given a set of these instruments to distribute to his team members along with a cover letter explaining the purpose of the program, ensuring anonymity, and describing where the completed surveys were to be sent for preparation of the feedback report. The consultant also told Sam that after all the instruments had been completed and returned, the two of them would meet to discuss the results and design a development plan that would be shared with Sam's boss.

When the feedback results became available, Sam met with the performance consultant to discuss them. The performance consultant helped Sam to understand how his team members viewed his management and leadership style. Sam learned that many team members experienced his style as extremely directive and task oriented, with a high need to follow up on decisions by "micromanaging" the actions resulting from those decisions.

Sam learned several other things about his behavior as perceived by others: he exhibited excellent technical knowledge; he expressed ideas openly and honestly; he interrupted people too often; he recognized good performance too infrequently; and he rarely involved the team members in planning, problem solving, and decision making. The performance consultant helped Sam to become more aware of his strengths as well as his areas for development. The two of them worked together to create a professional development plan that Sam could discuss with his boss.

Sam then discussed the plan and its implementation with his boss. He committed to work on very specific behaviors that would enhance his management ability in the new team-based culture. He also agreed to repeat the administration of the 360-degree-feedback instrument in approximately ten to twelve months to assess his progress.

Resources and References

Edwards, M., & Ewen, A. (1996). *360-degree feedback: A powerful new model for employee assessment and improvement.* New York: AMACOM.

Fleenor, J., & Leslie, J. (Eds.). *Feedback to managers: A review and comparison of multi-rater feedback instruments for management development* (3rd ed.). Greensboro, NC: Center for Creative Leadership (CCL) (phone: 336-286-4096). An excellent source of samples and objective comparisons of a wide variety of 360-degree-feedback assessments.

Lepsinger, R., & Lucia, A. (1997). *The art and science of 360-degree feedback.* San Francisco: Jossey-Bass/Pfeiffer.

Nowack, K. (1993). 360-degree feedback: The whole story. *Training & Development Journal, 47,* 69–72.

Shaver, W. (1995). *How to build and use a 360-degree-feedback system* (INFO-LINE No. 9508). Alexandria, VA: American Society for Training and Development (ASTD).

Wimer, S., & Nowack, K. (1998). 13 common mistakes using 360-degree feedback. *Training & Development Journal, 52,* 69–79.

Intervention Author

Kenneth M. Nowack, Ph.D.
President
Organizational Performance Dimensions
2621 6th St., Suite 2
Santa Monica, CA 90405
Phone: 310-450-8397
Fax: 310-450-8397
E-mail: knowack@opd.net
Web site: http://www.opd.net

■ ■ ■ ■ ■ ▪ ACCELERATED LEARNING

	Business Unit	Process	Work Group	Individual
Level of Performance				
Performance Change — Establish	○	○	○	●
Improve	○	○	○	●
Maintain	○	○	○	○
Extinguish	○	○	○	○

Alternative Names

Integrative learning
Enhanced learning

Definition

Accelerated learning consists of a variety of holistic learning techniques that seek to involve all a learner's resources (cognitive, physical, emotional, sensory, social, spiritual, and creative) in order to enhance the learning process.

Description

In the past twenty years, the accelerated learning movement has grown substantially as a response to perceived inadequacies in conventional education and training. It has drawn strength and direction from various late-twentieth-century sources including suggestology, humanistic psychology, cognitive science, quantum physics, the collapse of the Newtonian scientific worldview, the rise of systems thinking, and the unprecedented escalation of change. These sources and

47

others are forcing educators and trainers to reevaluate and reconceptualize the learning process.

Although rapid, nonstop learning is crucial today, the learning methods that people generally use were designed for life in the nineteenth and early twentieth centuries. That era's many influences included the assembly line; behaviorism; rote learning; bureaucratic control and measurement; paternalism; the lecture method as the de facto standard of delivery; individualism; and the almost exclusive emphasis on rational, verbal, compartmentalized thought processes. All of those influences tended to create relatively passive learners and stark learning environments.

Accelerated learning, in contrast, seeks to make learning natural again. It seeks to restore people to the openness, flexibility, sense of community, and whole-bodied intelligence that they had as children. Accelerated learning environments tend to be positive, colorful, collaborative, and stimulating to all the senses. Lectures are not necessarily eliminated but tend to be reduced in favor of activities that totally involve the learners. The aim is to appeal to all learning styles and to help learners exercise the full range of their rational, emotional, physical, social, intuitive, and creative intelligences as they learn.

Here are a few contrasts between what the traditional and accelerated learning approaches emphasize. (These are tendencies only and not pure, exclusive opposites.)

Traditional Learning	*Accelerated Learning*
Atomistic and fragmented	Holistic and relational
Cognitive	Cognitive/whole body
Words	Words, images, music
Materials based	Activity based
Teacher centered	Learner centered
Learner as consumer	Learner as creator
Abstract concepts	Concrete experiences
Emotionless	Expressive
Individualistic	Collaborative
Knowledge acquisition	Thinking skills
Teacher as dominant	Learners as co-teachers
Sober and serious	Playful and imaginative
Mechanistic	Humanistic
Inhibited, guarded	Open, relaxed
One-dish meal	Smorgasbord

The design of accelerated learning is also different from that of traditional learning. Because learners are given much more responsibility for their own learning, the teacher or trainer need not do as much for them ahead of time. Therefore, accelerated learning courses can be designed much more quickly. If accelerated learning designers do their jobs properly, they create a context in which the learners can co-create the content. The teacher, for trainer, then becomes a facilitator and orchestrator, not the exclusive fount and source of all knowledge. Participants become co-teachers as well as learners in a caring, option-rich, and results-oriented learning community.

As accelerated learning focuses on the results achieved and not the methods used, methods can vary widely. Learning can involve team-based activities, dialogue, peer tutoring, metaphors, learner-created mnemonic devices, music, problem solving, physically acting out processes, manipulating objects, building models and job aids, reflecting, creating pictograms, having and debriefing real-world experiences, and so on. What runs throughout all of these methods, however, is community, creativity, variety, immersion, and the involvement of the total learner.

The following are just a few of the many examples of success (Meier, 1985; Zemke, 1995):

- By creating an accelerated learning environment, Travelers Insurance improved test scores in one major training program by over 400 percent while reducing training time by 20 percent.
- Bell Atlantic reduced its failure rate in customer service training from 40 percent to 2 percent.
- American Airlines cut training time in half for one lesson while improving long-term retention.
- Chevron cut training time by 50 percent for a technical course while achieving the same or better learning.
- Florida Community College increased computer learning by nearly 300 percent while improving learner morale and virtually eliminating all absenteeism.

When to Use

Using the accelerated learning approach is appropriate in the following circumstances:

- When the subject matter is complex
- When it is critical that participants integrate and retain knowledge, concepts, and skills

- When the current mode of imparting new knowledge and skill is boring to the participants or when the participants have negative feelings about the learning process or their ability to learn.
- When it is necessary to reduce the time spent in designing the learning program as well as the time that the participants invest in learning

Case Study

A major cellular telephone company was routinely teaching cellular telephone concepts to newly hired customer service representatives. The instruction, based on conventional methods, took a verbal/cognitive approach that used lectures, black-and-white transparencies, and student workbooks in a typical classroom environment oriented toward individuals.

It soon became apparent that this approach was not working. Graduates were being released to the field lacking confidence and often confused about cellular concepts. (Their performance was checked by monitoring their calls.)

To improve job performance, the training department turned to accelerated learning methods. The training sessions became much more collaborative. The trainers established a learning community in which everyone was responsible for his or her own and everyone else's learning.

One technique they used was to have the participants act out the cellular concepts physically. After receiving a brief, high-level overview of cellular concepts, the participants played various roles in a cellular network. Wearing appropriate labels, some played the roles of cellular phones roaming about in automobiles; others acted as cell sites; still others took the roles of various kinds of land-line telephone equipment. Together they acted out various types of telephone calls, making connections with clothesline rope. Subsequently, the facilitator asked questions about the experience and engaged the group in dialogue.

Next, the participants were invited to suggest scenarios for the group to act out, concentrating on areas about which they were still somewhat confused. Afterward, pairs were formed, and the partners reinforced their learning by asking each other questions and explaining in detail how the total cellular system worked.

As a result of this collaborative approach, which emphasized total mental and physical involvement in learning, the participants' subsequent job performance improved dramatically. Monitored calls verified that they had a much better grasp of cellular concepts and were much more relaxed and confident when talking to customers than were those trained in the conventional way. Finally, the participants reported very positive attitudes toward this new, more active, *whole-learner* approach.

Resources and References

Caine, R., & Caine, G. (1991). *Making connections: Teaching and the human brain.* Alexandria, VA: American Society for Curriculum and Development (ASCD).

Hannaford, C. (1995). *Smart moves: Why learning is not all in your head.* Arlington, VA: Great Ocean.

Lawlor, M., & Handley, P. (1996). *The creative trainer: Holistic facilitation skills for accelerated learning.* New York: McGraw-Hill.

Meier, D. (1985, May). Accelerated learning: From linear to geodesic. *Training & Development Journal,* pp. 40–43.

Mellander, K. (1993). *The power of learning.* Burr Ridge, IL: Irwin.

Zemke, R. (1995, October). Accelerated learning: Madness with a method. *Training,* pp. 93–100.

Intervention Author

David Meier
Director
The Center for Accelerated Learning
1103 Wisconsin Street
Lake Geneva, WI 53147
Phone: 414-248-7070
Fax: 414-248-1912
E-mail: alcenter@execpc.com
Web site: www.execpc.com/~alcenter

▪ ▪ ▪ ▪ ▪ ▪ ACTION LEARNING

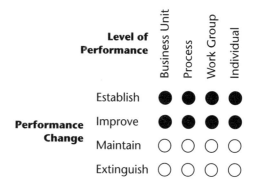

Level of Performance	Business Unit	Process	Work Group	Individual
Establish	●	●	●	●
Improve	●	●	●	●
Maintain	○	○	○	○
Extinguish	○	○	○	○

Performance Change labels the Improve/Maintain rows.

Definition

Action learning is a group problem-solving process built on diversity; reflective questioning; and commitment to individual, group, and organization-wide learning.

Description

Since its development by Reg Revans in the 1940s, action learning has become one of the most powerful problem-solving tools available to groups. It also serves as an individual, team, and organizational development intervention. It has gained popularity with organizations around the world, such as General Electric, British Airlines, Arthur Andersen, Exxon, and Rover.

Six Key Elements of an Action Learning Program

Element 1: Forming Action Learning Groups. One or more *action learning groups* (also known as *action learning sets*) are formed. Each group is composed of four to eight members from different functions or departments. By diversifying its membership in this way, the group can take advantage of different perspectives in addressing organizational problems. Each group includes people who care about the problem to be addressed, who know something about the problem, and who have the power to implement the solution recommended by the group or to monitor the work of others in implementing that solution.

Element 2: Undertaking Projects, Problems, or Tasks. One of the fundamental beliefs underlying action learning is that people learn best when they take meaningful action to solve important organizational problems and then reflect on and learn from the actions taken. Several criteria are used to determine whether a problem is appropriate for an action learning group to address:

- *Reality:* The problem must be current, be of genuine significance to the organization, and require a tangible result by a specific date so that the investment of time and funds is justified.
- *Feasibility:* The problem must be within the competence of the group to solve.
- *Richness in potential learning:* The problem must provide learning opportunities for the group members, and its solution must offer possible applications to other parts of the organization.

Element 3: Questioning and Reflecting. Action learning focuses on the right questions rather than the right answers. The assumption is that what people *do not know* is as important as what they *do* know. In action learning, the group members tackle a problem by first asking questions that clarify the exact nature of that problem; next they reflect on the problem and identify possible solutions; then they choose what action to take. The classic formula for action learning is $L = P + Q + R$, where L is learning, P is programmed instruction (knowledge in current use, in books, already in one's mind, and so on), Q is fresh questioning, and R is reflection (pulling apart, making sense of, trying to understand).

When the members of an action learning group begin to address a problem, they ask and answer the following key questions:

- What goal is the organization seeking to accomplish?
- What obstacles are keeping the organization from accomplishing this goal?
- What can the organization do about the obstacles?
- Who knows what information is needed?
- Who cares about having a solution implemented?
- Who has the power to implement the solution?

Element 4: Making a Commitment to Action. There is really no learning unless action is taken on the problem that a group addresses, and no action should be taken without learning from it. The group members either must have the power to implement their solution(s) or must be assured that others will assume responsibility for implementation. Action enhances the learning, as it provides a basis and anchor for the critical dimension of reflection.

Implementation is part of the contract between an action learning group and the organization. If the group members merely prepare reports and make recommendations, their commitment, effectiveness, and learning are diminished. Unless a solution is implemented and the group members reflect on that implementation and its effectiveness, there will be no evidence that something better or different can be done. Consequently, there will be no indication that real learning has taken place.

Element 5: Discussing What Has Been Learned. Solving an organizational problem provides immediate, short-term benefits to the organization. The greater, long-term benefit, however, is the learning that the group members acquire about themselves, about the effectiveness of their group, and about ways in which that learning can be applied throughout the organization. Therefore, time must be set aside for group member discussions about what they have learned as individuals and as a group and how that learning can be used in other parts of the organization.

Element 6: Analyzing the Learning Experience. It is advisable for each action learning group to have a *facilitator* (also known as a *set advisor*). This person may be either a member of the working group or a nonmember whose sole task is to help the group members reflect on what they are learning and how they are solving problems. The facilitator assists the group members in analyzing how they have listened, reframed the problem, provided feedback to one another, handled differences, fostered creativity, and so on. He or she should be competent in working with the processes vital to action learning: questioning, emphasizing learning, avoiding judgment, focusing on the task, and providing *air time* (time to talk) for every member.

If no facilitator is involved, the group members must still analyze their learning experience for themselves.

Phases of Action Learning

Action learning involves the following phases:

- *Introductory phase:* The group members determine what they are trying to do, what is preventing them from doing it, and how they can overcome those obstacles.

- *Diagnostic phase:* The group members examine the issues of who knows about the problem, who cares about the problem, and who can implement solutions.
- *Consultation phase:* The group members interview or observe outside resources.
- *Implementation phase:* The group members develop action plans, recommend a solution to senior management, and implement (or monitor the implementation of) the solution.
- *Review phase:* The group members share what they have learned and determine how to apply it in other parts of the organization.

Implementing Action Learning in an Organization

Action learning groups need not be implemented throughout an organization. Instead, they can be implemented in any area in which important problems exist and significant learning is possible and needed. Subsequently, action learning can be transferred to other parts of the organization, thus becoming a catalyst for organization-wide change.

The process of implementing action learning in an organization consists of the following six steps.

Step 1: Hold an Informational Workshop. An organization-wide workshop is conducted to show both managers and nonmanagerial employees how action learning works. External consultants or knowledgeable staff members explain and demonstrate the basic principles and dynamics of action learning.

Step 2: Establish Projects. One or more projects involving organizational problems are identified to be addressed by action learning groups. The projects chosen are ones that will be (1) meaningful to potential group members and their jobs and (2) important to the organization as a whole. The problems must be ones for which employees can offer several viable solutions, not ones that could be better solved by experts.

Step 3: Form Action Learning Groups. Action learning groups are formed, each consisting of four to eight members from diverse backgrounds and representing different kinds of functional expertise. A facilitator also may be assigned to each group, although this is not absolutely necessary. If a facilitator is assigned, that person should be someone whom the members do not already know, so that he or she can act independently of the group's culture.

Step 4: Work on Problems. Each action learning group meets on a periodic basis (daily, weekly, or every two weeks) over a period of several weeks to several months.

Each meeting requires a full day or a few hours, depending on the nature of the problem being addressed and the constraints of the members' schedules and responsibilities.

Step 5: Record Findings. An action group's learning is developed as a result of discussing and resolving its problem. In each group the members use such techniques as feedback, brainstorming, reflection, discussion, and analysis to reach a solution. What they discover and experience during this process is recorded.

Step 6: Reflecting on the Work. After a group completes its project, its members reflect on their work, either with or without the assistance of a facilitator. Their objective is to learn as much as possible about how they identified, assessed, and solved the problem; what increased their learning; how they communicated; and what assumptions shaped their actions.

When to Use

Action learning is an appropriate intervention in the following situations:

- When the organization wishes to solve complex problems with a comprehensive systems approach that focuses on causes and organizational assumptions.
- When the organization seeks to accelerate individual, group, and organizational learning.
- When the organization's leadership is willing to commit the necessary time, people, and resources to solving critical problems.
- When the organizational challenge being faced is a problem and not a puzzle (a puzzle is a perplexing question for which a single answer exists but is not yet known, whereas a problem has no single existing solution but is amenable to resolution in a variety of ways that people might devise).

Case Study

National Semiconductor, headquartered in Sunnyvale, California, is one of the leading global manufacturers of products that connect people to electronics and electronic networks. Its products include personal computers, cordless phones, computer security systems, automobile instrumentation, multimedia centers, and microwave ovens.

When poor delivery performance from National Semiconductor's South Portland, Maine, manufacturing plant resulted in an inability to provide quality service for one of its customers, AT&T, the plant's senior managers decided to do something about this situation. They selected eight people from different areas throughout the company to be the members of the Customer-Request Improvement Team, whose mission was to resolve the service problem.

The team members came from sales, marketing, engineering, manufacturing, and planning as well as from AT&T. They met as an action learning group two to three times a month over a ninety-day period.

The team members set out to resolve a real, feasible, and learning-rich problem: how to provide higher-quality service for AT&T. They began by asking questions to clarify and reframe the problem:

- What are we attempting to accomplish?
- What obstacles stand in the way of excellent service?
- What information and assistance do we need, and who can provide that?
- What action will we take between now and our next meeting?

Between meetings the members collected ideas and information from internal and external sources, tested action steps, and assessed improvement in the service being delivered to AT&T. All resulting information was shared at the subsequent meeting.

The action learning group also took time to reflect on its discussions and to make improvements in its work. In addition, time was spent in examining what individual members had learned and contributed to the team's success. The members took turns serving in the role of team facilitator so that each member would develop the necessary facilitation skills.

At the end of the ninety-day period, the team proposed more than forty ideas for resolving the service problem. Those ideas resulted in the following key action initiatives:

- Analyzing the delivery misses in new ways
- Increasing the frequency of lead-time updates
- Creating critical-device lists
- Developing *pre-alert* reports

After the implementation of the initiatives, AT&T recognized National Semiconductor as a "world-class" supplier. The action learning team was also seen as the key tool in increasing productivity and creativity at National Semiconductor.

Resources and References

Books

Marquardt, M. (1997). *Action learning.* Alexandria, VA: American Society for Training and Development (ASTD).

Pedler, M. (Ed.). (1996). *Action learning in practice.* Brookfield, VT: Gower.

Revans, R. (1982). *The ABC for action learning.* Bromley, England: Chartwell-Brat.

Weinstein, K. (1995). *Action learning: A journey in discovery and development.* New York: HarperCollins.

Foundation

International Foundation for Action Learning (Web site: http://www.mentat.co.uk/park/ifal).

International Foundation for Action Learning (in the U.S.) (Web site: http://www.metalearning.com/ifal-usa).

Intervention Author

Michael J. Marquardt
President
Global Learning Associates
1688 Moorings Drive
Reston, VA 22090
Phone: 703-437-0260
Fax: 703-437-3725
E-mail: mjmq@aol.com

ASSESSMENT CENTERS

Level of Performance		Business Unit	Process	Work Group	Individual
	Establish	○	○	○	●
Performance Change	Improve	○	○	○	●
	Maintain	○	○	○	●
	Extinguish	○	○	○	●

Definition

An *assessment center* is a process in which several different competencies of potential or existing employees are evaluated by more than one assessor using multiple techniques. These techniques include paper-and-pencil inventories, interviews, and role plays and simulations. The results of the assessment center process can be used for employee selection or development.

Description

Assessment centers were originally developed for military purposes, first by the German military and later by the U.S. Office of Strategic Services in World War II. The process was driven by the need to select officers and undercover agents. The competencies required of people entering these jobs were very complex and not appropriately measured by existing instruments.

The goal of the early assessment centers was to measure complex behavior accurately using several different kinds of measures. It was thought that competencies would be more reliably measured if observed more than once and by assessors with specially developed skills.

The key to a valid assessment center is the objective measurement of behaviors. If assessors are not extremely well trained, their assessments might be biased as a result of factors unrelated to performance, such as the attractiveness of the person whose behavior is being assessed.

In 1956, at AT&T, Douglas Bray first applied the assessment center technique in a business setting (described in Thornton & Byham, 1982). It is hard to imagine a more detailed study of individual behavior, attitudes, motivation, and success. More than four hundred entry-level employees participated in the AT&T assessment centers between 1956 and 1960. Five years later their assessment center scores were shown to be strongly correlated with different measures of managerial progress (for example, salary and number of promotions).

There is no such thing as a typical assessment center. However, some practices are more common than others, with 83 percent of assessment centers using in-basket activities, 78 percent using simulated coaching meetings, 70 percent using leaderless group discussions, 70 percent using structured interviews conducted by the assessors, and 68 percent using oral presentations (Kudisch et al., 1998). Nearly 90 percent of the organizations that administer assessment centers use them for employee selection, and 69 percent use them for employee development (Kudisch et al., 1998). A majority of development centers also use 360-degree, or multirater, feedback (Kudisch et al., 1998).

When to Use

Implementing assessment centers requires both time and financial resources. Therefore, assessment centers should be undertaken only when there is solid evidence that the organization can achieve a positive return on investment (ROI). The following three situations are appropriate opportunities for using assessment centers.

When Selecting Managers and Supervisors

Using the assessment center technique does add cost to the hiring process. However, Gaugler, Rosenthal, Thornton, and Bentson (1987) demonstrated that across many applications, there is a significant correlation between performance in an assessment center and performance on the job. Also, Cascio and Silbey (1982) demonstrated that even when assessment centers used to select supervisors result in less correlation between the two types of performance than that found by Gaugler et al., the organization can experience a positive ROI. This is because assessment centers can help organizations to hire better performers, even when written inventories or interviews are already part of the selection process. The performance difference between the new supervisory hires and those who would have been selected without the assessment center more than makes up for the additional cost.

Like any other selection technique, assessment centers should not be the sole source of data used in hiring. When considering the use of an assessment center for employee selection, an organization must consider four factors to calculate the ROI:

- The statistical relationship between assessment center scores and job performance (validity)
- The dollar value of the job performance differences between those who could potentially be selected using the assessment center and those who would have been selected using another method or randomly
- The number of applicants going through the assessment center for a given job opening
- The cost of administering the assessment center

Therefore an assessment center can be an excellent intervention as a selection tool when acquiring a high performer is critical and when the organization can choose among applicants.

When Developing Managers and Supervisors

Many assessment centers are run to give participants feedback about their behavior in critical situations. This feedback is often linked with development opportunities matched to an individual's performance in the assessment center (along with other performance-related data). In most assessment centers, feedback is delivered face-to-face by assessors (Spychalski, Quiñones, Gaugler, & Pohley, 1997), but it is not unusual for the feedback to come in a written form.

The feedback report might cover the following elements:

- The person's actions during the activity (or activities)
- The person's strengths and needs for development
- The recommended training or development opportunities that are likely to improve the person's performance

When Conducting a Needs Analysis

For the assessment center to be an effective needs analysis tool, the following conditions must be present:

- Adequate organizational resources to provide opportunities for training and development
- Management commitment to the development process
- Development goals that are part of performance planning for those who go through the assessment center and for their immediate supervisors

One example of using an assessment center for needs analysis occurs when an organization is implementing a new competency model. The assessment center can be used to benchmark the competence of incumbents. These data can be used to design training and development programs that would be used by the group. As mentioned earlier, participants would also receive specific feedback so that training could be individualized.

Combining the Three Uses

The three uses of assessment centers just discussed are not necessarily independent from one another. An organization can use all of the information from the assessment center to determine current training needs as well as to identify areas in which future development will be needed to meet competitive demands.

Both successful external and unsuccessful internal candidates who participate in assessment centers for selection should also receive feedback. Successful candidates can use the feedback to construct development plans to be implemented as soon as possible. Unsuccessful internal candidates can use the feedback to improve their skills so that they will be more competitive the next time they apply for a promotion. In both cases, employee skills are strengthened by the assessment center experience, thereby raising the bar within the organization.

Case Study

Human resource development (HRD) initiatives do not occur in a vacuum. They must be planned as part of an overall strategy. Figure 1 illustrates how different HRD programs fit into an overall organizational strategy, and the following case study shows how an assessment center is integrated into an overall strategy.

The telecommunications industry was being deregulated, and as a result one telecommunications company changed its business strategy. This company decided to expand its core business to include cable television, cellular phones, and so on. This change altered the critical skills and abilities needed by supervisors and managers to make the business successful. In particular, supervisors and managers needed to improve their performance in the areas of customer service and team-

FIGURE 1. HOW HR SUPPORTS ORGANIZATIONAL STRATEGY.

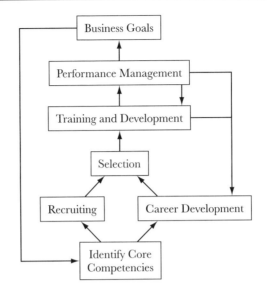

work. The company decided that one way to improve performance in these areas was to implement an assessment center.

The assessment center was seen as an appropriate solution because the company needed to accomplish two goals:

- Assess the skill levels of current supervisors and managers in order to create individual development plans for incumbents
- Ensure that future hires (and internal employees who were promoted) possessed the desired skill levels.

The assessment center exercises were based on competencies identified in the job analysis as critical. In the new environment, teamwork and customer service were criteria for successful job performance. The situations in the exercises were developed from critical incidents described by job experts in order to identify behaviors associated with the critical job dimensions, especially the new ones. Four exercises were developed:

- *In-basket:* In this exercise each participant responded to in-basket correspondence from customers, peers, subordinates, and his or her manager. Information in the in-basket was relevant to the other exercises.

- *Coaching:* In this exercise each participant resolved performance issues with a subordinate.
- *Angry customer:* Immediately after the coaching exercise, each participant proceeded to this exercise, in which he or she had to resolve a service issue with an upset customer.
- *Task force:* In this exercise all the participants interacted to solve an organizational problem.

In addition, a paper-and-pencil inventory assessing decision-making ability was completed by each participant.

A different trained assessor observed the participants in each of the four exercises. Each assessor also wrote narrative feedback for each participant assessed. The feedback included a summary of what the participant did during the exercise and a list of strengths and no more than three development needs. A copy of the feedback was also sent to each participant's direct supervisor. Subsequently, each participant and his or her supervisor created a plan to enhance the participant's skills and abilities in the areas that had been identified as needing development.

The data from the incumbents who participated were then used to set passing scores for the assessment center so that the center could be used in hiring and promoting future supervisors and managers. The same four activities were used for this purpose.

The impact of the assessment center has been felt in many ways. For example, the results from the incumbent participation served as an effective needs analysis; the assessment center identified the gaps between expected and actual performance levels in critical skills and abilities. This allowed the company to focus its training and development programs on these gaps. Previously, management training courses were arranged on request, rather than to fill gaps between actual performance and business needs.

The use of the assessment center for selection has also helped to move the company away from its entitlement mentality. Previously, the employees with the longest tenure expected to be promoted; now they have to demonstrate that they have the skills to do the job.

This change is particularly important. Like many companies, this one professed to appreciate the difference between the skills and abilities required to be an effective hourly associate (for example, lead technician) and those required to be an effective supervisor. However, in making decisions about whom to promote, the company often relied on past performance on a job that required completely different skills. Now that this practice has changed, those who want to become supervisors know that they must develop supervisory skills before going through the assessment center. The company has assisted these people by providing career development services.

The addition of new selection techniques meant that fewer people were successful during the hiring process, so it became necessary to have a larger pool of applicants to fill the same number of positions. Consequently, the use of the assessment center made the company rethink its recruiting tactics. It moved from relying on passive methods of recruiting to aggressive pursuit of qualified applicants.

The assessment center also affected the company's performance management system. Because the assessment center defined new critical skills and abilities and raised the bar in terms of current expectations, the performance management system had to reflect these changes. In addition, it had to account for the managers' responsibility of ensuring that people who went through the assessment center (either for selection or for development) received the necessary development so that their performance would improve. Without appropriate follow-up, many of the benefits of the assessment center would have been diminished.

In the end the change in business strategy affected how the company recruited, hired, developed, and managed its people. These changes were made so that HRD could support a new business strategy and add value to the organization.

Resources and References

Bobrow, W. S., & Leonards, J. S. (1997). Development and validation of an assessment center during organizational change. *Journal of Social Behavior and Personality, 12*(5), 217–236 (a special issue, edited by R. E. Riggio and B. T. Mayes and titled *Assessment Centers: Research & Applications*).

Cascio, W., & Silbey, V. (1982). Utility of the assessment center as a selection device. *Journal of Applied Psychology, 65,* 135–138.

Gaugler, B. B., Rosenthal, D. B., Thornton, G. C., III, & Bentson, C. (1987). Meta-analysis of assessment center validity. *Journal of Applied Psychology, 72*(3), 493–511.

Kudisch, J. D., Rotolo, C. T., Avis, J. M., Fallon, J. D., Roberts, F. E., Rollier, T. J., & Thibodeaux, H. F., III. (1998, May). *A preliminary look at assessment center practices world-wide: What's hot and what's not.* Paper presented at the 26th annual meeting of the International Congress on Assessment Center Methods, Pittsburgh, PA.

Spychalski, A. C., Quiñones, M. A., Gaugler, B. B., & Pohley, K. (1997). A survey of assessment center practices in organizations in the United States. *Personnel Psychology, 50,* 71–90.

considered for job opportunities. These efforts do not guarantee jobs to internal candidates, but commit assistance to employees in finding available jobs based on their knowledge, skills, and abilities.

One software vehicle that supports an organization's commitment to promoting from within is a system that evaluates a job seeker's knowledge, skills, ability, and education and matches those characteristics with a position requisition that includes job specifications and requirements. Such systems support staff members by making it easy for them to retrieve employment data on thousands of applicants.

These software systems typically use resume-scanning hardware, optical character recognition (OCR), and other imaging technologies to capture an on-line image of an original resume. Critical elements of the resume are extracted and stored in a resume database.

Experts familiar with a position's requirements, tasks, technology, and other features help to develop selection criteria. These criteria are then used by the system to determine whether a resume matches those requirements and any additional characteristics desired by the hiring authority. In most cases, instant on-line access to the resume and a summary are available.

The resume summary is composed of key information extracted directly from the resume:

- Contact information, including name, address, and telephone number
- Work history, including dates, organizations, job titles, and cumulative years of experience in given positions
- Educational information, including degrees, schools, grades, and year(s) of graduation
- Specific skills

Someone in the organization's HRD unit creates an on-line requisition for a particular job. The requisition contains specific criteria for the skills and experience desired by the hiring authority. The information from the job requisition is integrated with that from the on-line job descriptions for position requirements and experience factors. Then an HRD specialist conducts a search for a prioritized list of resumes that best meet the specifications stated in the requisition and in the job description. Such a search requires the use of a search button or mouse-activated hardware. This procedure allows the specialist to search through thousands of resumes in less than an hour to find all qualified candidates for the job.

On-line faxing to hiring authorities allows these authorities to review resumes immediately and to make decisions within hours of receipt. Because the on-line system builds in additional tracking fields, the HRD staff and managers can quickly access data on current search activity and applicant status. Personnel in the HRD unit find such tracking features helpful in several ways:

- They can fill positions quickly because requests are not lost in piles of paper.
- They can more easily address affirmative action plan requirements as well as the requirements of hiring authorities.
- They can identify a candidate's continued availability when he or she might fill any of several positions.

Another advantage is that as new resumes are scanned into the database, they can be automatically matched to open requisitions. Within twenty-four hours of resume receipt, any resume that matches an open requisition is highlighted for the HRD recruiter. Other valuable products can be created with the software as well: automatically generated offer and rejection letters and many standard and ad hoc management reports. Access to all these features means that HRD performance is faster and better and line managers can have qualified people on the job faster.

When to Use

Use of the automated resume tracking system is appropriate under the following circumstances:

- When there is a need to eliminate manual and extremely paper-intensive processes for reviewing, sorting, categorizing, and filing resumes
- When there is a need to match quickly applicable knowledge, skills, and abilities required for a job with candidate pools
- When there is a need to identify the number of resumes received and people hired using various kinds of recruitment, job fairs, advertising, and other sourcing efforts
- When there is a need to meet affirmative action plan requirements and capture equal employment opportunity (EEO) data (note that good automated systems generate postage-paid return cards to all applicants for tracking purposes)
- When there is a need to reduce advertising costs (note that the tracking system has the ability to assess quickly a database of qualified people, including internal candidates and former applicants, for open positions so that costly advertisements can be avoided or delayed)
- When there is a requirement to measure and improve on the time required to fill a position, the cost per hire, and other employment measures

- When there is a need for management to have many just-in-time updates on the status of any search

Case Study

Because of a false media report about the closing of a hospital, the hospital staff turnover increased to a painful level. The hospital's HRD unit was asked to fill approximately sixty positions immediately to ensure that satisfactory care could be provided to patients and to compensate for the resignations.

The HRD personnel reviewed current openings in nursing positions to ascertain areas of specialty as well as the number of regional open positions and to set priorities for recruitment efforts. Two searches of the resume computer database were conducted for staff nurses. The first search focused on finding resumes of candidates who had indicated an interest in working in the specific region involved; this fact was designated by a predetermined source code. A second search was conducted to identify resumes received with no specific regional preference. Out of the thousands of resumes stored in the database, for both internal and external applicants, approximately 170 resumes were determined to represent potential candidates.

Targeted advertising efforts resulted in the receipt of an additional fifty resumes. These fifty were coded and scanned into the database, allowing quick retrieval. Because source codes identified whether each resume came as a result of television advertisements, radio spots, journals, job fairs, college recruitment, walk-ins, internal employee interest, or other referral sources or whether it was a hot-line response or an unsolicited fax, the HRD personnel were able to determine the cost-effectiveness of each recruitment effort. The HRD assistants contacted all potential candidates by phone and prescreened them for current interest, regional and hospital preference, hour and shift preferences, and specialty areas of experience. This initial effort was achieved within a seven-day period.

The hiring authorities for the nursing positions met with HRD personnel to review resumes with prescreened information; the goal was to leave with a plan for scheduling interviews. Sixty-two staff nurses were hired within a three-month period—approximately twice the usual hire rate.

Use of the automated resume tracking system was the key component in providing a quick initial response to the HRD unit's customers (line managers in nursing). By automatically identifying and sorting resumes by specialty skills and experience, HRD personnel were able to respond very quickly to a serious need.

The ability to use source codes to track the cost-effectiveness of various recruiting efforts has long-term savings implications for the hospital. The HRD unit will know what works and what does not and will be better able to invest its time in expediting recruiting.

Resources and References

RESUMIX (890 Ross Drive, Sunnyvale, CA 94089, phone: 770-551-2650 or 408-744-3936, Web site: www.resumix.com). A skills management system.

Intervention Author

Eugene B. Kaminski
Director, Employment and Workforce Transitions
Detroit Medical Center
Employment Center
McLaughlin Hall
3740 John R.
Detroit, MI 48201
Phone: 313-966-7839
Fax: 313-966-7531

■ ■ ■ ■ ■ ■ CHALLENGE EDUCATION

	Business Unit	Process	Work Group	Individual
Level of Performance				
Establish	○	●	●	●
Improve	○	●	●	●
Maintain	○	●	●	●
Extinguish	○	●	●	●

Performance Change: Establish, Improve, Maintain, Extinguish

Alternative Names

Adventure education
Corporate experiential learning (CEL)

Definition

Challenge education is a process through which a learner constructs knowledge, skill, and value from direct experiences in specially designed indoor and outdoor environments. This intervention typically incorporates such activities as ropes courses, rock climbing, rappeling, sailing, rafting, and wilderness exploration.

Description

One of the roots of challenge education is outdoor education based on the philosophies of Jean-Jacques Rousseau in France, Johann Heinrich Pestalozzi in Switzerland, and John Dewey in the United States. Another root is survival training for seamen as practiced by Outward Bound, a group founded by Kurt Hahn in Wales during World War II. Worldwide expansion of this movement in the

1960s followed the establishment of an Outward Bound program in Colorado. Several other movements that have contributed to challenge education include somatic education, new games, counseling, and values clarification. Since the 1970s, challenge education has a become a major intervention in management and leadership development programs.

Most challenge education activities combine elements of training and therapy and are aimed at performance improvement. Participants engage in an intense activity that involves appropriate risk taking and relies on a combination of physical, emotional, intellectual, social, and spiritual elements. Typical activities incorporate physical challenges constructed from ropes and wood. These activities are divided into high- and low-ropes courses, depending on the height at which the physical structure for the activity is placed. Rock climbing, rappeling, and white-water rafting are other examples of deep experiences that help the participants to acquire knowledge and values in such soft skills as taking initiative, making decisions, trusting, and being accountable.

Contrary to the popular myth, raw experience does not guarantee learning. A key element in challenge education is group processing, which enables the participants to reflect on their experiences and share their insights with one another. A trained facilitator conducts these debriefing discussions midway through the activity and at the conclusion.

When to Use

Here are some criteria for identifying situations in which challenge education is an appropriate intervention:

- *When soft skills need to be learned:* The instructional objectives should relate to such areas as teamwork, communication, and interpersonal skills. The instructional topics should involve values, beliefs, attitudes, and emotions.
- *When self-awareness needs to be developed:* The participants need to increase awareness of dysfunctional behavior patterns, incorrect assumptions, and illogical stereotypes.
- *When facilitators are competent in the necessary skills:* The challenge education activities must be coordinated by facilitators who are capable of briefing, conducting, and debriefing the program in an effective and efficient manner.
- *When ample time is available:* The schedule must permit comfortable pacing of the activity and reflective discussion at the conclusion.
- *When the client and participants accept the validity of challenge education:* Both the client and the participants should value in-depth, holistic learning and should support

the philosophical basis of challenge education (that people can and do learn most effectively from hands-on experience).

• *When arrangements for measuring progress are appropriate:* Instruments and strategies used for collecting and presenting performance improvement data should maintain a balance between immediate and long-term results and between quantitative and qualitative outcomes.

Case Study

Although a particular client organization decided to jump on the knowledge management bandwagon, very few of its employees understood the concept and its rationale. Even fewer actually implemented the new information-archiving procedures that the organization adopted. Analysis of the client organization's situation identified deficits in both knowledge and motivation. Because of this unique combination of deficits, challenge education was chosen as the most appropriate intervention.

The Intervention

Labyrinth, a challenge education activity designed to explore the topic of knowledge management, was used in this intervention. Like other challenge education programs, *Labyrinth* requires the participants to work and learn in teams, undertake physical activities, and share their insights during the debriefing process. However, two features make *Labyrinth* different from the typical challenge education program: it uses electronic equipment and it is usually conducted indoors.

Labyrinth uses the Sentinel action learning device manufactured by Interel, Inc. The Sentinel system consists of eight free-standing tubular columns. Four of these columns contain vertical arrays of motion detectors that can be activated at a high or low level. The other four columns appear identical but are decoys without electronic components. The four active columns are arranged in a large room to create an invisible three-dimensional labyrinth. The other four columns are placed at strategic locations to mislead the participants about the layout of the labyrinth.

The participants are assembled in a separate room and provided with a science-fiction scenario involving the discovery of an alien labyrinth on a remote island. A team of five people is sent to the room with the labyrinth to retrieve a document within forty-five minutes. Certain areas of the labyrinth are radioactive, as indicated by an alarm sound. If the alarm is set off, all team members are to return to a safe zone before trying again. Members of the team cannot stay in the labyrinth room for more than seven minutes. After seven minutes they return to the base for a debriefing. Another five-member team is sent to the labyrinth room to continue the mission.

Through trial and error, the participants discover that they have to step over certain areas and crouch under other areas to avoid setting off the alarm. They also discover the importance of capturing and using the knowledge of the teams that participated earlier.

The Outcomes

Data were collected on performance outcomes both at the conclusion of the activity and three weeks later. In both cases group debriefing interviews were used as the data collection technique. During the debriefing that was conducted at the conclusion of the activity, the participants reflected on teamwork, communication, and interdependence. Their comments suggested the big-picture understanding of the principles and rationale for knowledge management. During the same debriefing, the participants demonstrated their intention to transfer knowledge by developing strategies for establishing and maintaining appropriate knowledge management systems in the workplace.

In the debriefing that took place three weeks later, the participants were asked to discuss how they had been able to use their new understanding in the workplace and what types of obstacles they faced in their application attempts. The comments from the participants confirmed that appropriate behaviors were being maintained.

Resources and References

Books and Articles

Agran, A., Garvey, D., Miner, T., & Priest, S. (1993). *Experience-based training and development programs* (3rd ed.). Boulder, CO: Association for Experiential Education.

Consalvo, C. M. (1993). *Experiential training activities for outside and in.* Amherst, MA: HRD Press.

Jackson, L., & Caffarella, R. (1994). *Experiential learning: A new approach.* San Francisco: Jossey-Bass.

Journal of Experiential Education (published three times per year [May, September, and December] by the Association for Experiential Education [AEE]).

Roland, C. C., Wagner, R. J., & Weigand, R. J. (1995). *Do it . . . and understand: The bottom line on corporate experiential learning.* Dubuque, IA: Kendall/Hunt.

Smith, T., Roland, C. C., Havens, M., & Hoyt, J. (1992). *The theory and practice of challenge education*. Dubuque, IA: Kendall/Hunt.

Association

Association for Experiential Education (AEE) (2305 Canyon Boulevard, Suite 100, Boulder, CO 80302-5651, phone: 303-440-8844, fax: 303-440-9581, Web site: http://www.princeton.edu/~rcurtis/aee.html). Founded in the early 1970s, AEE is a not-for-profit, international professional association with roots in adventure education. It is committed to the development, practice, and evaluation of experiential learning in all settings. Membership benefits include a subscription to the *Journal for Experiential Education* and to the AEE newsletter, reduced fees for regional and international conferences, discounts on books and directories published by AEE, and the opportunity to purchase outdoor gear and services at reduced prices.

Intervention Author

Sivasailam "Thiagi" Thiagarajan, Ph.D.
President
Workshops by Thiagi, Inc.
4423 East Trailridge Road
Bloomington, IN 47408-9633
Phone: 812-332-1478
E-mail: thiagi@thiagi.com
Web site: http://www.thiagi.com

Case Study Author

Boyd Watkins
Interel, Inc.
140 Carl Street
San Francisco, CA 94117
Phone: 415-566-0554

CHANGE STYLE
PREFERENCE MODELS

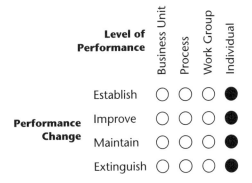

Level of Performance	Business Unit	Process	Work Group	Individual
Performance Change Establish	○	○	○	●
Improve	○	○	○	●
Maintain	○	○	○	●
Extinguish	○	○	○	●

Alternative Name

Change style indicators

Definition

Change style preference models help people to understand their own and others' preferences and reactions when experiencing organizational change. The underlying theory for such models is that people are able to handle significant changes—for example, reorganization, reengineering, layoffs, acquisitions and mergers, and company transfers—most effectively when they have a prior understanding of their own and others' patterns of response to such changes.

Description

Several models describe predictable responses to change; however, only three of them attempt to make a connection between individual personality preferences and reaction to change. Two of these three, the Creative Systems Theory by Charles Johnson and the Adaptive Innovative Model by Michael Kirton, actually address creativity and problem solving. The Change Style Indicator by Christopher Musselwhite is the only model that focuses specifically on the relationship between change and personality preference and is accompanied by a psychometrically sound assessment instrument.

Actual response to any change situation is always the choice of the individual, regardless of change style preference. However, change style preference is believed to reflect an aspect of personality, meaning that an individual may be, in effect, drawn to respond in a particular way, regardless of whether that response is the most effective choice at the time. Understanding this theory can be useful when navigating the waters of change that are so common in today's organizations.

The Change Style Indicator (CSI) is a self-assessment instrument designed to measure change style preference along a continuum of options. The score on this instrument places the respondent on a continuum of styles ranging from *conserver* to *originator*. A third style, *pragmatist*, occupies the middle of the continuum. The three styles represent distinct differences in approaches to change.

Conservers, on one end of the continuum, are characterized as preferring a gradual but continual approach to change. They also prefer the current circumstances over the unknown. The goal of the conserver is to use the organization's resources to best effect while preserving the existing system. When this approach is applied over time, the outcome can be significant change that does not threaten or disrupt the stability of the organization. Conservers can be thought of as representing the Total Quality Management (TQM) approach to change.

At the other end of the continuum are originators, who are characterized as preferring a quicker and more radical approach to change. If conservers represent TQM, then originators represent reengineering. When this approach is applied effectively, the outcome can be significant change that occurs quickly throughout the organization. Originators challenge existing organizational structures and promote fundamental systemic change.

Pragmatists, in the middle of the continuum, account for approximately 50 percent of the general population. On the one hand, they may appear to be reasonable, practical, agreeable, and flexible; on the other hand, they may appear to be noncommittal and indecisive. Pragmatists have a tendency to solve problems in ways that emphasize practical, workable outcomes; they focus more on results than on preserving or challenging organizational structure.

When to Use

Identifying people's change style preferences with an assessment instrument such as the CSI can be useful when the following change-related questions need to be answered:

- Why do some people appear to be threatened by change and intent on preserving the status quo?
- Why do some people appear constantly dissatisfied with the status quo and ready to challenge any existing paradigm?
- Why are some people reluctant to take even small, calculated risks while others seem eager to take dangerous, unexplored risks?
- Why are some people able to see both sides of an issue while others cannot?
- Why do some people respond so effectively to gradual, incremental change while others thrive on radical, systemic change?
- Why do some people appear unable to take a position in a change situation?

Case Study

In a typical reengineering effort, a core redesign team is selected to plan the reengineering strategy. Team members are generally selected because they are perceived to be open to change and are thought of as outside-the-box thinkers. People who are perceived to be resistant to change are generally excluded from membership, as it is assumed that they will obstruct team efforts. The subsequent implementation of the reengineering effort typically results in interpersonal dynamics that attribute "good" or "bad" and "right" or "wrong" behaviors to people, depending on the degree to which they are willing to go along with proposed changes.

In a large health care company, the CEO had initiated a reengineering effort that was meeting with considerable employee resistance. Soon after arriving in her new job, the CEO hired several new people for the senior executive team; all of the new executives, including the CEO, came from industries other than health care.

The CEO and the senior executives believed that the radical change created by the reengineering effort was logical and necessary. They perceived the resistance to be coming from employees who just did not like change, even when that change was obviously better for the organization. They further believed that employees were expending more effort in resisting the change than would be required to implement the change.

However, interviews with the employees who were perceived as resisting the change revealed a very different perspective. It turned out that this change effort was just the latest in a series that dated back to the CEO's arrival. The employees who were interviewed believed that the CEO and the senior executives had some good ideas, and these employees were willing to engage in some level of change. They described the problem to be too many changes at once with no follow-through and integration. Typical comments ran like this:

She announces a new way of doing something, and we start to implement that idea. But she's not realistic about the time and resources we need. Then, just as we're making progress, she dumps that idea or comes up with another. We don't have time to iron out the wrinkles before another change hits us. All of these changes have significant impact on our day-to-day effectiveness, but she just doesn't seem to understand that. Here we are trying to implement the changes and still keep up with our daily work so that the place doesn't fall apart, and we get blamed for the failure of the change effort because we're "resistant."

After the interviews, a half-day workshop was recommended and conducted for the top hundred managers in the organization. The Change Style Indicator was introduced, and each manager completed and scored the CSI. The managers discussed the need for a balanced perspective when dealing with organizational change and the value of hearing and respecting input from conservers, pragmatists, and originators. It was discovered that in the executive team, 45 percent of the members were originators, 40 percent were pragmatists, and 15 percent were conservers. The managers also learned that these percentages differed greatly from those of the general population, in which 25 percent were originators, 25 percent were conservers, and 50 percent were pragmatists.

Through the dialogue that followed, the managers significantly reframed the conflict that had developed over the organizational changes. The individual managers abandoned the notion that they were "right" and those with differing viewpoints were "wrong," and they began to respect and value opinions other than their own.

As a result of this intervention the managers reconsidered their approach to the reengineering effort. They clarified their justification of the effort, and they addressed people's concerns about the details of implementation. Subsequent discussions about the reengineering effort focused on the organizational benefits and problems it created rather than on interpersonal conflicts.

Resources and References

Johnston, C. M. (1994). *Pattern and reality: A brief introduction to creative systems theory.* Seattle, WA: ICD (Institute for Creative Development) Press.

Kirton, M. J. (1989). *Adaptors and innovators: Styles of creativity and problem-solving.* New York: Routledge.

Musselwhite, C. (1997, Winter). Measuring preference for change. *Creative Connections Newsletter,* pp. 5–8.

Musselwhite, C., & Ingram, R. (1996). *Change Style Indicator facilitator's guide.* San Francisco: Jossey-Bass.

Intervention Authors

W. Christopher Musselwhite, Ed.D.
President
Discovery Learning, Inc.
P.O. Box 41320
Greensboro, NC 27404
Phone: 336-272-9530
Fax: 336-273-4090
E-mail: DLI@discoverync.com

Robyn P. Ingram, Ed.D.
Partner
Associates for Psychotherapy
604 Green Valley Road
Suite 408
Greensboro, NC 27408
Phone: 336-854-4450

■ ■ ■ ■ ■ ■ COGNITIVE ERGONOMICS

	Business Unit	Process	Work Group	Individual
Level of Performance				
Establish	●	●	●	●
Performance Change Improve	●	●	●	●
Maintain	●	●	●	●
Extinguish	●	●	●	●

Alternative Names

Facilities design
Workplace design
Ergonomics

Definition

Cognitive ergonomics involves intervening in the physical workplace to improve both individual and group performance. It employs both physical and cognitive principles (such as preventing physical discomfort and random noise from distracting performers) to ensure that the workplace configuration, equipment, and furnishings facilitate employee performance.

Description

The invisible process of mental work, or thinking, is the first step of performance; it precedes the visible process of physical work. Interference with physical work is now widely recognized as a problem. The solution to this problem is offered by *physical ergonomics:* improving the design of furnishings and equipment and then training people to adjust furnishings and equipment to their physical frames.

However, interference with mental work—which tends to involve sensory interruptions—is a significant problem that is not yet widely acknowledged. The solution lies in *cognitive ergonomics.*

The environment affects thinking in a number of ways, exacting high performance costs when it creates interference. The sensory environment consists of the sensations, sights, and sounds that either help people to do their work or interfere with work. Knowledge workers are especially vulnerable to the sensory environment. Distractions coming from feelings (such as temperature fluctuations), sights (such as reflections on computer screens), and sounds (such as random noise from equipment and conversations) interfere with productive thinking. Poor environmental design can also have a major impact on team members' ability to think and work collaboratively.

Organizations now have an important opportunity to use what is known about the impact of the sensory environment on the quality of thinking. As the bulk of an organization's payroll goes toward purchasing knowledge work, this opportunity should not be missed.

Human performance is influenced by two major cognitive ergonomic variables: the type of mental work (routine or complex) involved and the employees' individual abilities to block out distractions (screening behavior). Routine mental work requires one kind of environment, whereas complex mental work requires another. In addition, because individuals vary in screening ability, they also vary in their need for supportive cognitive ergonomics.

It is important to realize that the attention capacity of the human mind is limited. When sensory distractions demand attention and consistently interrupt a train of thought, a person may be unable to provide value through complete, accurate, or innovative thinking. Reducing the need to screen distractions or providing workers with options for reducing distractions will improve the performance of knowledge workers.

In contrast, people who do routine work may not receive enough stimulation from their jobs. They may need distractions from the environment (such as interesting sights and sounds) to stay focused and productive. Employees who are understimulated may get up and wander around, looking for the stimulation that their work environment fails to provide.

The intervention begins with an initial question to performers: "What about your work environment gets in the way of doing your best work?" (For additional questions, see Exhibit 1, a sample data-gathering instrument that lists a number of questions that need to be asked in this first step.)

EXHIBIT 1. SAMPLE DATA-GATHERING INSTRUMENT FOR GROUP AND INDIVIDUAL ORAL INTERVIEWING.

Employee's name:
Title:

Job or Product

  1. What is your job? What do you produce?

  2. How do you do your job? (What physical actions are required to do your job and to produce the product for which you are responsible?)

  3. What percentage of your time is spent on routine work?

  4. What percentage is spent on complex work?

Furnishings and Equipment

  1. What furnishings and equipment do you need in order to do your job?

  2. What obstacles keep you from using furnishings and equipment to your best advantage?

  3. Are these obstacles stressful for you, either physically or emotionally?

  4. How do you handle the stress?

  5. What kind of support would help you to use furnishings and equipment most effectively?

Sensory Environment

  1. What elements of the sensory environment distract you and keep you from thinking as effectively as possible?

     • Lighting—what you see:

     • Sound—what you hear:

     • Temperature and air quality—what you feel and smell:

EXHIBIT 1. (CONTINUED).

2. Are these elements of the sensory environment stressful for you, either physically or emotionally?

3. How do you handle the stress?

4. What kind of support would help you to deal with the sensory environment most effectively?

Interactions with Others

1. For each of the following kinds of interactions with others, consider how often it occurs, where it occurs, and what obstacles keep you from using the interaction to your best advantage.

Chance encounters
- How often?

- Where?

- What obstacles get in your way?

Planned one-on-one meetings
- How often?

- Where?

- What obstacles get in your way?

Informal one-on-one meetings
- How often?

- Where?

- What obstacles get in your way?

Planned team meetings
- How often?

- Where?

- What obstacles get in your way?

EXHIBIT 1. (CONTINUED).

Informal team meetings
- How often?

- Where?

- What obstacles get in your way?

2. Are these interactions stressful for you, either physically or emotionally?

3. How do you handle the stress?

4. What kind of support would help you to interact with others most effectively?

General Issues
1. What is your greatest support need?

2. What is most important to you? What would you most like to see happen?

Procedures include the following:

- Assessing how the work environment places demands on people's attention, resulting in reduced productivity
- Directly gathering data from both groups and individuals about what interferes with performance
- Recommending changes in the work environment itself, such as changing where individuals or groups are located or changing furnishings and equipment (possibly with different furnishings and equipment for different individuals)
- Estimating costs
- Implementing solutions
- Monitoring the effectiveness of the implemented solutions

Immediate interventions to improve performance can include the following:

- Relocating work areas to improve interaction or to increase focus
- Providing areas to confer that have adequate privacy and work surface to spread out materials

- Moving equipment, resources, and activities that generate noise into a common area and screening that area to reduce noise and distractions
- Altering work spaces by reorienting seating toward or away from visual and auditory distractions
- Substituting higher panels to block distractions and aid focus
- Adding shelving and drawers to clear crowded work surfaces
- Providing adjustable task lighting and personal temperature controls (for example, small area fans and heaters)

When to Use

The use of cognitive ergonomics is an appropriate consideration under the following conditions:

- When there have been many complaints about the work area or its furnishings and equipment
- When individuals or groups are producing below expectations, either in quality or quantity
- When managers are saying that people need training in organization, time management, and self-management skills
- When people work independently despite the fact that they should be working collaboratively
- When there is a high level of irritability, friction, or conflict among work group members located in the same area
- When individuals frequently wander away from their work areas and socialize or take frequent or extended breaks and trips to vending machines, restrooms, and so on
- When there is a high incidence of lateness, absences, and illness (individual or work group)
- When people frequently work everywhere except in their assigned work areas (in conference rooms, cafeterias, at home, and so on)
- When a work area is crowded, cluttered, and noisy and work surfaces are piled high

Case Study

A department responsible for developing and tracking financial gifts to a very large academic institution had long suffered from an inadequate system that resulted in errors and poor-quality work. The manager had established a better work flow and data-processing system, which improved performance somewhat but problems remained. A needs assessment conducted by a performance technologist identified the following forms of interference from the work environment:

- Supervisors were too remote from visitors.
- Physical work flow patterns were poor, crisscrossing the work area.
- Too many distracting casual conversations took place in the open area.
- People who did data input work needed stimulation but not in-and-out traffic.
- People wasted time using the equipment.
- The image communicated by the crowded, messy office was too casual, unprofessional, and sloppy.
- Morale was negatively affected by crowded, noisy work conditions and dilapidated furnishings.

Before an intervention was designed, individual workers were interviewed and asked two questions: "What work do you need to do?" and, "What gets in the way of your doing it most easily?" Individuals were asked about specific needs concerning the following:

- The flow of work within and among work groups
- The types of work to be done (routine or complex)
- The furniture and equipment needed by groups and individuals
- The relative group and individual needs for interaction, for quiet, and for privacy
- Their individual screening tendencies

Intervention

Recognizing the nature and scale of the performance needs to be addressed, the performance technologist recommended an overall workplace redesign by a professional workplace designer. The performance technologist was careful to find a workplace designer who was knowledgeable about how the workplace affects human performance, in addition to the technical, economic, and aesthetic considerations of interior design.

The designer used the performance-based interview data provided by the performance technologist as the basic programming data for the redesign. The changes included relocating the supervisor's office, moving the four accountants into a quieter area together, moving the data-processing group out of the stream of traffic, using acoustic panels to reduce the noise levels, and adding spaces for meetings and discussions. The open work area was converted into private cubicles, people doing similar work were grouped together, and a pleasant break area was established.

When the staff members no longer had to adjust to workplace interference, their released energy was invested in producing the higher-quality work that the organization required. Employees were very proud of their new area and began dressing more professionally and taking greater pride in their work. The more organized look of their workplace resulted in the professional image they needed in order to showcase their increased potential.

Outcomes

Implementing the redesign required a day of downtime. The increase in output of accurate work was estimated at 20 percent. Turnover was decreased dramatically. Awareness of individual screening needs allowed those with high screening abilities who did routine work to listen to music with headphones and to take conversations to an outside courtyard. Those with low screening abilities became aware of how easily distracted they were; they relinquished their window views to obtain quiet spaces in the rear of the office.

The manager also reported an unanticipated benefit: his staff members learned to be much more self-managing. They learned how to match their cognitive ergonomic needs with the type of work they did and to respect one another's differences. They identified time that was respected as quiet time; they communicated comfortably with one another about the frequency of interruptions they could comfortably handle, they used headphones and lowered voices to muffle telephone noise, and they held meetings in the new common work spaces. These changes reduced both work delays and infighting.

Resources and References

Card, S. K ., Moran, T. P., & Newell, A. (1986). An engineering model of human performance. In K. R. Roff, L. Kaufman, & J. P. Thomas (Eds.), *Handbook of perception and human performance* (Vol. 2). New York: Wiley.

DeMarco, T., & Lister, T. (1987). *Peopleware.* New York: Dorset House.

Smith, P., & Kearny, L. (1994). *Creating workplaces where people can think.* San Francisco: Jossey-Bass.

Steele, F., & Becker, F. (1995). *Workplace by design.* San Francisco: Jossey-Bass.

Wineman, J. (1986). The importance of office design to organizational effectiveness and productivity. In J. Wineman (Ed.), *Behavioral issues in office design* (pp. xvi–xvii). New York: Van Nostrand Reinhold.

Intervention Authors

Lynn Kearny
Consultant
Human Performance Improvement
5379 Broadway
Oakland, CA 94618
Phone: 510-547-1896
Fax: 510-601-7480
E-mail: lkearny@sprintmail.com

Phyl Smith
Designer and Consultant
Working Spaces
1228 Montgomery Street
San Francisco, CA 94133
Phone/fax: 415-421-6139
E-mail: Pswrkgspce@aol.com

▪ ▪ ▪ ▪ ▪ ▪ COMMUNICATION

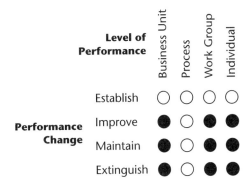

Level of Performance	Business Unit	Process	Work Group	Individual
Establish	○	○	○	○
Performance Change Improve	●	○	●	●
Maintain	●	○	●	●
Extinguish	●	○	●	●

Definition

Organizational *communication* is an interchange of ideas, opinions, information, instructions, and the like, presented personally or impersonally, by symbol or signal, for the purpose of attaining the goals of the organization (Rosenblatt, Cheatham, & Watt, 1977).

Description

What we now call the science of communication resulted from the combination of at least four lines of inquiry:

- Message content, structure, and audience effects
- Propaganda and media effects
- Transmission and reception of information
- Group dynamics and the processes by which meaning is created and shared

Throughout the twentieth century, each of these ways of looking at communication has left its mark on organizational communications. Influential work at Bell Labs in 1949 assumed that *encoders* design messages that influence passive *receivers* and that the purpose is to send a message with low interference and high clarity. With the onset of developmental psychology in the middle of the century, the classic communication theory was embellished with personal or organizational values and ways in which such values may affect individuals' reception of message cues. In the last decade, however, the paradigm has shifted significantly to viewing communication as the process through which people use messages to create, maintain, and alter social order, relationships, and identities.

The underlying principle that ties communication to performance in organizations is that people develop, change, and use verbal and nonverbal information to guide behavior and to create a shared social reality. The wide range of interventions used to improve performance within an organization can be categorized into the following types:

- *System interventions:* These interventions involve mechanisms to change the direction, amount, frequency, availability, and usability of exchanged information.
- *Interactive interventions:* These interventions influence direct or indirect communication patterns.
- *Message campaign interventions:* These interventions create unifying themes that direct performance. At their best, they are based on declared values that form the basis for all information dispersed throughout the organization. In their most limited form, they are used simply to create awareness.

When to Use

The process of choosing, designing, and implementing any communication intervention must be completed carefully and with a great deal of thought, as any type of communication effort leaves a residue of interaction patterns, experiences, ideas, and feelings that become a part of subsequent encounters. The assumption underlying a communication intervention is that the practitioner believes current organizational performance to be related to a communication issue of some kind, such as information flow, cross-functional cooperation, or conveyance of organizational values.

A communication intervention is best used under the following circumstances.

When a True Communication Issue Is Identified

Communication is invariably cited by organizational members as a generic area in need of improvement, so the practitioner should use methods to determine whether a specific communication concern is involved. A true communication need is indicated when it can be determined that a change in information flow or availability or in communication style or an increase in awareness or enthusiasm for an idea will affect behavior *even when the actual content of a message is not substantially changed.* For example, if *communicating* the need for downsizing in a certain way would help to maintain performance, even though the plan to downsize was not changed, then a communication intervention is necessary.

When There Is Willingness to Make Authentic Changes

Too often communication interventions are undertaken without real commitment on the part of those who must implement those interventions. A practitioner must look carefully at the implications of choosing a particular communication intervention, such as the organizational changes required, to ensure that the organization is willing to make all the necessary concessions.

When There Is Willingness to Receive Feedback

If an organization's leaders truly want to change the current forms of communication, they must be willing to accept employee feedback about the change. They also must be willing to persist in the change and not abandon it, even if employee reactions make them extremely uncomfortable. They should be helped to realize that all reactions—from vocal protests to absolute silence—provide useful information that is worthy of attention.

Case Study

The Chemistry Division of a nuclear power plant was identified in a report issued by the Nuclear Regulatory Commission (NRC) as having "performance and morale problems" that were resulting in chemical testing errors. The report generated a great deal of attention to the division and an enormous amount of pressure on the division manager to revise current work processes and improve performance.

The Chemistry Division is the heart of the plant's twenty-four-hour operation. The tests conducted there are vital to the safety of all personnel and the surrounding environment. No plant operation can be started, stopped, or continued without the completion of the Chemistry Division's daily tasks. Another complication is that the time constraints involved in processing and completing those tasks and the division's numerous work shifts do not allow for thorough or regular interaction between employees.

The division manager believed that poor communication and low levels of trust between the lab technicians and supervisors were causing the performance problems. *Communication* had not been carefully defined, nor had a firm project goal (other than "improve communication") been established. The manager consulted a communication consultant, who set out to determine the current state of both interpersonal and system communications by interviewing every division employee (four direct report managers, ten labor supervisors, and forty chemical technicians) and analyzing the flow of work orders.

It was important to interview everyone in the division because of the high level of distrust between individuals as well as between union and nonunion members. The consultant obtained the division manager's commitment to listen to all feedback—no matter how brutal. He also encouraged all employees to be honest, as all comments would remain anonymous. To increase the reliability of the data that were obtained, the consultant spent two months observing organizational communication behaviors to confirm these data.

Interview questions were designed to address the following issues:

- *Information flow:* Did people have the information necessary to do the work to the performance level expected?
- *Organizational loyalty:* Were people and their opinions valued so that participation and hard work were encouraged?
- *Performance expectations:* Did people understand the division's goals and believe in their roles in the division?

Findings revealed that there were serious problems in all three areas: (1) people did not feel that they had adequate or reliable information for making decisions; (2) they did not feel valued, and attrition was extremely high in the organization; and (3) they did not have a clear idea of the division's goals or their own roles in attaining those goals.

To address the communication-oriented issues, a multifaceted communication strategy was created from the following interventions.

System Intervention

The position of *supervising coordinator* was created, the responsibilities of which were to receive work requests, distribute projects equally between the labs, handle client concerns, and recommend work changes to increase client satisfaction. In addition, a Web page was created and promoted within the plant so that employees could review and print status reports.

These two changes yielded important benefits:

- The chemistry lab technicians no longer had to interrupt their work to answer phone calls.
- Information to clients was increased.
- Work was distributed more fairly in the labs, thereby reducing the number of union grievances filed.

Another positive outcome was the use of the Web page to recognize one employee per month for exceptional work or a project completed in addition to regular work goals.

Interaction Intervention

The division managers and supervisors were instructed in effective listening and conflict resolution techniques so that they could develop better relationships with their colleagues and direct reports. Also, meeting guidelines were established to encourage participation and to include time for cooperative problem solving. In addition, a schedule of regular, division-wide meetings was established to assemble all personnel for the purpose of sharing information and answering questions.

Message Campaign Intervention

A division communication policy was established to delineate communication values and to incorporate those values into the frequency, distribution, content, and style of all communications. A group of employees designed and garnered support for this policy and then saw to it that the policy was used in conveying all information within the division. The purpose of this intervention was to ensure that the different units within the division were given equal and consistent information and to unify the different work of the units under common objectives.

In addition, many performance issues—an unclear and subjective performance management process, career advancement problems, lack of a reward structure that was acceptable to the union, and so on—were identified. After working with a performance technologist, the communication consultant was able to provide recommendations in these areas in order to provide the division with a holistic performance improvement strategy.

After six months the number of testing errors decreased to a rate considered to be within normal levels, prompting the NRC to commend the efforts of the Chemistry Division in improving work-related communications. They also recommended that other plant divisions conduct similar research or improvement projects.

Opening up lines of communication by no means *solved* all of the performance-related problems, but it did provide an interactive structure that allows employees to work on issues. For instance, *work committees* within the division are currently creating a performance management and appraisal program intended to increase trust and the perceived value of employees' work contributions. Also, fewer grievances have been filed now that supervisors are more willing to listen to and deal with issues as they are communicated.

The overall communication policy that has been developed ensures that every employee has a protocol for the following tasks:

- Providing performance feedback to subordinates
- Submitting ideas for improving the work process
- Tracking the results of solutions proposed by the work committees
- Updating goals and lab status at the end of every work cycle

Finally, a recent survey of clients indicates that there has been an increase in understanding of lab projects and lab procedures as well as an increase in the belief that work is being completed accurately. Not only have current communication patterns helped to improve performance, but the new patterns have also laid the foundation for addressing other issues as they arise.

Resources and References

Books

Heath, R., & Bryant, J. (1992). *Human communication theory and research.* Hillsdale, NJ: Hove & London.

Infante, D., Rancer, A., & Womack, D. (1993). *Building communication theory.* Prospect Heights, IL: Waveland Press.

Jabin, F., Putnam, L., Putnam, K., & Porter, L. (Eds.). (1987). *Handbook of organizational communication: An interdisciplinary perspective.* Newbury Park, CA: Sage.

Knapp, M., & Miller, G. (Eds.). (1985). *Handbook of interpersonal communication.* Newbury Park, CA: Sage.

Rosenblatt, S., Cheatham, T., & Watt, J. (1977). *Communication in business.* Upper Saddle River, NJ: Prentice Hall.

Association

International Association of Business Communicators (Web sites: www.iabc.com and www.iabc.com/products). Practical manuals on different kinds of communication strategies for organizations.

Intervention Author

Joy Swenson
President
j. Swenson Communications
10 Atlantic Avenue, Suite 802
Long Beach, CA 90802
Phone: 562-436-2770
E-mail: swensonco@aol.com

▪ ▪ ▪ ▪ ▪ ▪ COMPENSATION SYSTEMS

Level of Performance	Business Unit	Process	Work Group	Individual
Establish	○	○	○	○
Performance Change — Improve	○	○	●	●
Maintain	○	○	●	●
Extinguish	○	○	○	○

Definition

The term *compensation* refers to monetary and in-kind payments that organizations make for work completed on their behalf. It typically includes direct pay and benefits such as medical insurance, disability income protection, family income protection on death, retirement contributions, and employee stock ownership plans.

An organization's *compensation system*—the system by which it makes monetary and in-kind payments—usually reflects differences in the fundamental market value of the different kinds of work being performed. The compensation system identifies rules on hiring rates and promotion increases; defines promotion, demotion, and lateral movement; and specifies the timing of and reasons for pay increases.

Description

Organized compensation systems began in the 1940s with the work of Edward N. Hay of the Pennsylvania Company and with Samuel L. H. Burk and Eugene J. Benge of the Atlantic Refining Company. These people did the research that resulted in the first job evaluation plan. Hay, Burk, and Benge theorized that the economic value of work is related to four factors: (1) skill, (2) effort, (3) responsibility, and (4) working conditions. When two jobs are similar with regard to three factors, but one requires a higher level of knowledge or performance on the fourth factor, that job will require a higher wage to draw labor. This theory is the basis for grading systems, which are used to determine pay ranges for jobs.

Today large organizations usually have elaborate compensation programs. For the performance technologist who works primarily with large organizations, use of this intervention is limited. But for those working with smaller organizations, establishing or modifying a compensation system may prove to be valuable.

Step 1: Describing the Work

The first step in creating a compensation system is to describe the work of each job so that it can be related to similar work in the labor market. Then the relationship between the work and that of other jobs in the organization can be documented.

Each job is described in a way that distinguishes it from other jobs. Good job descriptions are written simply and contain a general statement of job responsibilities. For example, the general statement for an accountant might read, "Performs accounting functions according to generally accepted accounting principles."

The brief statement is then followed by a listing of specific responsibilities associated with the job, such as, for the accountant, classifying expenses, trial closings, producing statements of income and expense, analyzing accounts, and so on. The list consists of concrete tasks and allows the reader or performer to distinguish the job in question from other, related ones. In this case, for example, the job of accountant is readily distinguishable from that of bookkeeper or controller. The list does not include philosophical statements about how the work is performed. In addition, it is not an exhaustive list. But it does give the reader or performer a good understanding of what the job incumbent accomplishes (and, by implication, what he or she does not do).

Usually a job description includes sections on other compensable factors, such as required skills: for example, the abilities to communicate effectively (both in writing and orally), to solve problems, to organize and coordinate the work of others, and to manage conflict.

Also included in the job description are the working conditions and the bona fide occupational qualifications—the minimum qualifications that a candidate usually possesses in order to perform satisfactorily, such as the possession of a certified public accountant (CPA) certificate.

Step 2: Discovering How Similar Jobs Are Paid

The second step is to use the job description to find out how similar jobs are paid in the market. There are many excellent salary surveys that offer information about the prevailing wage for a given job. It is important to have a good job description for this purpose; job titles are usually inadequate because they rarely match.

Step 3: Determining How to Price the Job in the Organization

The third step is to determine how the job will be priced in the organization. There are two major methods:

- *Direct market pricing of jobs:* This method, which is useful if there are few jobs, consists of finding salary surveys that provide information on the jobs and obtaining an average of the rates paid. This average becomes the target rate for a fully experienced job incumbent.
- *Job grading:* This method uses systems that present a set of core jobs ranked according to the jobs' perceived internal equity. These jobs are market priced and are arrayed in order of their rankings so that a statistical relationship between the rankings and the market price can be derived. A midpoint value is established for each rank. The midpoints should be highly correlated with the market values for the core jobs. All other jobs are related in responsibility to the core jobs, and their values are derived from their relationships (higher than or lower than).

Step 4: Establishing Pay for Groups of Jobs

This step consists of establishing the rate of pay for groups of jobs. A range of rates is built around the market rate, so that the *market* is the target average paid rate for the employees in that job. A range of 20 percent on either side of the midpoint is typical, but ranges can vary depending on the market. The minimum should allow the hiring of entry-level employees; the midpoint should be the target rate for most employees, as it is the market rate; and the maximum should allow recognition of the higher economic value of certain employees who have made extraordinary contributions to the organization.

Step 5: Establishing Rules for Hiring, Promoting, Laterally Transferring, Rehiring, and So On

In this step, rules for hiring rates, promotions, lateral transfers, and rehires are established based on the grading system. Rules for merit or seniority increases define how an employee will move through the wage or salary range and should relate to the organization's philosophy of what it intends to reward. The rules should be established in such a way that those employees who accomplish the tasks achieve a competitive rate for their work. This method helps ensure that those employees will be retained.

Benefit decisions can also help to retain employees. Several relatively new benefit categories related to quality-of-life issues have become popular recently. These benefits include flexible schedules, group rates on insurance (such as homeowners, automobile, and long-term care), part-time options, telecommuting options (working from home), child care, financial planning services, errand services, employee activities, recognition events, discounts for employees, and counseling services. Rules regulating the use of these newer forms of benefits need to be included in the compensation system as well.

Organizations that are small or cash poor may not be able to compete with direct wages for talent. Thus they frequently compensate employees with other benefits, such as improved or flexible working conditions (hours, dress code, access to resources, exciting work) and stock or company ownership opportunities.

Step 6: Reviewing Wage and Salary Ranges Annually

This step consists of looking at wage and salary ranges annually to ensure that they maintain a competitive position. Individual employee rates usually do not change automatically; instead, when performance is reviewed the rates are set according to the organization's pay philosophy.

When to Use

The general principles of a compensation system can be used informally when employees other than owners are hired. A more formal system may have to be adopted when several employees doing the same work are hired and the organization has been in existence for several years.

A formal system is useful in explaining differences in pay to employees and in determining whether there are inequities based on prohibited discrimination (sex, race, religious affiliation, or disability, for example). A formal system can help in constructing responses when an employee says something like, "Why is my pay lower than his? I do the same thing," or, "I've been here longer; why does he get paid more than I do?"

A formal system is also useful when recruiting programs are adopted because they give newly hired employees an idea of how their pay relates to that of others inside and outside the organization, how their pay will change in the future, and what their promotional opportunities are.

Case Study

The following case is typical of the use of compensation as a performance improvement intervention in small organizations. A small consulting firm was founded by two moneyed partners, neither of whom had skills or interest in management. However, both possessed a great deal of technical expertise and knowledge of the businesses run by their clients, Wall Street brokerages. They had a successful formula for providing feedback and performance indicators to these clients.

For six years after founding the company, the partners went without salaries and paid their employees comparatively low salaries. Then they called on the services of a performance technologist to help them improve their processes and procedures. As a result, they created several new products, got out of debt, began to pay themselves, and grew their staff to twenty-five employees.

The Problem

During an organization-wide meeting, several complaints were raised. Employees felt that compensation was not fair. In addition, the owners were displeased with the level of initiative shown by some employees; the vital energy displayed a few years before seemed to have been replaced with malaise and an attitude of "you owe me."

After the meeting the controller and performance technologist conducted research that showed that the organization's rate of pay and commission structure were determined on a case-by-case basis, resulting in several inequities:

- The squeaky wheels were given more attention.
- Women had to fight to receive the same pay awarded their male colleagues.
- Bonus payments were made periodically when the company did well, but they were unpredictable, were not tied to individual performance in any way, and did not affect future performance.

The Intervention

The solution was to design a compensation program that met the owners' needs while addressing the employees' concerns about fairness and predictability. The performance technologist held a meeting with employee representatives and developed a list of fourteen questions that employees wanted answered, including such items as, "How is my rate of pay determined?" and, "How do I get a promotion here?" There were also questions about how the *marketplace* was determined, as some jobs were generic (that of programmer, for example) and others were specific to the Wall Street firms. In addition, employees wanted to know whether additional compensation should be provided as new clients were added to individuals' workloads.

Subsequently, the performance technologist worked with a compensation expert to develop a compensation program. They based their work on the list of employee questions, and the resulting program accomplished the following:

- It addressed the owners' need to improve performance through compensation (in this case, by removing the perceived arbitrariness of pay).
- It established a compensation plan that addressed the employees' needs to understand how they were paid and how they could be paid more in the future.
- It was based on real data from employer sources rather than on information from advertisements and the Internet.

The final program included the following elements:

- Communication of the compensation plan to all employees
- Training for supervisors in giving feedback and performance evaluations
- A written plan with published ranges of pay
- A means for the owners to determine bonuses based on company performance

The intervention was implemented only with some difficulty. One of the founders was concerned that a compensation system would make employees feel entitled to raises and take away his right to reward people liberally for helping the organization to grow. The solution was (1) to limit the population affected by the program to those in generic jobs (administrative and programming positions) and (2) to write the compensation plan in language that conveyed the one founder's intent.

As a result of implementing the compensation system, management received fewer complaints about money and employee morale increased. The organization grew and substantial bonuses were given based on company growth. Innovation and hard work were amply rewarded. Employees who remained uncomfortable with an entrepreneurial environment left gradually, but a cadre of highly motivated and energetic employees remained. In addition, the founder who had been concerned was no longer presented with requests for pay raises without substantiating evidence of merit.

Resources and References

Books

Armstrong, M., & Brown, A. (1995). *The job evaluation handbook*. London: Institute of Personnel & Development.

Henrici, S. B. (1980). *Salary management for the nonspecialist*. New York: AMACOM.

Schuster, J. R., & Zingheim, P. K. (1996). *The new pay: Linking employee and organizational performance*. San Francisco: Jossey-Bass.

Salary Survey Sources

The following sources offer numerous surveys covering both general and special labor markets.

William M. Mercer, Inc. (1500 Meidinger Tower, Louisville, KY 40202, phone: 800-333-3070). Financial services, health care, and information services.

Watson Wyatt Data Services (218 Route 17 North, Rochelle Park, NJ 07662, phone: 201-843-1177). General labor markets and many industry and geographical breakouts.

Hay Group (The Wanamaker Building, 100 Penn Square East, Philadelphia, PA 19103, phone: 215-861-2000, E-mail: marketing_NAmerica@ hay-group.com). Information services, hospitals, banking.

Associations

Most states have an employers' association that supports member employers with excellent information on salary trends in local areas and on legislative issues.

American Compensation Association (P.O. Box 29312, Phoenix, AZ 85038-9312, phone: 602-922-2020). Courses and numerous educational publications.

International Foundation of Employee Benefit Plans, 18700 W. Buemound Road (P.O. Box 1270, Brookfield, WI 53008-1270, phone: 414-786-6700). Courses and publications.

Intervention Author

Carolyn J. Beeman
Director of Compensation Planning
Detroit Medical Center
4201 St. Antoine
Detroit, MI 48201
Phone: 313-745-5063
Fax: 313-745-0993

▪ ▪ ▮ ▮ ▮ ▮ COMPETENCY MODELING

Level of Performance	Business Unit	Process	Work Group	Individual
Establish	○	○	●	●
Performance Change Improve	○	○	●	●
Maintain	○	○	●	●
Extinguish	○	○	●	●

Alternative Names

Competency-based performance improvement
Competency-based performance management
Competency-based human resource management

Definition

Competency modeling is the practice of identifying or demonstrating the use of the characteristics held and consistently used by exemplary performers. In specific contexts it includes illustrating the level of efficiency and effectiveness needed by all performers if they are to achieve exemplary performance outputs or results.

Description

Competency modeling started more than twenty-five years ago with the work of David McClelland and others who were interested in the nature of *human intelligence,* factors that contributed to it, and how to measure it. McClelland believed that human ability was not accurately measured by "intelligence tests" of the day.

Instead, he advanced the notion that successful performance depended on how well individuals used their numerous characteristics or traits, both singularly and in combination with one another, in order to perform successfully.

Since McClelland's initial work, practitioners have interpreted competency terms and practices in a variety of ways and with varying degrees of success. Terms that are commonly used in connection with competency modeling and their definitions are as follows:

- *Competency:* Any characteristic that an individual uses correctly, either singularly or in combination with other characteristics, to perform fully successfully (effectively and efficiently). Competencies include knowledge, skills, thought patterns, mind-sets, ways of thinking, and so forth.
- *Behavioral indicators:* Behaviors that signify that a performer is appropriately using a competency in a performance context. Behavioral indicators are identified for each competency definition or statement.
- *Competency model:* A model that includes the competencies needed to achieve fully successful or exemplary performance within the context of existing environmental constraints.
- *Job output:* A product or service that an employee produces for or renders to a customer, client, or coworker.
- *Job task:* A unit of work that contributes, either entirely or in part, to the achievement of one or more job outputs. Performers use their competencies to perform tasks, the successful completion of which results in expected or desired outputs or results.
- *Fully successful performer:* One who achieves, consistently and within the context of existing environmental constraints, all the required job outputs or results in a manner that meets or exceeds established quality requirements.
- *Exemplary performer:* One who performs consistently and within the context of existing environmental constraints, in a manner that exceeds expectations with regard to outputs, quality, or success.

A variety of competency and competency modeling research practices have evolved over the past thirty years. The choice of practice appears to depend on the use that is made of the competencies and the degree of reliability and validity that are needed in application. The foundation research method, created and perfected by McClelland and his associates, consists of using behavioral-event interviews (BEIs) to collect competency data (Boyatzis, 1986; Dubois, 1993). When BEI data are scientifically analyzed and reported, the analysis outputs result in competency models with high reliability and validity, assuming that the job requirements remain stable once the competencies have been researched. Research based on BEIs facilitates the identification of those competencies used by exemplary performers in outperforming fully successful performers.

Figure 1 illustrates the distinctions between the competencies of an exemplary performer and those of a fully successful performer. The circle on the left represents the competencies of an exemplary performer (EC) identified during a BEI. The circle on the right represents the competencies of a fully successful performer (X) identified during a BEI. The section where the circles intersect represents the competencies used by both types of performers; these are the minimum competencies required for fully successful performance. Also in this section are the technical competencies (T) that have been identified by processes other than BEI, such as interviewing technical experts and identifying industry standards.

FIGURE 1. DISTINCTIONS BETWEEN COMPETENCIES.

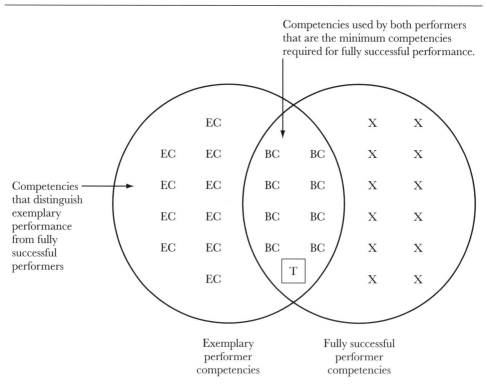

EC = Competencies of exemplary performers
 X = Competencies of fully successful performers only
 T = Technical competencies
BC = Competencies that both performers share

By studying the competencies of an exemplary performer (EC), the organization can learn much about what distinguishes this person from the fully successful performer. By analyzing the resulting data, the organization can design a competency model that will work best for its employees. Many organizations today are in the process of setting goals to make major improvements in their performance. The more often ECs are integrated into their competency models, the more likely it is that these organizations will reach their performance goals.

Carefully researched job tasks and competencies are a powerful resource with numerous applications in the arena of organizational performance. At the operations level, competencies can be used in conjunction with job task lists and information about outputs or results to improve performance. They provide the raw materials that help managers and their subordinates discuss performance and the results that the organization needs. The information from job competency research can immediately be used to accomplish the following:

- Create and implement opportunities for on-the-job performance enhancement
- Identify formal and informal training opportunities for acquiring and practicing competencies
- Implement external programs for developing competencies

At the organizational level, competency modeling is rapidly becoming a unifying theme that links virtually all human resource subsystems, such as recruitment and selection, performance management (including appraisal subsystems), human resource planning, employee reward and recognition programs, career management, and compensation. Competency-based compensation is in a developmental stage at the time of this writing.

When to Use

The use of competency modeling strategies and practices requires an organization to commit resources to the development and maintenance of competency-driven interventions. The organization must commit to using the intervention long term and must be patient about obtaining the desired results. As is the case with any developmental intervention, competency modeling requires acceptance on the part of those who will eventually be affected by its use.

Thus the organization's leaders must not only educate employees about the intervention but also actively involve them in the design, development, and implementation of the intervention. If any one of these elements—commitment, patience, and employee acceptance and involvement—is lacking, only limited success will be achieved in competency modeling. Consequently, any competency intervention must be conceived and planned both carefully and realistically. It also must be *strategically appealing* in terms of its ability to help the organization achieve its strategic objectives.

Case Study

Carmen Hegge-Kleiser (1998) describes how a competency-based approach to reengineered training delivery at American Express was successfully used to increase the business impact of the training while also achieving best-in-class economics. A competency model was built for training delivery, using information obtained from BEIs. "The model's design reflected not only specific role requirements but also the strategic direction of the company, major business challenges, corporate culture, and organizational dynamics," noted Hegge-Kleiser (p. 225). The BEIs established the foundation for developing a future-oriented competency model. The competencies included in the model were classroom instruction, facilitation, technical/functional expertise, knowledge of the customer, and personal effectiveness. A team of American Express training professionals with cross–business unit representation from around the world used the competency model as they redesigned processes for trainer selection, certification, and evaluation.

Although it is still in its early stages of application, the model has already had significant impact on how American Express delivers training. Hegge-Kleiser (p. 242) reported the following results:

> In the leadership course, where the certification model and training certification process have been used extensively, trainers give the process high marks. Line managers feel more confident about both the course content and their facilitation skills. . . . Human resources professionals report that the process is "the most effective trainer certification process" they've been through inside or outside the company. Most importantly, the class participants are giving the trainers high ratings and content mastery scores have markedly increased.

In summary, as this case study illustrates, competencies that are used as a foundation for performance improvement are a powerful tool for achieving employee and organizational success.

Resources and References

Boyatzis, R. E. (1986). *The competent manager.* New York: Wiley.
Dubois, D. D. (1993). *Competency-based performance improvement: A strategy for organizational change.* Amherst, MA: HRD Press.

Dubois, D. D. (1995). *Competency-based performance improvement: Organizational assessment package.* Amherst, MA: HRD Press.

Dubois, D. D. (1995). *The executive's guide to competency-based performance improvement.* Amherst, MA: HRD Press.

Hegge-Kleiser, C. (1998). A competency-based approach to training delivery: The American Express experience. In D. D. Dubois (Ed.), *The competency case book: Twelve studies in competency-based performance improvement* (pp. 223–242). Amherst, MA: HRD Press.

Spencer, L. M., Jr., & Spencer, S. M. (1993). *Competence at work: Models for superior performance.* New York: Wiley.

Intervention Author

David D. Dubois, Ph.D.
President
Dubois & Associates
P.O. Box 10340
Rockville, MD 20849-0340
Phone: 301-762-5026
Fax: 301-762-5026
E-mail: ddubois@tidalwave.net
Web site: call for information

Case Study Author

The case study was adapted by David D. Dubois from "A Competency-Based Approach to Training Delivery: The American Express Experience," by Carmen Hegge-Kleiser, 1998 (used by permission of the publisher, HRD Press, Inc., 22 Amherst Road, Amherst, MA 01002, phone: 800-822-2801 or 413-253-3480, fax: 413-253-3498).

▪ ▪ ▪ ▎ ▏ CONFLICT MANAGEMENT

	Level of Performance	Business Unit	Process	Work Group	Individual
	Establish	○	○	●	●
Performance	Improve	○	○	●	●
Change	Maintain	○	○	○	○
	Extinguish	○	○	●	●

Alternative Name

Conflict resolution

Definition

Conflict management includes interventions that

- Identify the methods typically used by people to handle conflict
- Determine whether those methods tend to be creative or dysfunctional
- Provide a model and training for the constructive handling of conflict

Description

Conflict is inevitable but need not be debilitating; instead, people can and must learn from it. Conflict occurs in an organization when interaction difficulties arise during task work and when people do not get what they need or want in order to perform well.

Conflict also arises in the following circumstances:

- The work styles of a group leader and one or more members differ.
- People have hidden agendas and will not reveal their true opinions and feelings.
- People's contributions are ignored so that they feel slighted and subsequently withdraw or complain about others.
- The amount of work creates a conflict between personal goals and the organization's expectations.
- People ignore disagreements and problems, hoping that they will simply go away.
- Resources are scarce, pitting colleagues against one another.
- Strategies are agreed on, but critical tactics are fought over.
- The appropriate parties have not agreed on critical business strategies.

Many people want to avoid conflict and the uncomfortable feelings associated with it. The consequences of conflict can damage people's health; can cause performance problems, turnover, and business losses; and ultimately can ruin an organization. Consequently, performance technologists need to understand and be able to ameliorate conflict.

A number of models for dealing with conflict exist. One model, the Conflict Cycle (Hart, 1991), outlines the responsibilities of the performance technologist in helping people to manage conflict effectively:

1. Familiarize people with the phases of the conflict cycle
2. Develop people's ability to identify the particular phase they are in when experiencing conflict
3. Facilitate a discussion about a current conflict, its causes, and its impact on performance
4. Help those experiencing conflict to identify and apply a resolution
5. Facilitate a discussion about what was learned from the conflict and the implemented resolution

According to Hart (1991), the conflict cycle consists of seven phases:

Phase 1: Anticipation

People anticipate conflict because it is a normal part of human existence. No one relishes confronting it, but everyone knows it will occur.

Phase 2: Wait and See

Once a conflict emerges, people generally take time to examine the situation, assess what is happening, and determine how serious the conflict is.

Phase 3: Growing

If a conflict is not resolved immediately, it generally escalates.

Phase 4: In the Open

After the conflict has grown into a full-scale problem, it is in the open; there is no denying its existence. At this point some people retreat, either because they want to avoid the conflict or because they want more time to assess the situation.

Phase 5: Resolution

Once the conflict is in the open, those involved can seek a resolution. They may decide to experiment, trying out various resolutions until the right one is applied successfully. For example, they may try such approaches as negotiating to reach a compromise, collaborating to reach consensus, or using position power to impose a resolution.

Phase 6: Settlement

After the successful application of a resolution, the parties involved proceed to settlement, ensuring that everyone is satisfied with the resolution. This phase alleviates stress and helps people to redirect their energy to other activities and to recapture the good feelings they previously had for one another.

Phase 7: Reflection

The last phase, although critical, is often neglected. Those involved reflect on the conflict and analyze what happened so that they can learn from it. They ask themselves the following questions:

- What was the cause of this conflict? Have we eliminated the cause so that another conflict will not emerge?
- How did each of us behave when it was obvious we had a conflict? How can we reduce our resistance to conflict?

- What did we do to resolve the conflict? How effective were the approaches we tried?

When to Use

Most groups go through several stages in the quest for high performance. For example, Tuckman (1965) proposed that each group goes through the developmental stages of *forming, storming, norming,* and *performing.* As suggested by the term *storming,* in this stage the team members can become frustrated with one another, their processes, inadequate support from the organization, or whatever. Often they do not yet have the necessary skills or tenacity to get through this difficult time by themselves. In short, they need conflict management intervention.

Conflict management also may be needed in the following situations:

- When there is a noticeable increase in the stress being experienced by individuals or by the whole group
- When the group is performing poorly
- When some members withdraw from group discussions or activities

Case Study

Many conflicts can be avoided if group members take the time at the forming stage to discuss their expectations and to establish behavioral guidelines.

The members of one project team did not establish guidelines in the beginning. They shared a common vision and mission; they all felt a sense of belonging; they were enthusiastic and ready to move ahead with their tasks; and their early meetings were productive. They did not feel the need to make provisions for the management of conflict.

However, after six months the goals of the project had expanded, but the team's resources had stayed the same. One member raised what appeared to be a simple question about her role. The leader gave her a hasty, impatient reply. Suddenly the other members became quiet, obviously taken aback by the leader's response.

A two-hour discussion ensued. Several members admitted that they had been going along with decisions even though they had reservations. After feelings were heard and examples given, the members realized that this conflict had occurred partly because they had never established guidelines on how they would work together. Therefore they did not have a plan for dealing with issues as they arose. Instead, months later they were finding out about hidden agendas and concerns.

Their resolution was to create a set of team guidelines. They came up with some initial ideas and then modified, deleted, and added guidelines to fit their needs. They agreed to use consensus as their decision-making method, as it would indicate that everyone was committed to the team's efforts.

They wrote a final list of guidelines (Exhibit 1) and all of them signed it to indicate commitment. They also agreed to keep the list posted prominently during each meeting. They established the role of *guidelines monitor* to ensure adherence to the guidelines, decided to take turns in this role, and agreed that everyone would watch for violation of the guidelines.

EXHIBIT 1. TEAM GUIDELINES.

Team Guidelines

- We will be as open as possible but honor the right of privacy.
- Unless we agree otherwise, what is discussed in our team will remain confidential.
- We will respect differences of opinion. We will not discount others' ideas.
- We will be supportive rather than judgmental.
- We will give feedback directly, openly, and in a timely fashion. We will provide information that is specific and focuses on the task and process rather than on personalities.
- As we all have resources to offer (our experiences, knowledge, and training), we will tell others what we can offer and will contribute freely.
- Each of us is responsible for what is derived from this team experience. We will ask for what we need from our sponsor, our facilitator, our team leader, and the other team members.
- We will try to get better acquainted with one another so that we can identify ways in which we can work better together and develop professionally.
- We will use our time well. We will start our meetings on time, return from breaks on time, and end our meetings promptly.
- When members miss a meeting, we will share the responsibility of letting them know what happened.
- We will keep our focus on our goals and avoid sidetracking, personality conflicts, and hidden agendas. We will acknowledge problems and deal with them.
- We will not make phone calls during meetings or let others interrupt us with messages.

Team Member Signatures

_____   _____

_____   _____

_____   _____

They also set a date to review the guidelines and modify them as needed. They further agreed that each new member who joined would be introduced to the guidelines immediately.

Resources and References

Books and Articles

Hart, L. B. (1991). *Learning from conflict.* Amherst, MA: HRD Press.

Tannen, D. (1990). *You just don't understand.* New York: Ballantine.

Tuckman, B. W. (1965). Development sequences in small groups. *Psychological Bulletin, 53,* 384–399.

Videos

Conflict: Managing under pressure (available from CRM Films, 2215 Faraday Avenue, Carlsbad, CA 92008, phone: 800-421-0833). Shows managers how to handle conflicts caused by rumors, misinformation, and differing points of view. In addition, it identifies the causes and stages of conflict.

Dealing with conflict (available from Xicom Films, RR #2, Woods Road, Tuxedo, NY 10987, phone: 800-759-4266). Based on the Thomas-Kilman Conflict Mode Instrument, it illustrates how to recognize and resolve conflict.

How to resolve conflicts on the job (available from Communication Briefings, 1101 King Street, Suite 110, Alexandria, VA 22314, phone: 703-548-3800). Covers the causes of conflict, the role of personality in conflict, ways to influence others, and methods for settling disagreements.

Self-Administered Feedback Instruments

Sashkin, M. *Conflict-Style Inventory.* Amherst, MA: HRD Press (22 Amherst Street, Amherst, MA 01002, phone: 800-822-2801). Assesses one's approaches to conflict management.

Thomas-Kilman Conflict Mode Instrument. Tuxedo, NY: Xicom (RR #2, Woods Road, Tuxedo, NY 10987, phone: 800-759-4266). Assesses one's preferred conflict-handling style and offers suggestions for increasing one's comfort level with infrequently used styles.

Intervention Author

Lois B. Hart, Ed.D.
President
Leadership Dynamics
10951 Isabelle Road
Lafayette, CO 80026
Phone: 303-666-4046
Fax: 303-666-4074
E-mail: lhart@seqnet.net

CRITICAL THINKING SYSTEMS

Level of Performance	Business Unit	Process	Work Group	Individual
Establish	○	●	●	●
Improve	○	●	●	●
Maintain	○	○	○	○
Extinguish	○	○	○	○

Performance Change is shown on the left side of the Establish/Improve/Maintain/Extinguish rows.

Alternative Names

Work systems
Embedded performance elements

Definition

Critical thinking is a process that involves the application of judgment. A *critical thinking system* consists of procedures that foster the proper application of that judgment to organizational issues.

Description

The goal of a critical thinking intervention is to help an organization behave more intelligently, adapting to reality quickly and effectively. Such thinking needs to be made an expected and natural part of the organization's culture so that issues that require attention can be identified and resolved. One way to embed such thinking in the organizational culture is to create systems that require it.

System in this context means a mandated series of concrete, observable steps performed by people in the organization (as opposed to mental activities that cannot be observed and are completed at the discretion of an individual thinker). When critical thinking is embedded in the organization, all people who share the same role adhere to the same system and behave similarly. The policies, procedures, and steps of the system are not subject to individual choice or motivation.

Here is an example of critical thinking: as a child I sometimes asked my father for money beyond what I had "earned." His invariable response was "Why?" This question conveyed certain information to me and thereby channeled my thinking in a direction of his choosing. In effect, he conveyed to me that it was his right to ask why I was requesting the money, that he cared about what purpose the money was meant to accomplish, and that he cared about what thought I had given the issue.

Similarly, what an organization asks of employees in order to navigate its formal systems channels their thinking in particular directions, focuses that thinking, and communicates what is valued. The right question stimulates thinking to search for relevant information to formulate an answer. The thinker is made more sensitive to what is known that may be relevant and more alert to what additional information is needed. The right question can also trigger the right type of analysis. For example, if you identify a problem and are then asked to name the cause of the problem, you will attempt to answer the question using the available information and what you know about cause and effect. Training might expand your ability to answer cause-and-effect questions, but it is the system that triggers and supports the effort.

Specific roles played by organizational members are what establish and keep a system in place. One person is given the authority to manage the system and is held accountable for the results that the system is intended to produce. After specific procedures are designed into a system, people should be given the responsibility of following those procedures. Lasting change will not occur unless authority and accountability are changed deliberately as part of the implementation of the critical thinking process.

When to Use

Any of the following conditions may indicate that a critical thinking system needs to be implemented to support and encourage clear thinking and intelligent action:

- Programs and organizational initiatives come and go, but the performance indicators remain untouched, awaiting the next *slogram* (slogan plus program).

- A large number of employees have completed and responded very well to training that emphasizes clear, rational thinking, but the training has had very little impact on thinking performance on the job.
- It is common for two or more projects to be initiated to address the same issue without mutual knowledge or coordination and with counterproductive results.
- Real corrective action is rarely taken; instead, a number of quick, stopgap actions are used.
- Many initiatives are dropped before completion.
- Decisions are of poor quality.
- The organization repeats failed programs on a cyclical basis; little or no use is made of historical information.
- Meetings about the same issues drag on and on like a soap opera, with very little change and no meaningful action.

Case Study

A West Coast factory of a national company employed eight hundred people. A training project was created as part of the factory's response to a corporate mandate to use teams across the organization. The local factory's training included the in-house certification of six instructor-facilitators and their subsequent training of three hundred members of various corrective action teams (CATs) in critical thinking. The purpose of the two-day workshop was to teach team members how to think critically and collaboratively.

One instructor documented cost savings and cost-avoidance results that totaled $3 million in two to three years. Therefore, by training standards, this was a very successful intervention averaging a $10,000 savings for each person trained.

The internal critical thinking experts noticed that the impact of the training on the performance of the CATs—impressive as it was for a training intervention—was just a drop in the bucket compared to what was possible. Some of the CATs performed better than others, and other problems surrounding the use of the CATs were surfacing. The following comments were typical of employee reactions across the organization after the training was completed:

"CATs are only instigated for external problems, not internal ones. How can we focus on some of our internal problems?"

"Members of CATs say they don't know which issue to work on."

"We overuse immediate action and almost never take corrective action."

"It's hard to find historical data when we're trying to determine the root causes of problems."

"We don't have the necessary details to be able to respond to customer complaints that are forwarded to us."

"After the fact we find out that the same issues have been addressed simultaneously by several different units. We end up producing incompatible solutions and wasting time."

"I need people to be working, not in meetings."

"We don't solve problems—we adapt to them."

After several years of lobbying on the part of in-house facilitators, the senior managers agreed that the plant could improve its response to problems. They decided that a problem resolution system (PRS) should be developed. A team was formed and given responsibility for recommending a PRS for adoption. The team members applied the same critical thinking methods that were presented during the original training. Their analysis established the needs for a PRS. These needs were then used to create design objectives for the new system. It was decided that the ideal system would have these characteristics:

- Early problem identification
- Easy stakeholder access to action status
- Timely and appropriate response to problems
- Accessibility to all employees
- Ability to create high-quality historical information
- Usefulness in areas other than problem resolution

The system was composed of a problem identification method that funneled problem descriptions to four different types of action units. These units were responsible for setting priority, deciding who should be involved, facilitating analysis, taking action, and documenting results. The four types of action units were *customer, department, interdepartment,* and *ISO.*[1] These four types of units already existed in one form or another. All that needed to happen was the redefinition of roles and the adoption of specific procedures for dealing with problems in a plantwide system.

The strategy was based on using embedded critical thinking elements within the plant's systems. For example, any employee could record a problem (a noncompliance) by entering answers to two questions on a data terminal; the answers

1.   The ISO unit focused on obtaining ISO certification. The International Organization for Standardization (ISO) is the publisher of the ISO 9000 Series of technical standards for business and industry.

would enable the system to determine which action unit had jurisdiction. Next the employee could use the data terminal to answer another series of questions designed to help the employee describe the problem (by revealing information about it, what documents had been consulted, and what actions had already been taken). The problem description questions were adapted from the original critical thinking training and were made part of the formal PRS in this way.

Once the problem description arrived (electronically) at the appropriate action unit, priority-setting information would be entered. The demand for this and other information was built into the system. For example, answers to questions such as, "What is the cause of this problem?" and, "How was this cause verified?" were made a permanent part of the record for each problem. A method of conducting cause analysis was not specified by the system, and verifying the cause of the problem was not specified. But the system asked that the cause be determined and verified and the results documented.

Training now teaches employees to perform within the system. It is left up to the individual or team (with the help of the action unit leaders) to determine what analysis may be needed. Training also teaches employees how to conduct a proper analysis. The action units select team members, including a representative from the training department, by matching experience and skills with the demands of the current problem.

This system is an improvement for several reasons. Problem identification, analysis, and resolution are now a formal part of the plant's systems. Problems have been elevated to job-duty status and consequently are resolved sooner. Formal record keeping reveals high-order problems. For example, in the pilot test of this system the overuse of first-response action and the underuse of corrective action were made very visible. Making people responsible for tracking and resolving issues of noncompliance resulted in improvements in all plant systems—both technical and human. Departments now have a clear way to initiate action on problems that they used to tolerate, and departments that create problems for other departments are under daily pressure to resolve them.

Resources and References

Fritz, R. (1996). *Corporate tides: The inescapable laws of organizational structure.* San Francisco, CA: Berrett-Koehler. See especially the discussion on the importance of a clear purpose.

Jacques, E., & Clement, S. (1994). *Executive leadership: A practical guide to managing complexity.* Arlington, VA: Carson Hall & Co. See especially the discussion of authority and accountability with regard to making a hierarchy work.

Larson, C. E., & LaFasto, F.M.J. (1989). *TeamWork: What must go right/what can go wrong.* Thousand Oaks, CA: Sage. Note an important point made in this book: only two of eight factors found to be associated with successful teams can be directly affected by training.

Intervention Author

Richard C. Wells
Vice President-R&D
Business Processes Inc.
Research & Development Office
P.O. Box 1456
La Jolla, CA 92038
Phone: 619-459-7600
Fax: 619-459-2390
E-mail: Think-BPI@msn.com
Web site: www.critical-thinking.com

■ ■ ■ I I I CULTURAL CHANGE

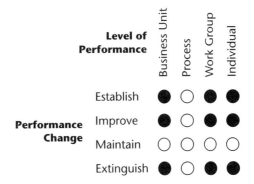

	Level of Performance	Business Unit	Process	Work Group	Individual
Performance Change	Establish	●	○	●	●
	Improve	●	○	●	●
	Maintain	○	○	○	○
	Extinguish	●	○	●	●

Alternative Name

Managing change

Definition

A cultural change intervention is an activity on the part of a change agent to influence the shared basic assumptions of a group or organization (Schein, 1992).

Description

Culture can be defined as the learned, shared assumptions that the members of a group or organization hold with respect to the following issues:

- How to deal with problems of external survival in the environment (how to fulfill the basic mission or primary task of the group or organization).
- How to organize internal relationships to facilitate effective functioning (if the members have a history of shared experience, they will have developed shared assumptions about external and internal relationships).

A group's basic assumptions will manifest themselves at the level of overt artifacts and behavior, at the level of espoused values and principles, and at the tacit level of shared assumptions. The existence of the tacit level can be inferred from the observation that a group's espoused values often contradict its members' behavior, which implies that there is a deeper level of shared assumptions driving the behavior. For example, many organizations officially espouse teamwork, but the tacit, shared assumption is that career progress is the result of individualistic, competitive behavior.

Many so-called cultural interventions concentrate on changing the overt behavior of group members or changing the espoused values of the group. For instance, an organization may encourage its employees to change in the direction of becoming more team oriented. However, if the changes made by employees do not influence the tacit, individualistic assumptions that they share and that govern their functioning, the culture will not change. Cultural change, by definition, must produce a change in the shared tacit assumptions.

A change in shared basic assumptions can occur only if the members of the organization have a new set of shared experiences—some new learning that will lead to their acceptance of a new assumption as valid. In other words, the culture cannot be said to have changed until the employees' new way of behaving, thinking, and feeling has led to consistent success and thereby comes to be taken for granted as a new way of perceiving reality.

New shared experiences that lead to new assumptions about the nature of external and internal reality can come about through *natural evolution, guided evolution, managed cultural change,* or *revolutionary changes from within.*

Natural Evolution

Every group or organization exists in a changing environment and must gradually adapt to that environment. This usually happens through normal adaptive processes and through the learning of new ways of perceiving and thinking introduced by new members. Even though new members are socialized into the existing culture, they always bring with them some new elements that will change the existing culture to some degree.

Guided Evolution

Guided evolution occurs either through the conscious efforts of founders and leaders or through a process by which the organizational members gain insight into their own culture and consciously reinforce those elements that they value. What leaders pay attention to and reward, the kinds of people they hire and promote, and the values they consistently communicate to their organization influence the direction of the culture's evolution—provided that the behaviors based on those values and assumptions lead to success in the external environment.

Managed Cultural Change

Managed cultural change either seeks to enhance assumptions and values that are thought to be valuable in helping the organization to achieve its goals or seeks to eliminate assumptions and values that are thought to inhibit the organization's ability to achieve its goals. Insofar as culture provides meaning and stability to members, it will always be easier to build on and enhance the present cultural elements than to remove ones that are seen as dysfunctional.

However, if leaders or organizational members decide to eliminate dysfunctional elements, they can launch a specific change program. The program must have the following elements, which help to alleviate the anxiety and resistance to change that inevitably accompany any such program.

- *Clear vision of the future:* A consistent, clear vision of the future must be articulated by leaders, change agents, and opinion leaders within the organization. This vision must show how changing some aspects of the culture will promote the organization's survival or success.
- *Education and training programs:* These programs must assist employees in learning whatever new behaviors will be required to implement the new vision.
- *Structural changes in the organization:* Such changes align authority and communication systems with the new vision.
- *Redesign of organizational systems:* The incentive, reward, control, and discipline systems must be redesigned to reflect and support the new vision.
- *Coaching and other informal learning opportunities:* Informal learning helps employees to internalize the new behavior, values, and vision.
- *Employee participation in the design of the change and learning process:* Those whose behavior, values, and assumptions must change need to participate in designing the change and learning process. Their participation lessens their anxiety and promotes their acceptance of the changes.

What makes managed cultural change so difficult and time-consuming is that all of these elements must be present and several of them require long periods of learning and restructuring.

Revolutionary Change

Drastic changes in cultural assumptions can occur if the major culture carriers—usually the formal and opinion leaders—are removed, either through a change in top management or through a revolutionary coup-d'etat engineered by employees. New leaders with new values and assumptions institute new policies and procedures; as those new policies and procedures bring about success, the culture gradually changes in ways that are consistent with the new tacit assumptions.

When to Use

Cultural change works at the level of thoughts, values, attitudes, and perceptions, which in turn affect behavior. It is rare to launch a cultural change program to extinguish some undesirable behavior. Instead, the desire to change behavior leads to other kinds of interventions, which, if successful, ultimately change the culture. However, if the needs listed below exist in an organization, cultural change interventions may be the best solution.

- The need to preserve cultural elements that have been associated with the past success of the group or organization
- The need to change cultural elements that are perceived to be dysfunctional in the present or future
- The need to build new shared assumptions in a group or an organization that has just been formed

Case Study

One large oil company decided to move all of its engineers from the various business units into one central service organization. Instead of working as part of a regular unit, the engineers would be required to sell their services to the business units, which meant that they would have to learn a whole new set of behaviors based on very different assumptions. The cultural change effort required the top management of the new service unit to define and articulate a new vision of what it meant to be an engineer who sells his or her services.

A *culture task force* was set up to determine the day-to-day behaviors and self-image that would enable the engineers to function effectively under the new circumstances. The members of the task force defined what it meant to be successful in selling enough services to cover costs (as had been mandated by management). They then designed the change program.

The program linked a number of interventions. An outside consultant was employed to educate the top management of the engineering group about the cultural change and to help these managers articulate their new vision of how the organization would work. The head of the task force functioned as the key change agent, designing the educational interventions and contracting with the outside consultant to implement them.

As a result of these efforts, the members of the top management of the engineering group realized that they had to involve direct reports, the next level of managers, in the same tasks of first understanding the new culture and then designing what the "new way of working" would be. Representatives of this level worked closely with the culture task force and the outside consultant to design a program that would appropriately involve the next layers of management and the working engineers, whose self-images had to adjust to the new structure.

Role models were identified and new stories and myths developed to show how it was possible to work effectively in this new way. Without these examples the working engineers would not have been able to develop the necessary images of themselves as consultants who sell their services for fees. The reward and promotion system had to be examined and redesigned to take into account who the new heroes were. In addition, provisions had to be made for the retraining, early retirement, or layoffs of employees who could not adapt to the new way of working.

The top management of the engineering group now realizes that it has to remain clear in articulating the vision of the future and that it has to be entirely supportive, despite high levels of anxiety about the changes. The ultimate success of the change program depends on whether the company buys enough engineering services to make the new way of working cost-effective. If that does not happen, the old culture will have been partly destroyed, but a new culture will not have been created. This case illustrates the fact that a final assessment of any cultural change program cannot be made until long after the program has been launched.

Resources and References

Collins, J. C., & Porras, J. I. (1994). *Built to last.* New York: Harper Business.

Cook, S.D.N., & Yanow, D. (1993). Culture and organizational learning. *Journal of Management Inquiry, 2*(4), 373–390.

After each contact with an organization, customers mentally compare their expectations of what should have happened with their experiences of what did happen. For every customer, the difference—positive or negative—forms the basis of that customer's evaluation of the organization. Some parts of a customer's experience are readily measurable. For example, it is possible to track the number of rings before a customer's call is answered or the number of days before an episode of poor service is resolved. Other aspects of customer experience, such as the customer's perception of courtesy or of the value of service, are more difficult to measure.

Adding to the challenge of understanding the customer's perception of how well the organization is performing is the fact that customer needs, wants, and expectations do not remain the same. They change with time, experience, and circumstance.

There are many useful approaches to gathering information about current and potential customers' wants, needs, and priorities and also information about improvement opportunities. Following are brief explanations of ten of these methods.

Method 1: Traditional Market Research

Traditional market research is done to assess the needs of current customers, former customers, noncustomers, and competitors' customers. It focuses on the good, bad, and missing features of current, competitive, or proposed products and services. Following are the most commonly used market research tools:

- Surveys (telephone, mail, intercept)
- Focus groups (open ended, discussion, product prototype evaluation, facilitated by instrument administration, decision making)
- Demographic and psychographic analysis (generally a statistical analysis of usage patterns or buyer characteristics or observations of shopper or user behaviors)

Method 2: Customer Hotlines and Toll-Free, or "800," Numbers

Used primarily to track customer questions, complaints, problem reports, and assistance calls, customer hotlines also may be used to ask customers questions and to give instructions on assembly, installation, and simple repair. For example, Pillsbury and General Mills include toll-free numbers on their food products so that they can collect customer complaints and concerns and so that they can add value to the products by offering additional usage advice and directions.

Method 3: Employee-Visit Teams

Employees who normally do not call on customers directly visit customer sites to see how the organization's product or service is being used, what problems are being experienced, and what needs are not being met. Generally, an employee-visit team is a cross-disciplinary group whose members come from approximately the same level in the organization. An extreme example is that of Japanese automobile manufacturers, who send members of their design teams to live with the target audience for a new automobile.

Method 4: Customer-Visit Teams

Small groups of end users, buyers, and customers are invited to tour the company, ask questions, audit operations, or in some way become *consultants* in the design, development, and delivery process. For example, Ben and Jerry's Ice Cream regularly invites customers to submit their ideas for new flavors and products and to test new product prototypes.

Method 5: Customer Advisory Panels

Retailers often use panels of customers to anticipate fashion trends, as do electronics manufacturers, who look for feedback on design, standards, and pricing. In addition, several major airlines identify their most frequent flyers and invite these individuals to test new seat designs and to comment on current service levels.

Method 6: User Groups

Computer owners often form groups to share information and ideas about the use of their equipment and software. Manufacturers often use these groups to obtain information and design assistance. When Apple introduced its first Macintosh, it made its presentation to the Boston Computer Club.

Method 7: User Conferences and Seminars

Many business-to-business organizations sponsor educational events for customers and potential customers. Many organizations use these events as opportunities to listen as well as tell. Bringing in an expert on some developing area—technological or social—and then listening to the news with this person can be an opportunity to create new products and services.

Method 8: Face-to-Face Fact Finding

The simplest method of questioning customers about products and services (including those desired as well as those received) is one-to-one conversation. Many senior managers in large organizations seldom see customers. By going into stores, talking with customers, and visiting their offices, these managers can gain a fresh perspective.

Method 9: Working the Front Line

Executives and managers who do not see customers are increasingly spending time serving customers on the phone or at the counter, making deliveries, taking deposits, making loans, and dispatching repair calls. They do so for many reasons, but one key reason is to learn more about customers and how they are and are not being served.

A related technique consists of debriefing the front line. Employees on the front line have a tremendous amount of information about customers' wants and needs. Debriefing them means asking them regularly what they are learning. This process generally occurs through focus groups and programs in which *notes to management* are constructed.

Method 10: Benchmarking

Benchmarking started as a way for an organization to compare its operational efficiencies with those of companies in a different business but with parallel problems. Today benchmarking is more broadly interpreted as a way of searching for breakthrough ideas by observing how other organizations see their customers. This practice is sometimes referred to as *industrial tourism*.

When to Use

When to Use Traditional Market Research

Every organization should have a market research plan. Regularly mailed survey forms and *bounce-back cards* (brief surveys written on postcards and distributed to customers at the time the service is delivered or the product is purchased) allow an organization to monitor the quality of its products and services.

Although it is important not to overgeneralize from the information provided, using focus groups can give depth and meaning to survey results. In most organizations, focus groups should be conducted at least twice a year. For example, if customer satisfaction surveys show increasing dissatisfaction with repair services, focus groups may help to determine whether the cause of the dissatisfaction is an actual drop in service performance or an increase in customer expectations. Focus groups also allow an organization to preview potential new products or service improvements.

Demographic and psychographic analysis can be costly and complex. However, the insights gained from such analysis are well worth the expense and effort. This approach is particularly useful in helping an organization to identify and develop profiles of its most important customer segments. It also may suggest more profitable ways to reach other customer segments, such as through catalogues or direct marketing.

When to Use Customer Hotlines and Toll-Free, or "800," Numbers

Studies by the Technical Assistance Research Project (TARP) and Coca-Cola (cited in Technical Assistance Research Project, 1986) suggest that having a hotline or toll-free phone number is seen by customers as important. However, it is important to realize that customers also expect around-the-clock availability. Consequently, this intervention should not be implemented unless the phone line can be staffed with an adequate number of appropriately knowledgeable employees. The immediacy offered by this method gives an organization an opportunity to correct or eliminate unsatisfactory performance before large numbers of customers are dissatisfied. This intervention should be used whenever time is critical for the customer. For example, a customer with a question about a baking product, such as a cake mix, expects an immediate response.

In addition, an increasing number of organizations are using the Internet or modem-accessed *bulletin boards* to listen to and respond to their customers electronically.

When to Use Employee-Visit Teams

Employee-visit teams should be used when employees are not familiar with how their work affects the end user of the organization's products or services. For example, members of the Gillette manufacturing staff visit retail outlets to view Gillette products on display and to watch customers evaluate and purchase them. Members of the team learn firsthand how important the package look and display are to customers.

When to Use Customer-Visit Teams

Customer-visit teams should be used when customers are greatly invested in the product or service delivery process. For example, some customers are really internal partners to the delivery team, such as the retail stores who are the customers of the corporate finance area. Another example is a situation in which a product or service is delivered via a long-term contract, such as when a bank contracts with another organization for data-processing services. Customer-visit teams allow customers to participate in the process, thereby increasing customer loyalty as well as the organization's understanding of what its customers want and need.

When to Use Customer Advisory Panels

Customer advisory panels typically require less time and energy than customer-visit teams. The members of the advisory panel may not even meet as a formal group, instead agreeing to participate in regular mail or telephone interviews.

This intervention can be used to create a "board of directors" for the front line. Several utility companies have successfully invited the same public interest advocates who once dogged their every step to bring their interest and energy to bear inside the organization, where these assets can be applied in useful ways.

When to Employ User Groups

User groups are similar to customer-visit teams except that they are controlled by customers and are more convenient for customers. They are particularly useful in service areas in which users must continually work to keep up with information and technology. The organization that provides products or services in such an area—for example, computers—would do well to find out what user groups already exist. If none or few do, customers should be asked whether they would like to have such groups and how the organization might facilitate their formation. If a number of groups already exist, the organization should explore ways in which it can be a resource to these groups and should consider offering information about the groups to new and existing customers.

Occasionally, organizations are reluctant to have their customers form or join user groups, fearing that communication among customers will increase customer dissatisfaction. That fear is, unfortunately, legitimate for some organizations. However, the best response is to address and correct any sources of dissatisfaction. Customers always talk with other customers, regardless of whether they have access to formal user groups; they connect with one another through a variety of means, including industry association and casual acquaintance.

When to Employ User Conferences and Seminars

User conferences and seminars offer an excellent opportunity to introduce new product and service lines. An alternative is to sponsor sessions, booths, or receptions at regularly scheduled industry conferences.

When to Use Face-to-Face Fact Finding

Years ago researchers discovered that customers were more apt to complete and return comment cards when those cards featured a picture of the company president. Apparently, customers felt that their comments were actually going to be heard by someone who wanted to listen and who was in a position to respond.

This experience illustrates the power of face-to-face contact with customers. Such contact is especially important when customers have been reluctant to voice their concerns and when customers have an underlying cynical attitude that "nothing will change anyway." Of course, for face-to-face fact finding to work, those who participate in gathering information must believe in the importance of customer feedback and must commit to taking appropriate actions based on what they hear.

When to Work the Front Line

Every manager or executive should schedule time on a weekly, monthly, or quarterly basis to be in direct contact with customers. This experience offers insight into not only what customers experience but also—equally important—what fronting employees experience.

When to Use Benchmarking

Any service process for which there is an industry standard, such as delivery time, should be benchmarked. Benchmarking allows the organization to determine how it is performing as compared to the best in class and why its own performance may be lagging. For example, Federal Express's hub-and-spoke system has become the standard for those in the delivery business. Understanding how and why the Federal Express system works and then comparing it to their own systems has allowed organizations in other industries to improve their delivery times.

Case Study

A company that conducts traditional market research often relies primarily on surveys, failing to obtain a clear understanding of how customers are currently experiencing the organization. Surveys written without the insight of qualitative input, such as focus group information, frequently miss vital areas of concern to customers.

One large Midwest hospital recognized this weakness in its existing customer feedback plan and decided to conduct regular patient and family member focus groups. One goal was to try to see the hospital experience from the customer's point of view—what patients and family members found unexpectedly good or disappointing. Another goal was to ensure that the right questions were being asked on the written customer surveys. (Exhibit 1 is a copy of the original focus group discussion guide.)

The focus group process was conducted by a team of people from the functions of marketing, human resources, and operations. It included the following eight steps.

Step 1: Holding the Initial Planning Meeting

The purpose of this initial meeting was to examine the problem and its parameters. The first step was to identify which customers to interview. The hospital created a screening guide and contracted with a professional focus group recruiting firm to select participants.

Step 2: Developing the Discussion Guide

The discussion guide is an outline of what to say and questions to ask. It focuses on the issues and helps keep the discussion on track.

Step 3: Holding the Second Planning Meeting

This meeting was held for the purposes of cross-checking and verification. The hospital met with the recruiting firm to ensure that appropriate customers were being chosen as participants. During this meeting, those in attendance also solidified the details of the focus group effort.

Step 4: Conducting the Focus Groups

The hospital chose to conduct its own focus groups, using an internal moderator who was trained in group facilitation skills. (This option is not always appropriate,

EXHIBIT 1. CUSTOMER FEEDBACK.

Welcome and Setting the Stage

"Thank you for coming. We're here today to find out more about how our patients—you folks—experience the work we do in the Surgical Unit. We've been doing a lot to address this topic internally, but now we need to talk with you—people who've spent time with us and who have direct experience with the Surgical Unit from the patient perspective."

Permission to Record and Confidentiality

"You're probably wondering about the microphone and tape recorder. We record these sessions so that we can listen to you better and not have to rely on notes. After we've used the tapes to do our analysis, we destroy them. Your comments will be synthesized; nothing you say will be identified with you by name."

Purpose

"We'll use the information and insight you provide to try to improve what we do—to learn how we can better serve you and all of our patients. Any questions?"

Introductions

"I'd like to start by finding out who each of you is. Just first names are fine. If you'd like to say something about yourself, that would be great. Add, too, a bit about your contact with the Surgical Unit."

Imagine with Me . . .

"I've got great news for you: all of you have a new and wonderful job as 'partner companions' for Surgical Unit patients. Your task is to help new patients—people who've never had a hospital stay—know what to expect from their experience with us.

"Think about that for a moment. You have a big responsibility to prepare these new patients for what is to come.

"[*Name—choose one participant*], what will you tell them will happen? Just start at the beginning and lead them through their hospital stay."

[*Pause while the participant speaks.*]

"What about the rest of you? What would you add in your role as partner companions that would prepare a new patient for his or her experience in the Surgical Unit?

[*Pause while participants comment.*]

"What steps or events did someone else experience that we've left out?"

[*Pause while participants comment.*]

Group Interview Questions

1. Were there things that you expected the Surgical Unit staff to do for you that weren't done? Were there things that you expected the staff to provide for you that you didn't receive?
2. How would you describe your relationship with your RN or NA?
3. How "connected" did you feel to the Surgical Unit staff?
4. What should you expect from the staff?
5. [Name], you mentioned call lights. Tell me more about that.
   - How long did you wait for a response?
   - How long do you feel you should have waited for a response?

EXHIBIT 1. (CONTINUED).

6. I heard [Name] mention the noise level. Can you tell me more about that?
   • When did you experience quiet time?
   • When did you expect quiet time?
7. What's the most unexpected thing that happened to you?
8. What things did happen to you?
9. What single piece of advice would you give to someone who is about to become a patient in the Surgical Unit?

as it presents a temptation to respond to participant comments with explanations or defensiveness. Generally, a third-party moderator is retained.)

Step 5: Transcribing Tapes and Reading Transcripts

The taped records of the focus group meetings were transcribed. In this way the moderator, other observers, and some nonparticipants were able to read what was actually said; they did not have to rely on notes or impressions. Reading the transcripts also aided theme analysis and group comparisons.

Step 6: Analyzing and Internalizing the Results

Results are never determined in the hallway or on the run. In this case the moderator spent a week analyzing the tapes and transcripts and making a list of key ideas. The moderator included quotations from the transcripts that supported each key idea.

Step 7: Writing a Report

The moderator wrote a report that included a brief description of what was done, a list and explanation of the main ideas brought out, and recommendations based on the focus group findings. The report and transcripts then were placed in the medical library for all staff members to review.

Step 8: Reporting the Findings

The most important part of any information-gathering effort is doing something with the data. In this case recommendations were presented to the hospital administration, and an action team was assigned to address each key idea or improvement opportunity.

Resources and References

Berry, L. L. (1995). *On great service: A framework for action.* New York: Free Press.

Breen, G., & Blankenship, A. B. (1989). Do-it-yourself marketing research (3rd ed.). New York: McGraw-Hill.

Dillman, D. A. (1978). *Mail and telephone surveys: The total design method.* New York: Wiley.

Kessler, S. (1996). *Measuring and managing customer satisfaction: Going for the gold.* Milwaukee, WI: ASQ (American Society for Quality) Quality Press.

Technical Assistance Research Project (TARP). 1986. *Increasing customer satisfaction through effective complaint handling: An updated study.* Washington, DC: U.S. Office of Consumer Affairs.

Worchester, R. M., & Downham, J. (1978). *Consumer market research handbook.* New York: Van Nostrand Reinhold.

Zemke, R., & Bell, C. R. (1992). *Managing knock your socks off service.* New York: AMACOM.

Zemke, R., & Connellan, T. K. (1993). *Sustaining knock your socks off service.* New York: AMACOM.

Intervention Author

Ron Zemke
President
Performance Research Associates, Inc.
821 Marquette Avenue South, Suite 1820
Minneapolis, MN 55402
Phone: 800-359-2576
Fax: 612-338-8536
E-mail: Zemke@aol.com
Web site: http://www.socksoff.com

ELECTRONIC PERFORMANCE
∎ ∎ ∎ ∎ ∎ ∎ SUPPORT SYSTEM (EPSS)

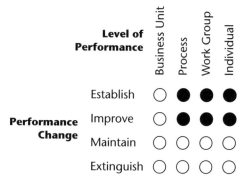

Level of Performance	Business Unit	Process	Work Group	Individual
Establish	○	●	●	●
Improve	○	●	●	●
Maintain	○	○	○	○
Extinguish	○	○	○	○

(Performance Change — rows Improve, Maintain, Extinguish)

Alternative Names

Integrated performance support
Just-in-time training
Performance-centered systems
Wizards
Coaches
Assistants

Definition

An *electronic performance support system* (EPSS) is software that provides integrated, on-demand access to information, advice, learning experiences, and tools to enable a high level of job performance with a minimum of training and support from other people.

Description

Initially used for general purpose applications (for example, word processing), computers have increasingly become part of everyone's system for *work* processing. As their capabilities increased and their prices decreased, computers quickly established a secure place in the working world. By providing quick and easy access to vast amounts of data, computers have provided knowledge workers with an opportunity to perform many functions more efficiently. However, the initial use of computers in the training field merely automated the existing models that trainers had at that time.

Today our view of what an EPSS can do to enhance performance goes well beyond the traditional approach of training and data-processing systems. Instead of concentrating on training individuals to perform a given task, the implementation of an EPSS supports the performer in accomplishing the task with information, tools, reminders, and other forms of support.

At its simplest level, an EPSS guides performers through a task, enabling them to learn a process while they use it—a virtual coach and an explicit task model. A more complex EPSS provides the performer with on-line help, a searchable reference database with live updates, and electronic access to expert users. It may even be possible to design an EPSS that combines elements of interactive learning, electronic communications, and expert systems that not only coach but also modify functions to meet the needs of the operator.

For example, as a user becomes proficient in a system, cues and support structures no longer needed are concealed, thus supporting expert performance. If the user makes repeated errors, the computer can provide tips or instruction to prevent recurrence. If the EPSS detects that some functions are being repeated—for example, entering a return address—the computer will complete the task for the user automatically.

An EPSS, because it is incorporated into the work process, enables individuals to get up to speed quickly and work more efficiently. It manages complexity and work flow for the user, and it is capable of supporting diverse working styles. In addition, it enables performers to share knowledge.

In short an EPSS has the explicit goal of supporting expert work performance on the part of people who know neither the work nor the software. It accomplishes this by binding the following elements:

- *Task structuring:* Representing and sequencing the activities necessary for accomplishing a task or procedure. Optimizing the work process is a major contributor to performance improvement.
- *Knowledge:* Content; rules; and relationships associated with the task, thinking, or process. Knowledge may be represented through some combination of text, graphics, sound, and animation. Examples, explanations, tips, facts, and numerous other methods can depict knowledge. Rules are typically embedded in the system logic.

- *Data:* Quantitative information related to the task. This could include such elements as sales volumes, demographics, population growth, and temperature.
- *Tools:* Programs that support (or perform) specific functions. Given the performers' input, the EPSS will provide information or carry out a task. This may range from something as simple as built-in calculating fields to more complex programs for analyzing variables, performing database queries, or operating peripheral equipment.
- *Communications:* Ways for performers to share information among themselves or with experts. This could be something as simple as an *electronic watercooler* that allows performers to swap anecdotes and experiences. Using e-mail, chat, video conferencing, or other tools, people can interact to allow faster and more accurate responses to situations. Sophisticated groupware applications permit collaborative work across time and space.

An EPSS is intended to improve performance by affecting the work as well as the worker. By providing performers with the tools they need and improving the work flow, an EPSS can provide a significant return on investment.

When to Use

An EPSS is best used in the circumstances described in the following list. After reading about these uses, one might get the impression that an EPSS is a panacea for improving performance. However, it should be remembered that this intervention may require a significant hardware investment, almost always requires a software investment, and is intended for people working with machines.

- *When a computer is fundamental to the task:* The computer may not need to be a personal computer; it can be part of a machine or a personal digital assistant (PDA).
- *When the task complexity is wide and deep:* If there are many paths that a user can conceivably navigate or many variables to control, a system to manage the experience is highly advantageous.
- *When system maintenance can handle process and task stability issues:* An EPSS is a software program that must be designed, programmed, and maintained. Process and task stability is a consideration in evaluating cost-effectiveness as compared to trying to change people's performance through ongoing training or announcements of changes that may or may not be incorporated into work performance. Designing for ongoing maintenance by using object-oriented developmental approaches can make the software solution more appropriate

than not. This maintenance requirement must be evaluated in relation to the number of performers and the consequences of people's failure to implement required performance changes.

- *When the system must support both novice and advanced performers:* The needs of novices are quite different from those of experts. A system designed to accommodate one will frustrate the other. An EPSS must be capable of handling all levels of performers by dynamically modifying its interface or permitting performers to select among alternatives.
- *When inadequate performers present significant business consequences:* Even if there are few performers, the impact of inadequate performance on the business may be sufficient justification for an EPSS.
- *When turnover is high:* If new performers are introduced on a regular basis, a considerable amount of training may be necessary. An EPSS can bring new employees up to speed without extensive training.
- *When redesigning an old system or developing a new system:* An EPSS is most effective when it is incorporated into the work system itself and not added as an afterthought.
- *When there is a large performer population:* The more people using the EPSS, the greater the return on investment (for example, if the development cost can be spread over hundreds or thousands of operators).
- *When performers must create and share knowledge:* If a job requires developing and gathering information, a system that enables people to share this information with colleagues will allow them to leverage this knowledge.

When Not to Use

An EPSS should not be used in the following circumstances:

- *When a computer is not practical:* there are some tasks for which a computer may simply hamper performance. A day-care worker, for example, is unlikely to consult a computer to find out how to deal with a crying child.
- *When sufficient development funds are not available:* developing any computer solution is rarely inexpensive. If funds are not available to create a *complete* product, creating anything less may frustrate performers and lead to poor performance.
- *When the task is simple and repetitive:* if the job can be learned quickly and easily and requires little support, an EPSS may prove far too costly.
- *When the task is constantly changing:* numerous changes severely affect the maintenance cost of an EPSS, possibly canceling out any performance gain.

Case Study

The employees of "MegaBank" are responsible for implementing numerous requests from customers. Some customers require simple, one-time transfers of funds from their accounts; others need periodic and ongoing transfers from their Mega-Bank accounts into accounts in other institutions.

For example, one client requests that $500 be transferred to her son's college checking account on the first of each month. Each transaction must conform to legal requirements and to the bank's policies (for example, account ownership and signatures must be correct; transfers cannot be made on accounts with court-ordered restrictions; tax withholdings and penalties must be considered). Furthermore, the employees must communicate these requirements to account owners or their financial planners.

Performance Development Problem

The tasks and rules are numerous and complex. Training staff members in these procedures is time-consuming; for example, introductory training on the administrative aspects of periodic transfers requires eleven hours of classroom instruction.

Also, retention of the training has so far been inadequate. Because the employees do not handle most of these requests on a regular basis, they tend to forget the proper procedures. Error rates following training are 20 percent; after twelve months errors drop to 10 percent. Consequently, all work must be double-checked.

Productivity levels are low. On the average, it takes an employee seventeen minutes to complete a transaction after training, nine minutes after two weeks of experience, and five minutes after twelve months of experience. Studies have shown that much of the time is spent correcting errors initially accepted by the computer system.

EPSS Solution

As MegaBank was upgrading its dumb terminals to computers with a graphical user interface, the company elected to implement an EPSS. Installing the new system would require that workers be retrained, but the bank hoped that the EPSS would reduce the training time and error rate for new hires.

After a year of development, the system was gradually brought on-line. The EPSS included a brief computer-based training module that gave employees an initial overview of the funds transfer process. The system was programmed to highlight mandatory fields and to disable fields that were not needed. In addition, there was a task-centered interface with embedded examples, explanations, rule checking of data on request, and so forth.

Outcomes

As a result of the implementation of the EPSS, introductory training on the administrative aspects of periodic transfers was reduced to seven hours. Error rates were initially recorded at 8 percent and then dropped to 4 percent after six months. New hires initially averaged ten minutes per transaction, but after two weeks on the job this rate dropped to five minutes. After six months they were averaging just under four minutes.

An additional benefit was realized when federal regulations were modified some months after the new system was in place. Instead of providing the staff with new training, MegaBank updated the EPSS and sent employees an e-mail message about the change. This approach saved the firm both time and money.

Resources and References

Books and Articles

Collis, B. A., & Verwijs, C. (1995). A human approach to electronic performance and learning support systems: Hybrid EPSSs. *Educational Technology, 35*(1), 5–21.

Foster, E. (1997, February 24). Training when you need it. *Infoworld*, pp. 51–52.

Ganzel, R. (1998, February). Getting a grip on the digital future. *Training*, pp. 62–68.

Gery, G. (1991). *Electronic performance support systems: How and why to remake the workplace through the strategic application of technology.* Tolland, MA: Gery Performance Press.

Gery, G. (1995). Attributes and behaviors of performance centered systems. *Performance Improvement Quarterly, 8*(1). This is a special issue on EPSS.

Gery, G. (1997). Traditional vs. performance centered systems (Web site: http://www.epss.com/lb/artonline;articles/gg1/htm).

Juechter, W. M. (1993). Learning by doing. *Training & Development Journal, 47*(10), 28–30.

Norman, D. (1993). *Things that make us smart.* Reading, MA: Addison-Wesley.

On-Line Information Sources

EPSS.com! (Web site: http://www.epss.com/). An on-line publication that is a comprehensive resource for those interested in EPSS.

EPSS Infosite (Web site: http://www.tgx.enhance.com). A well-maintained site.

EPSS-Net (Web site: http://sunflower.singnet.com.sg/~abanerji/). An information resource for EPSS-related design, development, and research. Abstracts and articles are located in the publications section of the site.

Georgia Tech Research Institute (Web site: mime1.marc.gatech.edu/EPSS/). Includes on-line papers; these researchers expect EPSS to shape the jobs of plant workers.

Conferences

Performance Support Conference, RMR Conferences (e-mail: rmrconf@aol.com, Web site: http://www.performancesupport.com).

Intervention Authors

Gloria Gery
Principal
Gery Associates
108 South Trail
Tolland, MA 01034-9403
Phone: 413-258-4693
Fax: 413-258-4890
E-mail: gloria_gery@msn.com

Louis Jezsik
President
Vitaebase, Inc.
2191 Melrose Ave.
Montreal, Quebec H4A 2R7
Canada
Phone: 514-489-4797
E-mail: jezsik@vitaebase.com

Level of Performance	Business Unit	Process	Work Group	Individual
Establish	○	○	○	●
Performance Change Improve	○	○	○	●
Maintain	○	○	○	○
Extinguish	○	○	○	○

Alternative Names

Induction

Indoctrination

Definition

Employee orientation is the process of introducing and welcoming a new employee to the organization and helping that employee to make a good start. Successful new employee orientation (NEO) is a planned process, not a one-day event. It encourages retention of the information presented and fosters quick and independent productivity on the part of the employee.

The twelve key points for a successful orientation process are copyright © 1986 by The Training Clinic and are used here by permission.

Description

Many organizations have an orientation day. Typically, the new employee fills out forms, is overwhelmed with information, tours the facility, and reports to his or her work area. New employees often complain that their orientation is boring and overwhelming or that nothing happens and they are left alone to sink or swim.

Successful NEO, in contrast, is characterized by an enthusiastic welcome, a great deal of variety, and timely information. When orientation is a process that occurs over a period of time, the new employee is presented with appropriate amounts of information delivered *just in time* (just when the employee needs it).

Most new employee orientations are designed to accomplish the following objectives:

• Provide critical information and resources in a timely manner
• Help to make the new employee independently productive as soon as possible
• Teach essential safety and job skills
• Truly welcome the new employee
• Help the new employee to feel secure, to fit in, and to get off to a good start by developing an understanding of the organization's culture (how business is done, the organization's mission, its vision, and so on)

How these objectives are accomplished in orientation depends on the following factors:

• How many people are oriented at the same time
• The type of job or level of experience that the new employee has
• When initial and follow-up orientation meetings are held (for example, on the first day, during the first week, or once a month)
• The type of business conducted by the organization
• The duration of the actual orientation process
• The amount of time and money budgeted to develop the orientation process

Research (Barbazette, 1994) indicates that successful new employee orientations share the twelve elements described in the following paragraphs. These elements suggest that NEO is a process that each organization needs to customize for its own particular situation. In addition, each organization needs to modify these elements in accordance with the timing of the first orientation meeting and the number of new employees oriented at one time.

Element 1: Orientation Is Viewed as a Process

Orientation usually begins with the hiring decision and continues well into the first year of employment. In fact, NEO becomes the umbrella program for other important developmental events in the employee's career with the organization, such as performance reviews and training.

Element 2: Information Is Given When Needed

Information is best assimilated by the new employee when it is provided close to the time it is needed. For example, if the employee's health benefits begin thirty days after the start date, it is not appropriate to give the employee information about those benefits during the first week of employment.

Element 3: Benefits of Orientation Are Clear to Everyone

The benefits of orientation should be visible not only to the new employee but also to the entire organization. For example, the organization can identify such factors as reduced turnover or improved productivity as benefits of a systematic orientation. In addition, the new employee can determine quickly whether he or she feels valued by the organization and is able to fit into the new job. The new employee who feels at home is more relaxed, and more relaxed employees tend to make fewer mistakes—another benefit that is readily apparent to everyone.

Element 4: Organizational Culture Is Shared

A successful orientation program includes detailed information about the organization's culture (its philosophy, how to get along, how business is done, and so on). New employees need to know the organization's norms, customs, and traditions. In some organizations, for example, all employees are addressed by their first names; in others there is a strong sense of formality that requires the use of surnames. To be successful, the orientation process should clarify expectations and common definitions of what is considered *normal*.

Element 5: Employee's First Day Is Welcoming

When the employee's first day is truly welcoming, that employee immediately begins to feel useful and productive. Welcoming an employee appropriately requires preparation. The employee's office, desk, phone, and supplies should be ready for use when he or she first arrives. Also, the welcome might include introductions and a tour that ends in the employee's work area.

The new employee may then be paired with an experienced *buddy,* who teaches the employee a simple task that can be completed during the first day. In this way the new employee can immediately contribute to his or her department's production and can feel a sense of accomplishment.

Element 6: Roles of the Supervisor and Human Resources Are Clear

The organization's human resource department or function should help the new employee's supervisor to understand and effectively execute his or her role in orientation. The supervisor and human resources share responsibility for the new employee's successful orientation. Together they need to identify which aspects of orientation are more specific to the employee's job and are therefore the supervisor's responsibility and also which aspects involve more general information and are therefore the responsibility of human resources. This division of tasks involves negotiation between the supervisor and human resources if the responsibility for orientation is to be shared successfully.

Element 7: Orientation Activities Focus on Knowledge, Skills, and Attitudes

A successful orientation is based on objectives that are measurable and that focus not only on knowledge but also on the skills and attitudes that the new employee must acquire. Some organizations focus their orientation efforts exclusively on knowledge, resulting in information overload. A better approach is to include discussions about necessary attitudes as well as training in necessary skills, such as operating the telephone system. A balance of different kinds of activities and pacing makes orientation interesting and helps avoid boredom and overload.

Element 8: Orientation Is Self-Directed

If an organization wants its employees to use their initiative and to exercise judgment, then self-directed new employee orientation is appropriate. Several successful NEO programs give the new employee a list of tasks to accomplish, a deadline for each task, and the time and resources necessary to complete the tasks. Many unsuccessful programs, in contrast, spoon-feed all information to the employee, thereby conveying the notion that the employee need not apply initiative and personal judgment in the new job. If employees are to work independently, at least part of their orientation should be their responsibility.

Element 9: Guest Speakers Are Used

Guest speakers may make either live or videotaped presentations. They should be well prepared, should present only essential information with specific objectives, and should use good presentation techniques. The human resource department may want to coach the speakers, prepare professional-looking visual aids for them to use, or even outline or script their presentations.

Element 10: Audiovisuals Are Used

Audiovisual components give emphasis to the orientation program and convey a positive message. For example, videos or slides may be used to describe the organization's culture, history, and philosophy. Although the temptation is to put as much as possible on video, it is important to remember that the content needs to be lasting.

Element 11: Orientation Is Evaluated

The orientation program should be evaluated by new employees, their supervisors, and the human resource department or function. The program participants can give their reactions and offer suggestions about ways to improve the process. Supervisors can assess whether the information presented in orientation is used on the job and to what extent the orientation content should be revised. The human resource department or function should evaluate the orientation program in terms of its results. A cost-benefit analysis is not easy to conduct, but it is well worth doing to prove the value of the program.

Element 12: Information Is Given to Employee's Family

Successful NEO programs involve the employee's family. For example, a welcome may be extended to the family, letters or copies of the organization's newsletter may be sent to the family, or family members may be included in some of the orientation activities. Many companies invite family members to come to work one day during the year; others schedule benefits orientations during the evening so that family members may attend. One organization even visits the home of a new employee in a gesture equivalent to a corporate welcome wagon.

When to Use

The following are circumstances under which it is useful to establish or improve the process of new employee orientation.

When New Employees' Productivity Is Not What It Should Be

New employees who are fully oriented and trained are more productive than those who are poorly oriented and trained. Every new employee reaches a point at which he or she becomes independently productive, and a systematic orientation can reduce the time required to reach this point.

New employees are productive only when they know how to do essential tasks such as the following:

- Sending and receiving e-mail
- Using the telephone system
- Obtaining needed supplies
- Finding their way around the facility
- Identifying who does what

In addition, it should be remembered that new employees who are clearing up family relocation issues have difficulty being fully productive at work.

When New Employees' Safety Records Are Poor

When training in basic safety and job skills is ignored or left to chance, accident rates are higher than when such training is made a systematic part of new employee orientation.

When New Employees Resign Within the First Year

If employees are left on their own to sink or swim, they sometimes leave the organization within the first year of employment, either because they do not fit in or because they do not know what is expected of them.

Case Study

In November 1997, Bechtel International, a global company in the business of project management, engineering, and construction management, decided to create a task force to develop a consistent NEO program in all of its offices worldwide. The members of the task force—employees from Bechtel's human resource functions in Southeast Asia, the United Kingdom, and three locations in the United States—were selected to represent a variety of tenures with the company. In addition, their parent offices all had different orientation programs.

The task force members were asked to complete their task during a two-day meeting at the company's headquarters in San Francisco. In preparation for this meeting, they completed the following activities:

- They gathered existing orientation materials from their respective offices to share with one another.
- Each of them researched the literature on new employee orientation and collected books and articles to share with one another (see "Resources and References").
- They invited a customer, a new employee at the San Francisco office, to meet with the task force to serve as a sounding board for their ideas and to test the NEO process as it developed.
- They invited an external consultant to facilitate their process.

The members' thorough preparation allowed efficient use of their two-day meeting. Their meeting process consisted of receiving extensive input from one another as they shared materials and ideas.

First, they identified the primary target population for NEO: new employees, existing employees who had not yet participated in NEO, employees who had transferred from one Bechtel facility to another, local site workers, and members of *secondary populations* (such as contract and temporary employees).

Next they brainstormed objectives and developed an outline for orientation. Then they identified content and methods for new employees at (1) the corporate level, (2) the regional level, (3) the site-specific, or local, level, and (4) the departmental or job level.

To ensure that orientation would be managed as a process, they identified when (and at what intervals) specific information would be delivered:

- On the first day
- During the first week, but not on the first day

- During the first month, but not the first week
- During the three-month follow-up
- During the six-month follow-up

Subsequently they identified specific employees (by job title) who would be responsible for delivering the orientation content at different times. Then they estimated the costs for developing or revising materials for each audience level.

They also considered the context of the information to be delivered. For example, they decided that during the first week the new employee's supervisor would make sure that the employee

- Had an understanding of the critical success factors
- Had resolved any relocation issues
- Had a grasp of the big picture
- Had all of the supplies and equipment necessary to do the job
- Had developed needed skills in specific areas

The program they developed is now in the approval process. Offices that currently have orientation programs will continue to use those programs until the new, uniform program has been approved and implemented in all offices worldwide.

Resources and References

Barbazette, J. (1994). *Successful new-employee orientation.* San Francisco: Jossey-Bass/Pfeiffer.

Berger, S., & Huchendord, K. (1989, December). Ongoing orientation at Metropolitan Life. *Personnel Journal,* pp. 48–50.

Bridges, K., Hawkins, G., & Elledge, K. (1993, August). From new recruit to team member. *Training & Development Journal,* pp. 55–58.

George, M., & Miller, K. (1996, July). Assimilating new employees. *Training & Development Journal,* pp. 49–50.

Klein, C. S., & Taylor, J. (1994, May). Employee orientation is an ongoing process at the DuPont Merck Pharmaceutical Co. *Personnel Journal,* p. 67.

Intervention Author

Jean Barbazette
President
The Training Clinic
645 Seabreeze Drive
Seal Beach, CA 90740
Phone: 562-430-2484
Fax: 562-430-9603
E-mail: trainu@apc.net
Web site: http://www.apc.net/trainu

Case Study Author

Jean Barbazette, with assistance from
Marty Jordan
Manager
Organizational Learning & Performance Improvement
Bechtel International
50 Beale Street
San Francisco, CA 94119

■ ■ ■ ■ ı ı EXPERT SYSTEMS

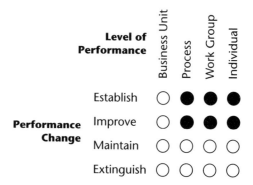

Level of Performance	Business Unit	Process	Work Group	Individual
Establish	○	●	●	●
Performance Change Improve	○	●	●	●
Maintain	○	○	○	○
Extinguish	○	○	○	○

Alternative Names

Knowledge management
Artificial intelligence
Knowledge-based systems
Rule-based systems
Heuristic systems
Intelligent tutoring system (ITS)
Electronic performance support system (EPSS)

Definition

An *expert system* (ES) is a computer program that simulates intelligent problem solving within a narrow area of expertise—an artificial decision maker (Romiszowski, 1987).

Description

There are three main types of artificial intelligence: robotics, natural language, and expert systems. Robotics engineers study how to make and operate robots.

Natural language researchers try to find ways to help computers understand everyday speech so that people can communicate with computers without using complicated programming languages (preferably by simply talking to them). Developers of expert systems, now often called *knowledge-based systems*, create programs that contain expert knowledge.

Expert systems offer people what they have always wanted from a computer: the ability to ask difficult questions and receive practical answers. The early expert systems most often provided diagnosis or classification in medical or scientific areas. During the 1970s various expert systems were developed for business applications, which proved that these systems could be competitive tools, not simply medical and scientific references (Feigenbaum, McCorduck, & Nii, 1989).

In a typical transaction, a human performer initiates a consultation when facing a decision requiring some highly specialized knowledge, such as diagnosis and treatment of rare blood infections. The performer provides relevant information, which the expert system then analyzes using a set of rules in its knowledge base to arrive at a recommendation. An expert system can also monitor a complex process and be triggered by an event, such as a dangerous combination of conditions in a nuclear power plant. An expert system can be thought of as an intelligent, electronic job aid.

There are expert systems for all types of business applications, and more are being built all the time. They range from systems that help farmers market their grain at the highest prices to systems that diagnose problems in telecommunication lines, to systems that train automobile mechanics. Early expert systems were stand-alone applications; today, however, they are usually embedded in large software systems, in performance support systems, or in intelligent tutoring systems.

Expert systems have several defining characteristics, as explained in the following paragraphs.

Ability to Handle Problems with Missing or Incomplete Information

Conventional programs cannot run if a key input is missing. For example, the cyclicity of an industry is an important factor in establishing that industry's overall credit risk. A seasoned credit reviewer can make a best guess (based on previous experience) at what he or she expects the cyclicity to be and then allow a wider margin of error in the rating to compensate for the missing data. An expert system will do the same thing. It will produce an answer based on the information available and will rate the level of confidence that should be placed in that answer.

Ability to Use Both Quantitative and Qualitative Data

Conventional computer programs written to help bankers assess credit risk were limited to calculating quantitative data, as in the computation of a borrower's financial ratios from financial statements. They were unable to handle information that was not numeric. A knowledge-based system asks a banker to describe the stage of development in an industry by selecting from a menu consisting of choices like "fast growth," "mature," or "declining." Moreover, these qualitative judgments made by the lender can be combined with the quantitative analysis to project how well a given borrower in a given industry will be able to sustain current revenue growth.

Ability to Indicate Amount of Uncertainty in an Assessment

Human experts often qualify their assessments by giving a range of probable outcomes. A well-constructed expert system will behave the same way, indicating uncertainty based on statistical techniques to provide confidence intervals.

Ability to Explain the Inferencing Process

Human experts can generally justify their conclusions, and the same is true for expert systems. A well-designed system is able to show how it arrives at its conclusions. The best systems are able to trace backward from the final conclusions to the original situation that was input by the user.

The distinctions between conventional data-processing systems and expert systems are most easily summarized in terms of the input accepted, the process of generating answers, and the certainty of the output. Conventional systems plug numerical data into formulas and apply step-by-step procedures (algorithms) to arrive at answers. Expert systems can accept qualitative information and make logical inferences based on a set of guiding principles or rules of thumb (heuristics) supplied by human experts. Algorithms are always correct, as they are calculations and deductions; heuristic answers, either from human experts or expert systems, involve some uncertainty because they are based on qualitative data and inductive reasoning derived from experience.

When to Use

Expert systems are an expensive, highly complex technology that can be very useful in the right situation. The first decision to make is whether an expert system is an appropriate intervention. This depends primarily on the task and the quality of problem solving and decision making involved. When all of the following conditions exist, the use of expert systems is appropriate.

- The task is so complex that human performers require many years of study and practice in order to achieve competence, with the result that human experts are scarce or very expensive
- The task has a high payoff value, either in terms of commercial value or social benefit, which justifies the high cost of development
- The decision requires contextual judgment (heuristics) rather than formulas or purely logical deductions
- The problem can be represented symbolically, involving a relatively narrow area of knowledge

Unless the task involves all of these elements, a cheaper and easier intervention will work. The cost and difficulty of developing an expert system requires that the task be both difficult and valuable. If the problem solving is driven purely by formulas, as in calculating the trajectories of space vehicles, then even though those calculations are complex, conventional algorithm-based programming is the right approach. Judging legal cases is an example of decision making that goes beyond logical application of the laws: it may be very complex and it requires interpreting the law and weighing complex matters of social justice, ethics, and morality. However, an expert system is not appropriate here because the technology has not yet enabled us to create useful knowledge bases that go beyond a narrow domain.

If all of the previously cited conditions exist, the next consideration is whether an expert system is possible for the task. This depends primarily on what people already know about the area involved:

- Genuine experts exist and their expertise can be demonstrated
- Experts have a high degree of agreement on the solutions
- Experts can articulate their methods

If these criteria are not met, then it is probably not possible to develop an expert system. For example, many people would like to develop an expert system for selecting stocks. (In fact, this has been tried.) The stock market, however, involves what economists call a *random walk*, which is just another way of saying that a monkey throwing darts will do as well. No true expertise in the field has been demonstrated; there is little agreement about solution methods; and those who claim a high success rate cannot explain how they do it.

If it is both possible and feasible to develop an expert system as an intervention, it is appropriate to do so under the following conditions:

- When valuable knowledge needs to be managed and preserved and human experts are scarce or might walk out the door to work for competitors

the time was one of the larger corporate distance education programs. Informal project newsletters provided information, tips, and hints, along with a strong dose of humor. Finally, the bank developed a professionally prepared video to show during the formal introduction of the system. These steps allayed people's natural concerns about being replaced or downgraded by the new computer system.

As is the case with all introductions of major systems, there was some resistance. However, the commitment of senior management and some early success stories resulted in a promising formal introduction. What made the expert system a good intervention in this instance was the need for performance support for many lenders and the regulatory necessity of improving consistency in lending policies. There was no way the bank could take the majority of its lenders out of service until their skill level reached an acceptable level, nor were there enough senior lenders to tutor all of the junior lenders. Also, keeping lending decisions consistent with the law avoided the wrath of customers and regulatory penalties, and keeping decisions consistent with the bank's strategy maximized profits.

The bank executives were pleased with the success of the Credit Management Project. They acknowledged the learning that resulted from defining a performance improvement strategy, examining a systemic problem in the bank's credit operations, developing an expert system model of a sound credit process, and implementing a comprehensive plan in which the ES was an integral element of a total organizational change strategy.

Resources and References

Feigenbaum, E., McCorduck, P., & Nii, H. P. (1989). *The rise of the expert company.* New York: Vintage Books.

Grabinger, R. S., Jonassen, D., & Wilson, B. (1992). The use of expert systems. In H. D. Stolovitch and E. J. Keeps (Eds.), *Handbook of human performance technology: A comprehensive guide for analyzing and solving performance problems in organizations* (pp. 365–380). San Francisco: Jossey-Bass.

Harmon, P. (1990). *Creating expert systems for business and industry.* New York: Wiley.

Romiszowski, A. J. (1987, October). Expert systems in education and training: Automated job aids or sophisticated instructional media? *Educational Technology*, pp. 22–30.

Waterman, D. (1986). *A guide to expert systems.* Reading, MA: Addison-Wesley.

Intervention Author

Fred Estes
Program Manager
The Hewlett-Packard Company
1417 Shoal Drive
San Mateo, CA 94404
Phone: 650-578-1503
Fax: 650-578-1071

▪ ▪ ▪ ▪ ▪ ▪ FLOWCHARTS

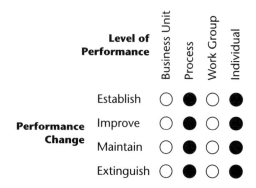

Level of Performance	Business Unit	Process	Work Group	Individual
Establish	○	●	○	●
Performance Change Improve	○	●	○	●
Maintain	○	●	○	●
Extinguish	○	●	○	●

Alternative Names

Macro flowcharts
Tops-down flowcharts
Work flow diagrams
Deployment flowcharts
Work process maps

Definition

A *flowchart* is a graphic representation of a work process. It represents all aspects of the process: the sequence of activities, the physical flow of materials or information involved, and the associated inputs and outputs. Flowcharts are used in connection with efforts to define or improve work processes.

Description

Although there are numerous types of flowcharts and flowcharting techniques, the primary purpose of all flowcharting is to define how work is performed and to improve the productivity of that work. Because flowcharts are generally easier to follow and interpret than narrative operating procedures, they have become valuable tools in improving the performance of job incumbents and in training new workers.

Flowcharts range in detail from macro-level charts that show major steps in a work process to charts that show all activities, material, documents, and information flow. It is common to begin with a macro-level chart.

Flowcharts were originally hand drawn, making changes difficult and messy. As computers became capable of producing graphic representations, flowcharting software emerged. Initially this software aided programmers who designed and analyzed information systems. Other early applications included the product flowcharts used in manufacturing processes and the PERT (program evaluation research technique) and CPM (critical path method) charts used in project management during the 1950s.

Today's software products simplify the creation of multiple levels of chart detail, in which a basic step is expanded into the detailed activities performed. Other features of current software packages include process simulation of cost and time, importing of pictures and clip art, hidden notes and annotation, what-if analysis, and statistical reports.

A flowchart documents a process by illustrating many of the following work process elements:

- Type and sequence of activities and decisions
- Flow of material, documents, and communication of information (including inputs to the process, steps within the process, and outputs from the process)
- Responsibility and geographical location of activities
- Process time to complete individual activities
- Value added by and costs of activities in the process
- Steps in the process in which data measurement occurs

Macro Flowcharts

A macro flowchart (see Figure 1) shows the sequence of major activities in a process and provides a good perspective of the total process. The development of a macro flowchart often precedes that of more detailed flowcharts. It shows the sequence of process steps in either columns or rows of rectangular blocks starting with the first step in the top-left corner. Each block includes a short description of the activity in a verb-noun format.

FIGURE 1. MACRO FLOWCHART: PROCESS IMPROVEMENT MODEL.

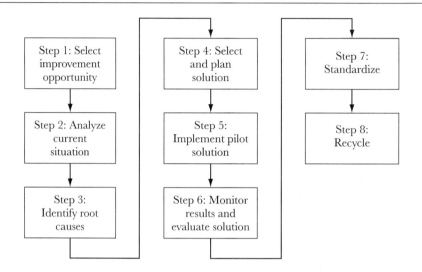

Tops-Down Flowcharts

A tops-down flowchart (see Figure 2) shows the major steps in a process and key activities within each step. The steps are listed in order across the top of the chart, starting with the first one on the left. The activities necessary to achieve each step are listed below that step. Activities are described using short statements in a verb-noun format. In order to avoid complexity, people who use tops-down flowcharts generally limit them to seven steps and to seven activities within each step. (Steps and activities may be combined to maintain these limits.)

Work Flow Diagrams

A work flow diagram (see Figure 3) graphically displays the physical movement of people, work, or information in a process. The chart is created by tracing movements on a floor plan or other spatial representation of a geographical location. This chart is helpful in illustrating illogical flows of work or information and in demonstrating the need to locate common activities together in an area. This kind of chart can be constructed to show not only the patterns of interaction and the work or information flows, but also the sequence of activities. Work flow diagrams, in conjunction with other detailed flowcharts, illustrate the need to change the sequence of steps or the physical arrangement of facilities.

FIGURE 2. TOPS-DOWN FLOWCHART: PREPARING A DEPLOYMENT FLOWCHART.

List Process Steps	Identify Responsibility	Place Post-It Notes	Complete Draft Flowchart	Add Timeline	Review Flowchart	Identify Improvement Opportunities
Identify process boundaries (input and output).	Identify organizations or people involved in the process.	Place the input Post-It note in the upper-left corner.	Add small symbols to Post-It notes to indicate decisions (diamond), documents, inputs, or outputs.	Add actual and theoretical process time for each step.	Review flowchart with process owner and stakeholders.	Non-value-added steps
Brainstorm steps in current process (verb-noun format).	Label columns (or rows) on flip-chart paper with the name of responsible organization or people	Arrange Post-it notes in sequence in columns (or rows).		Show non-value-added steps with a zero (0) theoretical process time.	Modify flowchart as required.	Sequential steps to be done concurrently
Prepare Post-It notes for each step.		Add remaining steps in sequence in appropriate columns (or rows).	Link steps in the sequence performed with lines ending in arrows.			Illogical flows
						Bottlenecks, critical steps, and failures requiring rework
						Manual steps, duplicate tasks, and unnecessary approvals and inspection

FIGURE 3. WORK FLOW DIAGRAM:
VIDEO STORE CHECKOUT PROCESS.

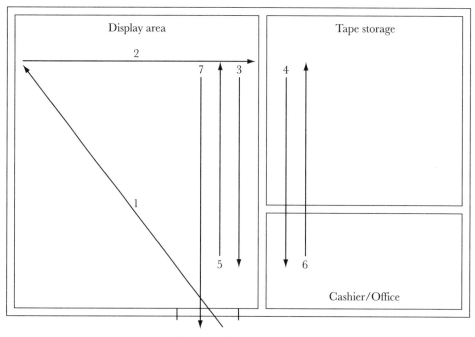

Deployment Flowcharts

A deployment flowchart is a detailed flowchart that maps a work process. It illustrates the sequence of work activities and the person or organization responsible for each task and decision. This level of detail highlights the interaction between individuals or organizations, including communication and other involvement such as document review and meetings. A deployment flowchart can be constructed with the organization or people as the header of either columns or rows.

In order to improve the analytical capability of a deployment flowchart, the person who creates it adds a timeline in the left column (or bottom row). This timeline usually includes the average actual time for each process activity and an estimated theoretical process time. Comparisons of the two times highlight process steps that need the greatest improvement.

Deployment flowcharts are often linked to performance measurement systems in which measurement points are located at key steps in the process. Cycle time measures can be used to measure elapsed time from the beginning to the end of the process or elapsed time between any two intermediate steps. Quality measures can be taken at any point at which inspection occurs. Steps to record labor and material charges and to document the timelines of the process to meet customer requirements are often included.

Process flowcharts generally use a standard set of symbols (see Figure 4) to reflect various activities or events.

When to Use

Flowcharts can be used effectively in the following circumstances:

• When the goal is to understand, manage, and improve a process
• When several people in a work group or several work groups perform a process consisting of a series of activities
• When there is uncertainty over what activities are performed, the sequence in which those activities are performed, where they are performed, and by whom

FIGURE 4. FLOWCHART SYMBOLS.

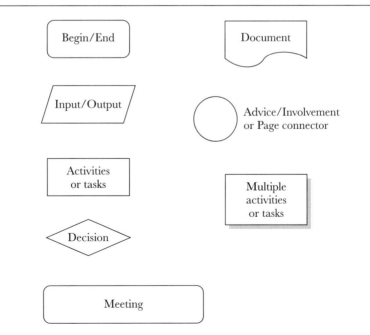

- When one or more of the activities in a process fails and the process does not produce the results expected
- When other forms of documenting activities, such as written procedures, do not provide a clear understanding of the process

Case Study

Organizations with strong functional departments often struggle with cross-functional processes. Work is performed in sequence, first in one department and then in the next. At best, errors created early in the process are discovered at final inspection. The results include delays, unnecessary rework, and dissatisfied customers.

In one company that designs new packaging materials for clients, employees discovered that the average job took more than fifteen work days (from the time the order was received until the customer received the printed packaging materials). In addition, customer complaints indicated that numerous corrections were required. To improve the process, the company's sales manager formed a team composed of representatives from sales, design/engineering, production control, and purchasing. The team's specific objective was to reduce the time required to complete the process and reduce the number of errors requiring correction.

The team members' first task was to define the existing process. To do this, they first created a macro flowchart showing the major steps. Next they created a tops-down flowchart using the major steps of the macro flowchart and adding all the detailed activities performed under each major step. Finally, they created a deployment flowchart (Figure 5) using the detailed activities from the tops-down flowchart.

Once the sequence and responsibility for each step was validated, the team members developed a timeline that showed the average actual process time and an estimated theoretical time for each step.

The team members then prepared a detailed action plan to analyze opportunities for improving the process. They decided to start recording the types of corrections required, the names of customers whose orders needed correction, and other details. They also agreed to record the date and time that each department received and completed each new order.

Next the team members explored ways to provide information in advance for design/engineering and production control in an attempt to perform activities concurrently rather than sequentially. Finally, each department agreed to streamline activities beginning with those tasks with the highest ratio of actual time to theoretical time. (Inefficient activities had high ratios of actual to theoretical times.

FIGURE 5. DEPLOYMENT FLOWCHART: PACKAGING PROCESS.

Average Process Time (Hr.)		Customer	Sales	Design/ Engineering	Production control	Purchasing	Printer
Actual	**Theoretical**						
1.0	0.5	Issue P.O.	Receive P.O.				
16.0	1.5		Verify order				
2.0	0.5	Make corrections	Corrections — Yes / No				
1.0	0.5		Enter order in computer				
8.0	1.0		Copy order for R&D	Review order			
16.0	8.0			Design new package			
16.0	1.5	Make corrections		Corrections — Yes / No			
2.0	0			Release design to product control			
2.0	1.0				Schedule job		

FIGURE 5. DEPLOYMENT FLOWCHART: PACKAGING PROCESS (CONTINUED).

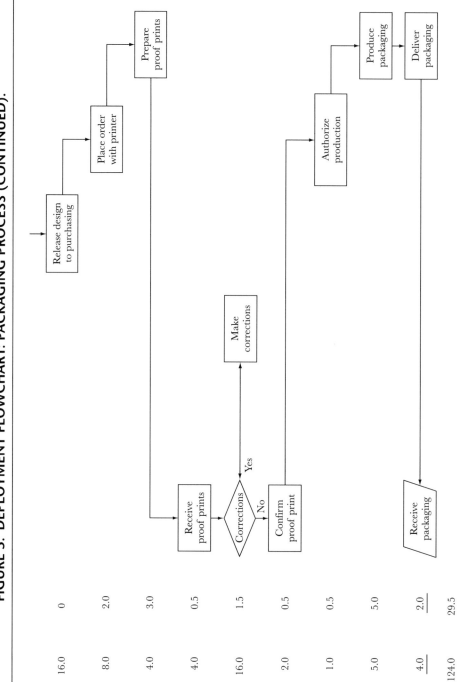

Non-value-added activities were assigned a zero theoretical time—meaning that these activities should not exist—and the ratio was a very large number, infinity.)

Resources and References

Brassard, M., & Ritter, D. (1994). *The Memory Jogger II*. Methuen, MA: Goal/QPC.

Buffa, E .S. (1963). *Models of production and operations management*. New York: Wiley.

Galloway, D. (1994). *Mapping work processes*. Milwaukee, WI: ASQ (American Society for Quality) Quality Press, 1994.

Swanson, R. C. (1995). *The quality improvement handbook: Team guide to tools and techniques*. Del Rey Beach, FL: St. Lucie Press.

Intervention Author

Roger C. Swanson
President
Competitive Dynamics, Inc.
650 Pacific St., #7
Santa Monica, CA 90405-2412
Phone: 310-399-4142
E-mail: rswanson@compdynamics.com
Web site: http://www.compdynamics.com

■ ■ ■ ■ ■ ¡ FLUENCY DEVELOPMENT

Level of Performance	Business Unit	Process	Work Group	Individual
Establish	○	○	○	●
Performance Improve	○	○	○	●
Change Maintain	○	○	○	○
Extinguish	○	○	○	○

Alternative Names

Practice
Fluency Building[1]

Definition

Fluency development consists of procedures and materials that enable performers to achieve fluency, which is the combination of accuracy and speed in performance that optimally supports retention, stability (resistance to distraction), and application (transfer of training).

Description

Educators in the 1960s and 1970s who applied a method known as *precision teaching* (Binder, 1996; Lindsley, 1997) discovered that the rate at which a learner can

---

1.   Fluency Building is a trademark of Binder Riha Associates.

accurately perform a given skill affects the retention and stability of the skill itself as well as the application of that skill to more complex skills. They recognized that daily practice—using brief, timed sessions and immediate performance feedback—enabled learners to achieve higher rates of performance, as long as the individual components of the target behavior were themselves capable of being performed at sufficiently high rates.

This work led to further research and application with schoolchildren and to the development of carefully sequenced learning objectives and materials for primary and secondary education, with a focus on basic skills. Use of this approach yielded dramatic improvements in students' standardized achievement scores.

Ogden Lindsley founded the movement of precision teaching. Other early pioneers in this method were Eric Haughton, Clay Starlin, Ann Starlin, and Ray Beck. In the early 1980s, Carl Binder, a researcher and trainer of teachers, decided to bring fluency-based instruction into the field of performance technology. In the process, he formulated a methodology for building behavioral fluency in adults that integrated the principles of precision teaching with the needs of the workplace.

The development and the support of fluent performance depend on both instructional and environmental factors.

Instructional Factors

One model of learning suggests that the learning process consists of three stages: *acquisition, practice,* and *application.* When learners first acquire a new skill, they achieve the ability to perform accurately but not necessarily rapidly. With efficient practice, though, they achieve the ability to perform quickly and without hesitation—and to do so for extended periods of time, so that they are relatively resistant to fatigue and distraction. By performing rapidly and without hesitation, they retain what they have learned. Finally, after achieving fluency, they are able to apply their skill to more complex performance, including improvisation and creative combinations of behavior. These effects are obvious in some kinds of performance, such as sports, but they are relatively unrecognized in academic and workplace training.

This three-stage model of learning indicates that a learning program should provide practice so that an individual can achieve fluency prior to applying the learning. A common error, however, is to arrange for acquisition, which does not produce fluency, and then to move into role plays, case study activities, or other application exercises. This means that practice is skipped and fluency cannot be obtained. Evidence suggests that skipping practice in this way may be one of the most significant reasons that educational and corporate training programs do not produce lasting performance change.

Environmental Factors

Environmental factors can either support or constrain performance. Ergonomics and user-interface design aim to ensure smooth, efficient interaction between performer and environment. In addition, structured writing produces reference and learning materials that support fluent access to information. The technology of fluency development, therefore, consists of removing any barriers to fluent performance and creating materials and environments that encourage and support fluency.

Fluency development methods are best used in situations in which learners can engage in *distributed* practice rather than in *cramming*, whether in learning modules that are parts of larger programs or in stand-alone interventions. A self-study program that allows for brief practice sessions each day over a period of several weeks is ideal, as are on-the-job training and self-managed learning labs that are part of longer classroom programs. Field-based coaching in sales and customer service organizations lends itself to informal practice activities involving managers or peers. Practice sessions that take place at larger events such as company conferences can be highly productive and motivating, as long as the scope of the practice is limited. Such sessions produce obvious improvements in skills and knowledge in a short time.

Jobs that require speaking with customers are among the most obvious applications of fluency development procedures (for example, sales and customer service). Those that involve specific physical skills are also good candidates (for example, keyboarding or developing the fine motor skills required in assembly or maintenance). In addition, jobs that involve typing as well as navigating through a system with complex cognitive behavior (for example, diagnosis, responding to requests, analyzing situations) can benefit from efficient practice during initial training. In general, if a task requires repetition to achieve genuine skill and if the criterion is truly mastery, then fluency development can make a practical difference.

See Figure 1 for factors that obstruct fluency as well as those that support it.

When to Use

Consider using fluency development methods when any of the following conditions exist.

FIGURE 1. FACTORS THAT OBSTRUCT AND SUPPORT FLUENCY.

Category	Factors That Prevent Fluency	Factors That Support Fluency
Measurement	Measurement procedures that ignore the time dimension Measurement procedures with too few response opportunities for the allotted time	Time-based performance measurement and evaluation More response opportunities than an expert can complete in the time allowed
Procedures	Too few practice opportunities Preventing learners from moving at their own pace Limited response opportunities per minute Emphasis on preventing errors during learning	Sufficient practice to attain fluency Self-paced learning and practice procedures Many opportunities per minute Treating errors as learning opportunities
Materials	Too few examples Materials that are difficult to use or that waste paper, movement, and so on Unnecessarily wordy work sheets and directions Difficult to read and comprehend	Many examples Easy to manipulate or use; efficient use of paper, space, and movement Succinct work sheets and directions Easy to read and comprehend
Skill elements	Critical steps in procedures or chained skills that are not fluent Tool skills or elements that are not fluent	Fluent steps in procedures Fluent tool skills or elements
Knowledge elements	Prerequisite knowledge that is not second nature or fluent Inability to fluently locate critical information	Fluent prerequisite knowledge (facts, concepts, structures, principles, classifications, or processes) Ability to use reference systems or job aids fluently, automatically

When Behavior Must Be Performed Without Hesitation

In situations in which the target behavior (including the use of job aids) must be performed smoothly and without hesitation, the person must be able to perform a skill or exhibit knowledge in a competent and confident manner. If the initial learning does not produce such predictably fluent performance, then efficient practice should enable the learner to achieve it. For example, salespeople must be able to deliver presentations confidently and smoothly and would therefore benefit from fluency development methods.

When Behavior Is Part of Activity to Be Performed Without Hesitation

When the target behavior is a component of a more complex activity that must be performed fluidly and without hesitation, fluency development methods are appropriate. Sometimes the acquisition of a complex behavior is difficult or impossible unless the person first acquires and then practices each separate component of that activity until fluency is achieved. For example, the inability to use touch typing fluently might keep customer service representatives from using service automation software while diagnosing and recording problems over the telephone.

When Behavior Must Be Performed at Length Without Fatigue or Loss of Attention

Achieving fluent performance in relatively short intervals increases *endurance* and resistance to distraction when the required duration of performance increases. For example, consider the case of beginning instructional designers, whose job is to produce modules of training day after day. To reduce the likelihood of mental fatigue in their first few weeks on the job, they can benefit from practice in writing clear instructional objectives, in matching types of learning activities to objectives, and in performing other key components of the process until they can do so for short intervals at a rate of five to fifteen items per minute (depending on the specific activity).

When Creative or Improvisational Behavior Must Be Produced

Research shows that creative or improvisational behavior benefits from fluent performance of the components of such behavior. By increasing their performance of components to high levels, learners increase the likelihood that these components will be available to them to combine in new ways. For example, being able to improvise playing the guitar depends on a fluent repertoire of playing scales, chord changes, and riffs. Similarly, supervisors who must provide feedback to difficult employees need a fluent repertoire of phrases and tactics that enable them to adapt effectively to a range of situations.

Case Studies

Two examples illustrate fluency development in different situations.

Fluency in Sales

Sales representatives in a medical equipment company needed to engage effectively in a number of behaviors: speaking about scientific topics with doctors, discussing health care economics with hospital administrators, identifying specific customer needs, matching those needs with features of their products that addressed those needs, presenting information about their products to groups of nurses, and answering a broad array of questions. The sales development department prepared a set of flash cards—easy-to-use, structured reference and self-study materials—to introduce the sales representatives to key information. The flash cards covered basic facts and bits of knowledge and the sales representatives practiced with them daily, with a goal of saying correct answers to thirty-five cards in one minute.

The sales representatives also engaged in rapid-recall exercises. They blurted out as many facts as they could about a particular topic, aiming to generate twenty to thirty such facts per minute, and practiced talking through selected overhead slides until they could combine what they knew into a confident, nicely paced presentation. They used practice sheets that required them to match dozens of statements reflecting specific customers' needs with product features.

Finally, in pairs the representatives practiced responding to tough questions written on the fronts of 3-by-5-inch cards until they could cover the key elements of agreed-on answers (represented by bullets on the backs of the cards) in their own words and at the same pace they would use in conversing on a familiar topic. In addition to these exercises, they completed timed multiple-choice tests before and after periods of self-study and practice to assess their knowledge of basic facts and associations.

The results of this program included the ability to complete fifteen to twenty multiple-choice test items per minute on a posttest (a criterion that has obvious face validity in relation to the time requirements of face-to-face sales). In addition, the sales representatives reported that they had never felt so confident about their ability to talk about their customers' situations and to present products in a competitive environment.

Fluency in a Factory Process

In a second case, factory maintenance technicians performed routine maintenance activities on the factory equipment. Procedural documentation was hard to understand and read, and some steps in the procedures (for example, placing rubber gaskets in hard-to-reach places) involved difficult manual skills. Improving the documentation with job aids and structured writing increased the ease with which technicians could find and follow directions (and the likelihood that they would use the documentation rather than simply experiment). Isolated practice in performing the difficult movements improved dexterity so that those steps no longer prevented the technicians from working smoothly and accurately through the procedures that included those steps. Results included the ability to find and use the correct procedural documentation and a more rapid acceleration to maintenance time and quality standards once new technicians were on the job.

Resources and References

Binder, C. (1990, September). Closing the confidence gap. *Training*, pp. 49–56.

Binder, C. (1996). Behavioral fluency: Evolution of a new paradigm. *The Behavior Analyst, 19*, 163–197.

Binder, C., & Bloom, C. (1989, February). Fluent product knowledge: Application in the financial services industry. *Performance and Instruction*, pp. 17–21.

Lindsley, O. R. (1997). Precise instructional design: Guidelines from precision teaching. In C. R. Dills & A. J. Romiszowski (Eds.), *Instructional development paradigms* (pp. 537–554). Englewood Cliffs, NJ: Educational Technology.

Snyder, G. (1992). Training to fluency: A real return on investment. *Performance Management, 10*, 16–22.

Intervention Author

Carl Binder
Partner
Binder Riha Associates
2300 Bethards Drive
Suite G
Santa Rosa, CA 95405
Phone: 707-578-7850
Fax: 707-578-7829
E-mail: carlbinder@aol.com
Web site: www.binder-riha.com

HUMAN RESOURCE INFORMATION SYSTEMS (HRIS)

Performance Change \ Level of Performance	Business Unit	Process	Work Group	Individual
Establish	●	○	●	○
Improve	●	○	●	○
Maintain	●	○	●	○
Extinguish	●	○	●	○

Definition

A *human resource information system* (HRIS) is a collection of employee information that is stored and retrieved electronically.

Description

A well-designed HRIS can be a powerful tool in helping managers improve their performance; and, as the performance of managers improves, so does that of the entire organization. A typical HRIS includes the following elements for every employee, current and past:

- Rate of pay
- Annual salary
- Sick (or absence) hours taken
- Vacation hours taken
- Hours worked
- Hours paid
- Date of last increase
- Date of last performance review

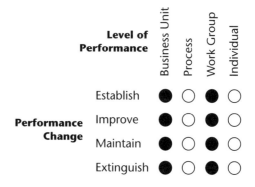

- Date of next performance review
- Reason for change (of status)
- Date of job (current)
- Date of hire (into original position)

The data retrieved from an HRIS can help managers answer many questions. For example, a report showing employees' performance appraisal dates, the amounts and percentages of their last increases, and their current wages can help a manager monitor the sizes of increases, conduct appraisals on time, and ensure equitable salaries. Also, certain performance mysteries, such as high error rates in a position, might be explained by looking at a report listing people's length of service, their reasons for leaving, and the number of new hires. When managers can obtain such personnel data easily, they can solve many of their problems on their own, without assistance from various experts. In fact, only the size of the computer on which the HRIS resides and the imagination of the HRIS designer can limit what can be collected and used.

Even unusual fields of data such as the following might be accessed:

- Orientation date (for use by accreditation agencies)
- Administered grade (the job market grade)
- Customer or stakeholder score (part of the merit review packet)
- Interaction behavior score (part of the merit review packet)
- Ethics manual signature code
- Foreign language code
- TB test date (if required by law)
- X-ray date (if required by law)
- Clerical testing scores
- Management mailing codes
- Registration or certification code
- Last discipline date
- Discipline reason
- Unexcused absence incidents and hours

In the 1980s human resource information systems were merely a statistical research function of an organization's human resource department. Application development was added as the need for more and different types of data increased. As the applications become more complex and data were duplicated within each different application, the role of the HRIS expanded to include administration of a consolidated, critical database.

A detailed analysis of the processes associated with employment and person-nel administration is needed to develop the requirements for redesigning a human resource system. This analysis answers important questions such as the following:

- What needs to be done?
- Who is involved in the process?
- How is the process initiated?
- What forms or data are passed from one process or activity to the next?
- Why is this done this way?

Essentially, the analysis questions everything about the way a process is done, with a focus on improving the process before automation (Berry, 1996).

For example, a hospital administrator had heard rumors that the employees in one of her reporting hospitals were quite unhappy and that many were re-signing. Before reacting, this administrator asked for a report from the HRIS to tell her the following:

- Employee terminations in that year, 1997
- Employee hire and termination dates
- Employee job titles
- Employee operating unit (department or division)
- Employee reason for internal change
- Employee reason for leaving the organization

Exhibit 1 is a reproduction of the report that she received. Exhibit 2 explains the report; it describes the kind of information that each field provided the ad-ministrator in terms of verifying whether employees were leaving in large num-bers. The administrator used the HRIS report, which gave her real data at a moment's notice, to analyze the situation.

When to Use

An HRIS is useful in the following situations:

- *When the number of employees exceeds fifty:* Data on as many as fifty employees can be collected and compiled in simple electronic and print files; however, when the number of employees is greater than fifty, an HRIS can expedite the process.
- *When special talents and skills need to be identified and searched for regularly:* For exam-ple, if the organization's work requires special talents, such as knowledge of

Date 12-31-97 Division DMC

EXHIBIT 1. HRIS REPORT: TERMINATIONS BY TYPE.

Terminations by Type

Type	Employee Name	Job Title	Change Reason	Term Reason	Term Date	Hire Date	Operating Unit
Term	David Giuld	ADMIN SEC I	701	501	11/26/97	11-16-72	4
Term	Bruce Mallstrom	AMB CARE HLTHSRC NRS	214	214	04/02/97	07-22-96	2
Term	Caroline Pamel	AMB CARE HLTHSRC NRS	501	501	11/19/97	04-20-92	2
Term	Dan Tamer	AMB SVCS REP	211	211	04/11/97	03-01-93	3
Term	Alan Hamilton	AMBULATORY ADMIN COORD	211	211	09/17/97	03-01-93	3
Term	Sharon Carris	AMBULATORY CARE CLERK	314	314	09/08/97	09-08-97	2
Term	Peter Hayden	BILLING/FOLLOW-UP REP	210	210	09/13/97	01-01-94	1
Term	Kurt Zelms	CARE MGMT SPECLST	236	236	11/22/97	09-22-90	4
Term	Craig Lemsen	CARE COORDINATOR	203	203	10/25/97	03-04-91	2
Term	Tammie Figgins	DIR MED REC/UTILIZ REV	210	210	08/15/97	06-07-82	4
Term	Ed Polson	ENVIRON SVCS WRKER II	406	406	04/08/97	07-06-92	5
Term	Jessi Cubbard	ENVIRON SVCS WRKER II	402	402	01/20/97	07-07-92	5
Term	Jake Hynes	ENVIRON SVCS WRKER II	214	214	03/20/97	02-01-93	5
Term	Mary Ingram	ENVIRON SVCS WRKER II	212	212	10/02/97	01-03-94	5
Term	Martin Kirwin	ENVIRON SVCS WRKER II	203	203	07/06/97	06-03-96	5
Term	Claus Jacob	ENVIRON SVCS WRKER II	212	212	07/19/97	06-17-96	5
Term	Steven Soel	ENVIRON SVCS WRKER II	314	314	01/27/97	09-30-96	5
Term	James Rohnson	ENVIRON SVCS WRKER II	408	408	01/28/97	11-04-96	5
Term	Chuck Noffee	ENVIRON SVCS WRKER II	314	314	01/27/97	09-16-96	5
Term	Trudi Vordan	ENVIRON SVCS WRKER II	303	303	10/22/97	09-29-97	5
Term	Jane Dudd	FILE CLERK	311	311	01/31/97	10-24-94	4
Term	Sally Tane	FILE CLERK	314	314	10/10/97	05-15-95	4
Term	Pat Kaufman	FILE CLERK	311	311	06/17/97	09-25-95	4
Term	Joanne Selly	FILE CLERK	203	203	06/11/97	07-01-96	4
Term	Michael Zerr	LICENSED PRACT NURSE-MED	208	208	01/15/97	09-06-88	2
Term	Marilyn Merwick	MEDICAL ASSISTANT	203	203	02/14/97	12-28-93	1

EXHIBIT 2. EXPLANATION OF HRIS REPORT.

Request	Reason for Looking at These Data
List of terminations in 1997	To confirm or deny the rumors.
Hire date and termination date	To determine whether employees leaving were long term or short term.
Job titles	To determine what levels of employees were leaving, as entry-level turnover is much less of a problem than turnover of professionals.
Operating unit	To determine location of turnover, perhaps indicating problems in leadership and supervision.
Reason for change	To determine the reasons employees gave: Were the reasons the same, did they form a pattern, or were they a normal and random set of reasons?
Reason for termination	To compare employee reasons with organization's reason for change; employees rarely state that they were terminated for cause.

certain software packages or languages, an HRIS can be used in place of costly manual searches.

- *When personnel problems recur:* If the same kinds of personnel problems tend to happen again and again, an HRIS can be especially useful.
- *When certain other problems regularly recur:* In the event that particular problems keep plaguing the organization, a solution might be found through the use of an HRIS. For example, if valued employees are leaving the organization regularly, one might want to either examine wage studies of exiting employees or review exit interview data.

Case Study

Several years ago, the human resource departments of seven operating units of a multihospital system were consolidated. The challenge was to develop a single, consistent HRIS that would meet the data needs of all seven human resource departments as well as the needs of all individual line managers in those departments.

A team of representatives from the seven units was assembled. After identifying the project scope, objectives, goals, and measurements, the team members completed more than thirty lists of data that could be used by human resource staff and line managers as well. The lists illustrated the differences in sophistication between the units. However, before long, every piece of data that could be used to improve performance at the individual or unit level was identified. Then strategies were developed for capturing the data in the least redundant fashion.

Once the database had been built, it became necessary to teach line managers how to write reports that would give them the data they needed in order to make important personnel decisions. After the managers learned how to get the data into the format they needed (a function called "writing a report"), they were able to accomplish several goals:

- Identify training needs (through the use of the reporting function of the database)
- Identify future staffing needs
- Predict shortfalls in staffing plans
- Do vacation planning in a more systematic and predictable way

Resources and References

Berry, W. E. (1996). Modern guidelines for HRIS requirements analysis: A new approach to match today's needs. In M. N. Thompson (Ed.), *Handbook of human resources information systems* (1996 supplement). Boston: Warren, Gorham, & Lamont.

Eli Broad Graduate School of Management. (1996). *Process Mapping: How to streamline and reengineer business processes.* East Lansing, MI: Author (Michigan State University, 424 Eppley Center, East Lansing, MI 48824, phone: 800-365-5705).

Rummler, G. A., & Brache, A. P. (1995). *Improving performance: How to manage the white space on the organization chart* (2nd ed.). San Francisco: Jossey-Bass.

Intervention Author

Susan B. Bristol
Director, Human Resources Information Systems
The Detroit Medical Center
3740 John R.
Detroit, MI 48201
Phone: 313-745-4572
Fax: 313-745-4592

▪ ▪ ▪ ▪ ▪ ▪ JOB AIDS

	Level of Performance	Business Unit	Process	Work Group	Individual
	Establish	○	●	●	●
Performance Change	Improve	○	●	●	●
	Maintain	○	●	●	●
	Extinguish	○	●	●	●

Alternative Name

Performance aids

Definition

A *job aid* is "anything that, when added to the work situation, improves job performance by guiding, facilitating, or reminding the performer in his or her accomplishment of job tasks" (Langdon, Lineberry, & Bullock, 1980, p. xi).

Description

Prior to the 1970s, training was prescribed as the solution to almost every performance issue that arose. In the early 1970s, however, trainers who were confronted with performance issues began conducting *needs analyses* to determine whether training was actually necessary or whether the issues might be resolved by means other than training. After the advent of needs analysis, it was discovered that many performance issues do not require a training resolution and can be addressed instead with a variety of job or performance aids. Thus the job aids movement began. Donald Bullock, Joe Harless, Claude Lineberry, Ivan Horabin, Brian Lewis, and Allison Rossett have been key contributors to our knowledge.

In the broad sense, anything that aids performance, decision making, evaluation, or documentation of desired results might be considered a job aid. One kind of job aid allows an employee to perform a task without any prior knowledge of how to perform it. For example, if an employee does not know how to assemble an item, the set of instructions provided with that item is a job aid. When prior knowledge does exist, another kind of job aid can help an employee to organize that knowledge so that he or she is able to perform more effectively or efficiently. For example, a work sheet that organizes information to be filled in, which, in turn, is used by an employee to make a decision, is a job aid.

Although a job aid is not generally thought of as an instructional means, it may be a precursor to, used within, or serve as a follow-up to an instructional activity. Thus an outline for a report might serve as a job aid in that it helps the user to organize conceptually what the report will be. Another job aid might be a checklist of the sequential steps of a task that an employee must learn to perform. Finally, a job aid might consist of a set of criteria to evaluate a skill that has been learned or is to be practiced for mastery and measurement, such as teaching or presenting.

Of course, the most widely known job aids are those that are independent of training or instruction. For example, most copying machines include a printed or electronic job aid that describes how to fix a jam or other problem without prior knowledge. Similarly, most computer software has a *help* function that the user can access to assist in completing a particular task. Labels on food products offer information on dietary and nutritional content that serves as an aid in selection and purchase.

Some common classes of job aids include the following:

- Step-by-step lists and procedures
- Flowcharts
- Algorithms
- Decision charts and tables
- Checklists
- Forms
- Work sheets
- Outlines
- Evaluation criteria

When to Use

The following criteria (Langdon, Lineberry, & Bullock, 1980) are useful in determining when to use job aids.

When the Performance Requires Guidance Rather Than Recall

A job aid is useful when the performer does not have to recall completely and immediately, but can rely instead on an external source to assist performance. For example, a benefits form provides information on what insurance coverage is provided and guides employees in completing the form. It would not be prudent to teach everyone the details of how to seek reimbursement, as recall is not necessary and performance is sporadic.

When Time Is Not a Critical Factor

If time is not critical, as in the case of fixing something that is broken or needs maintenance, the performer can turn to the use of a job aid to assist in performing the task. For example, if the performer wants to change a flat tire, he or she could benefit from the use of a job aid. In contrast, a job aid is not appropriate for a task such as driving a car because time is of the essence.

When the Task Is Performed Infrequently

If the performer seldom performs a procedure or needs to use information that he or she might forget over time, a job aid would be more appropriate than instruction. An infrequently performed activity can be guided by a job aid when required. For example, a project completion checklist would remind a project manager what things must be done at the completion of a construction project, which might occur only after lapses of months or years.

When Not to Use

Circumstances under which job aids may not be appropriate include the following:

- When face-to-face skills are important, such as those required for conducting a meeting

- When there are physical or psychosocial barriers (stressful conditions, safety factors, or physical limitations, for example)
- When emotional limitations exist, as they might in notifying an employee of a disciplinary write-up or layoff

Case Study

Very large construction companies often require employees from project management, engineering, and other technical fields to give oral presentations to prospective clients. Such prospective clients request these presentations so that they can better evaluate bids and project teams from the various companies who have proposed building factories, highways, and so forth.

The vice president of marketing in one construction company had long recognized that the company's technical and management personnel, although excellent performers in their own fields, did not generally possess adequate skills in organizing and delivering effective oral presentations. He also knew that their lack of comfort and experience in front of an audience might diminish their competence in the eyes of the would-be client.

In analyzing the performance need, the vice president became aware of the following specific conditions:

- With the exception of project managers, employees gave an average of fewer than three presentations apiece throughout their careers. Therefore, frequency of performance was very low, meaning that any presentation skills they learned now probably would not be used again for several months or even years.
- The personnel with the content knowledge necessary to give such presentations were located in different countries. Also, they generally received very short notice (usually less than seven days) that a presentation had to be made. Often they represented different companies on joint venture project proposals, had varying degrees of experience, and rarely had firsthand knowledge of one another.

After identifying the necessary skill requirements, the conditions for developing presentations, and the effective techniques for presentation based on observational analysis and client interviews, the vice president and his staff determined that the performance need for presentations could best be met with a series of job aids combined with interventions of coaching, modeling, standards, and video feedback. The job aids included the following:

- A thirteen-step procedural guideline describing the exact process to be followed by the members of the presentation team in preparing, visualizing, and practicing their presentation (including appropriate models such as visual layouts for each step of the process)
- A job aid that helped team members identify areas of responsibility and resources and schedule the development of the presentation
- Developmental job aids, such as forms and checklists for collecting client background information, and other resources, such as the request for proposal (RFP) and invitation letter
- Templates for visual development and presentation format (see Figure 1)
- An evaluation checklist for measuring practice sessions

Resources and References

Langdon, D. G. (Series Ed.), & Lineberry, C., & Bullock, D. (Vol. Author). (1980). *The instructional design library: Vol. 25. Job aids*. Englewood Cliffs, NJ: Educational Technology.

Lineberry, C. S. (1977, Summer–Fall). When to develop aids for on-the-job and when to provide instruction. *Improving Human Performance*, pp. 2–3.

Rossett, A., & Gautier-Downes, J. (1991). *A handbook of job aids*. San Francisco: Jossey-Bass/Pfeiffer.

Woods, J. (1997). *Job aids*. In R. Kaufman, S. Thiagarajan, & P. MacGillis (Eds.), *The guidebook for performance improvement: Working with individuals and organizations*. San Francisco: Jossey-Bass/Pfeiffer.

Intervention Author

Danny G. Langdon
Partner
Performance International
1330 Stanford Street, Suite D
Santa Monica, CA 90404
Phone: 310-453-8440
E-mail: PerformI@aol.com

FIGURE 1. OVERALL PRESENTATION STRATEGY TREE.

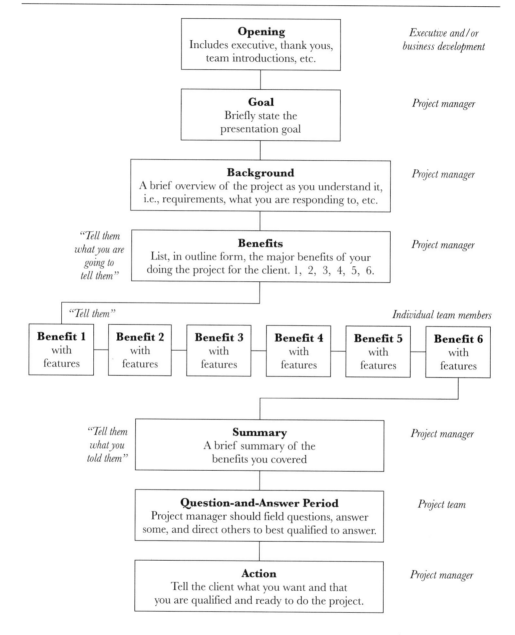

LEADERSHIP DEVELOPMENT
■ ■ ■ ■ ı PROGRAMS

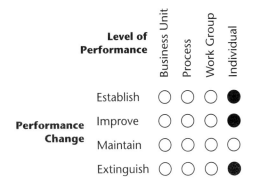

Performance Change	Level of Performance	Business Unit	Process	Work Group	Individual
	Establish	○	○	○	●
	Improve	○	○	○	●
	Maintain	○	○	○	○
	Extinguish	○	○	○	●

Definition

Leadership development programs are special opportunities for training and development designed to enhance the leadership capacity of high-potential employees and of the organization as a whole.

Description

Preparing individuals for leadership roles has been an important activity for centuries. One of the first leadership programs is attributed to Plato (cited in Conger, 1992), who in the *Republic* described his vision of a leadership development process for the ideal political state. Since then leadership as a topic of research has evolved and expanded widely. In the last two decades in particular there has been an explosion of interest in leadership and leadership development, especially in the business sector. Effective leadership is now seen as a necessity for dealing with a business environment that has become more competitive, complex, and turbulent and with an employee population that is more educated and diverse and that seeks a more empowering workplace.

In general, the purpose of leadership development programs is to enhance the capacity of employees to be effective in leadership roles—both formal and informal (McCauley, Moxley, & Van Velsor, 1998). Leadership is most widely understood as a social process that enables groups of people to work together in productive and meaningful ways. Thus, individuals who are seen as leaders are those who enable groups to interpret events, to choose objectives and strategies, to organize work activities, to motivate people to achieve objectives, to maintain cooperative relationships, to develop skills, and to enlist support and cooperation from people outside the group (Yukl, 1998).

A broad array of activities has been labeled as *leadership development programs*—everything from university-based educational programs that focus on conveying knowledge about leadership to outdoor adventure programs that focus on motivating people to discover and apply their leadership talents. But the most effective leadership development programs take a systemic approach (McCauley, Moxley, & Van Velsor, 1998) and share the characteristics described in the following paragraphs.

It is important to note that these characteristics are general rather than specific. The specific content and design of a particular leadership development program is shaped by *who* is being developed *for what purpose*. For example, a leadership development program for middle-level managers who are being groomed for senior leadership roles may be quite different from one for younger employees who are being targeted for leadership roles in the international part of the business.

They Focus on Broad Leadership Capacities

The most effective leadership development programs focus on developing the broad capacities that people need in order to be effective in leadership roles. Most programs are based on a model that describes the skills and abilities of effective leaders. This may be a research-based model taken from the literature on leadership, or it may be a competency model generated internally by the organization. Although there are numerous lists of leadership skills and competencies, underlying most of them are some core capacities that enable effective leadership: self-awareness; self-confidence; the ability to work in social systems; the ability to take a broad, systemic view; the ability to think creatively; and the ability to learn continually.

They Provide Assessment, Challenge, and Support

Effective leadership development programs provide three elements that are essential in stimulating and maintaining development: assessment, challenge, and support. To develop, people need to assess their current strengths and developmental needs, to take on challenge in the form of tasks and responsibilities that they have not yet mastered, and to know that others support and value their leadership development.

They Are Long-Term Processes

Leadership development programs that are effective are not single events. Instead, they are long-term processes that use multiple experiences to enhance learning and development. Four main categories of experiences are integrated into such programs:

- *Feedback:* Program participants need experiences that provide data about their strengths and weaknesses as leaders. Such feedback may come from performance appraisals, 360-degree-asssessment instruments, trained observers, or debriefs of group activities. At the conclusion of many feedback activities, participants identify their own developmental needs and design action plans to meet those needs.
- *Formal training and education:* Participants benefit from classroom-based experiences that offer models and frameworks for understanding leadership as well as opportunities (1) to practice leadership skills in a learning environment (for example, through role plays or simulations) and (2) to discuss leadership issues with colleagues who are experiencing similar challenges.
- *Work experiences:* Participants need experiences that require them to practice leadership in real work settings. These experiences might include moving individuals to new jobs, adding special assignments to their existing work, or having groups of them work on targeted, strategic projects for the organization. The goal is to provide opportunities that allow individual participants to apply their current strengths as they develop new ones.
- *Relationships:* Another beneficial kind of experience is that of learning from and through others. For example, participants may work with mentors or coaches, with peers who serve as learning partners, or with groups that meet periodically so that their members can learn from one another.

They Take Place in a Supportive Learning Environment

Leadership development programs must be embedded in an organizational context that encourages and supports learning and development. The organizational context should provide the following elements:

- The business strategy that leadership development is intended to support
- The pervasive belief that leadership development is an important and valued activity in the organization

- The systems and practices that reward taking on leadership roles (both formal and informal) and improving one's leadership capacities

When to Use

The following paragraphs explain when it is appropriate to use leadership development programs.

When Leadership Skills Are Missing in the Organization

A leadership development program is appropriate when the organization does not have enough individuals with the skills and capabilities to be successful in a particular type of leadership position. For example, there may not be people ready to move into senior management positions, project leader positions, or global leadership positions.

When More Employees Need to Exercise Leadership Skills

In this circumstance, the organization is moving to a flatter or more participative management structure. Today, most organizations are moving away from the idea that leadership is a *command-and-control* function to be held by very few and toward the idea that leadership knowledge and experience should be dispersed throughout the organization and shared among a larger number of employees. The thinking is that in this way more resources will be brought to bear on solving organizational issues or meeting new challenges. More employees are being asked to take on leadership roles or to participate in the direction-setting and decision-making work of the organization; consequently, more need development opportunities.

When Leaders Need to Expand Their Capabilities

A leadership development program is also appropriate when those already in leadership roles need to expand their capabilities in order to deal with new leadership challenges.

The organization may want its leaders to take a new approach to leadership or to develop new leadership skills. A frequent example is the shift in many organizations to a more team-based management approach. Also, any major change effort in an organization—for example, efforts to become more customer focused, more innovative, or more socially responsible—will confront leaders with new situations that require new responses.

Case Study

A national, nonprofit organization became concerned about whether it had sufficient leadership strength to fill a number of top management positions in its local offices in large cities. These were very complex jobs managing sizable organizations, and many of those currently serving in the positions were near retirement age. Also, there had never been a systematic effort to develop people for these large-city leadership positions.

Consequently, a leadership development program targeting high-potential employees was designed and launched. Individuals were nominated from across the organization, and a selection committee identified twenty to participate in the first program. The program spanned a two-year period and consisted of multiple integrated experiences.

The program was launched with a week-long, feedback-intensive event. During this week the participants received feedback about their strengths and developmental needs as leaders. Multiple sources of feedback were used: ratings of leadership behaviors from each participant's current boss, peers, and subordinates; assessments by trained observers who watched the participants in several leadership activities; videotapes of each participant's behavior in groups; observations by fellow participants; and psychological tests. In addition, the participants were also exposed to models, concepts, and research findings about effective leadership. At the conclusion of the week, they identified particular developmental goals that they wanted to achieve in the coming two years.

The participants experienced a number of educational events during the ensuring two-year period. For example, they attended a workshop on strategic planning and chose among several self-study courses on topics relevant to the organization's history and philosophy. The educational experiences focused on exposing the participants to knowledge that they would need as leaders of large-city organizations.

Groups of participants also were sent on special assignments to provide services to communities in a particular part of the world. These assignments provided the opportunity to practice leadership skills and to gain insights about the service challenges faced by nonprofit organizations. Working in another country, they were also exposed to different cultures and new perspectives.

The participants were assigned to two different learning relationships during the program. In the first of these, each was matched with an experienced large-city leader. The participant visited the leader, shadowed the leader throughout a workday, talked to the leader's staff members about his or her style and their response to it, and discussed the challenges of a large-city leader as well as strategies for dealing with those challenges. The leader was available to be a sounding board throughout the program. This relationship was created to help the participants obtain a better understanding of what a large-city leadership position entails.

The second relationship was one that each participant established with a recognized leader in his or her community, usually outside the nonprofit sector. The goal for each participant was to be exposed to new and different perspectives of effective leadership and to establish a relationship with someone who could coach the participant in his or her efforts to achieve developmental goals.

Both formal and informal evaluations of this leadership development program are yielding positive results (the first twenty participants just recently completed the program). The groups in which the participants currently work have noted enhanced leadership capabilities. The participants themselves express a renewed commitment to leadership and have, because of their common experience in the program, created a cohort group whose members will continue to advise and support one another. By the end of the program, three participants had been interviewed for a large-city leadership position and two had accepted positions. Although some participants learned that they did not want to pursue a large-city leadership position, the organization viewed this as a positive outcome, believing it was better both for the organization and for each individual to discover a mismatch in advance. Furthermore, the funder of the program wants to continue supporting this type of leadership development program.

Resources and References

Books and Articles

Conger, J. A. (1992). *Learning to lead: The art of transforming managers into leaders.* San Francisco: Jossey-Bass.

Dalton, M. A. (1996). *How to design an effective system for developing managers and executives.* Greensboro, NC: Center for Creative Leadership.

Fulmer, R. M. (1997). The evolving paradigm of leadership development. *Organizational Dynamics, 25*(4), 59–72.

McCauley, C. D., Moxley, R., & Van Velsor, E. (1998). *The Center for Creative Leadership handbook of leadership development.* San Francisco: Jossey-Bass.

Yukl, G. (1998). *Leadership in organizations* (4th ed.). Upper Saddle River, NJ: Prentice Hall.

Association

American Society for Training and Development (ASTD) (1640 King Street, Box 1443, Alexandria, VA 22313, phone: 703-683-8100, Web site: http//www.astd.org).

Intervention Author

Cynthia D. McCauley
Research Scientist
Center for Creative Leadership
P.O. Box 26300
Greensboro, NC 27438
Phone: 336-288-7210
E-mail: mccauley@leaders.ccl.org

LEARNER-CONTROLLED
∎ ∎ ∎ ∎ ∎ ∎ INSTRUCTION

Level of Performance	Business Unit	Process	Work Group	Individual
Establish	○	○	○	●
Improve	○	○	○	●
Maintain	○	○	○	○
Extinguish	○	○	○	●

Performance Change: Establish, Improve, Maintain, Extinguish

Alternative Name

Learner-centered instruction

Definition

Learner-controlled instruction (LCI) is an instructional strategy in which the learner has control of which resources (experts, learning materials or programs, and so on) will be used, when mastery will be tested, and what the sequence of learning will be. The learner must master prescribed objectives but has control over when to study, where, and with what and also over when to be tested.

Description

Learner-controlled instruction (LCI) is an instructional strategy that is an outgrowth of a number of forces. In the 1960s performance technologists were involved with programmed instruction, self-paced learning, computer-assisted instruction and other nontraditional teaching and learning strategies. Many of these strategies explored behavioral theory and its application in organizations outside the traditional school systems. These applications were experiments in building controls into the learning system instead of into the teacher.

This concept of returning control to the learner is a core concept of accelerated learning. Other principles of accelerated learning are also part of LCI interventions, such as discovery learning, teachers who serve as facilitators and resource people rather than as experts, and the creation of supportive learning environments.

The following three elements must exist in order for LCI to be successful:

- A variety of resources that cover the content requirements
- Learning objectives, stated in measurable terms
- Tools to measure the learning outcomes

These three elements allow the instructional designer to design learning systems that communicate to the learners what they will need to learn, what resources will be available to them, and how they will know when they have successfully acquired the requisite knowledge or skill.

The key benefit of LCI is that each learner takes control of his or her learning, tailoring the learning experience to fit how he or she learns best. This control can come in many forms. Often learners are involved in the following:

- Selecting the resources that match their individual learning styles
- Setting the pace with which they are most comfortable
- Using discovery learning, which most learners find motivating
- Measuring themselves against established standards with immediate feedback
- Selecting what forms of assistance they prefer and when they prefer assistance

Learner-controlled instruction provides a learner with many choices. With these choices come responsibility and accountability—two traits that organizations often need to recapture in their workforce.

In addition, as the pace of change increases for all organizations, the time needed to gather people in a classroom is harder to find. Learner-controlled instruction offers a flexible and creative alternative. It can be used with large numbers of people individually or in groups. It generally requires minimal facilities and is usually incorporated into a learner's workplace and workday activities.

As shown in the LCI Model (Figure 1), the instructional designer designs a learning environment that includes the learning objectives, entrance and exit requirements, management support requirements, and the development of measurements and standards for learning. Then the designer develops various performance experiences. For example, in the case of a grocery store management

FIGURE 1. LCI MODEL.

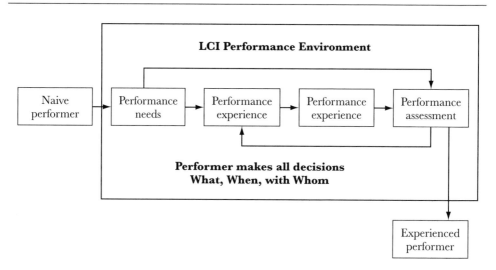

trainee, the learner may be asked to "set up a sales planning and merchandising in-store promotion."

A number of performance experiences, all of which directly address the performance needs for each specific learner, are developed and linked together. After the learner completes the performance experiences, his or her new skills are assessed and integrated into everyday performance on the job.

A strength of LCI is that when the investment is made in the design phase, there are substantial cost reductions in the application phase. The cost savings inherent in the approach make it an attractive strategy for developing a standard set of skills on the part of large numbers of people.

When to Use

Learner-controlled instruction is appropriate in the following situations:

- When the instructional content is complex and requires practice
- When it is difficult to assemble all learners in a room at the same time (for example, when people are hired one at a time or when people cannot all be taken from their job duties at the same time)
- When the learning population varies widely in knowledge and experience

- When large populations are required to perform a standard set of skills (for example, employees in organizations with redundant processes, such as retailers or manufacturers).
- When one instructor cannot teach all of the topics
- When it is desired that employees take responsibility for their own learning

Case Study

For a number of years, one of the largest banks in the United States had been training its operations officers using a combination of training classes and experiences that required approximately a year to complete. The bank decided to institute a learner-controlled instruction (LCI) program to capitalize on a variety of resources available within a live bank environment and to shorten the training time and produce more effective operations officers.

An operations officer serves as the lead manager of a bank, managing all segments except the loan department. Operations officers must be intimately familiar with all bank operations and positions, from the teller line to customer service management and bank transactions. The skills base that they need includes approximately two hundred and fifty competencies. People who fill these positions typically enter the job with varying levels of skill and experience. It is important to capitalize on their existing skills and experience rather than to engage in complete retraining. Of course, there are bank-specific requirements and experiences that cannot be transferred through experience in other bank settings.

Preparing to Use LCI

Following the LCI Model, the bank worked with a performance improvement consulting firm to identify all of the necessary skill requirements. From these requirements the bank developed a set of learner objectives and classified these objectives into the major job skills (teller operations, management, safety deposit boxes, statements, and so on) that were required of the operations officer. For each performance objective, all of the available resources (for example, audiovisuals, texts, videos, computers, training courses, and existing operations officer and staff members) were listed as potential resources for learning and practicing the necessary objectives. How the performance would be tested (written test, oral questioning, actual performance, or whatever) was also listed for each objective (see Exhibit 1).

One trainee operations officer was assigned to each of five ongoing bank environments especially structured to support an LCI experience. At each of these

EXHIBIT 1. BANK'S LIST OF LCI OBJECTIVES, RESOURCES, AND MEASURES.

Goal 1, Part 1 (continued) Objectives and Available Resources	Resources	Criterion Measure	Completion Date	Operations Officer Verification
6. Explain the procedure for locating, recording, and processing irregular checks discovered during the paying and filing process	Exec.[a] 142, SPM[b] 319	Written test		
7. Process rejected items that are listed on the Rejected-Items Register	SPM 315.1, 319	Written test		
8. Resubmit record-change forms when necessary	SPM 301, pg. 4, 151.1, IQ[c] pg. 12 #3	Written test		
9. Describe the purpose of carrier envelopes, substitute slip, and the overnight file; perform the audit to these records	SPM 313, 319	Performance test		
10. Describe the procedures for the preparation and mailing of depositor's checking-account statements	SPM 323	Oral test		
11. Process the non-read entries and prepare the Non-Read Register	SPM 319	Feedback		
C. Safe deposit and statement				
1. Assist customers who wish to enter their safe-deposit boxes and be able to explain the reason for each required precautionary measure	SPM 265.5	Performance test		
2. Explain procedures, identify forms, and determine fees relating to rentals, voluntary surrender, and delinquent rentals	SPM 265.1, 265.5	Written test		

[a]Exec. = *Executive Guidebook.*

[b]SPM = *Standards and Procedures Manual.*

[c]IQ = *Inquiries and Questions* (answers to most frequently asked customer questions).

environments the existing operations officer was trained as a facilitator, an information resource, a mentor, and an evaluator.

A Day in the Life of an LCI Trainee

When the trainees arrived in their assigned banks, each was oriented to the tasks and resources by the existing operations officer for the LCI program. Also, each received a job aid notebook containing all of the learning objectives, existing learning resources, and a description of the learning program. The program emphasized the learner's right to control when and how he or she would learn as well as when he or she could request testing of skills and knowledge.

After being oriented, each trainee made his or her own learning plan, evaluating skills and experience against the list of performance objectives and determining which ones he or she would attempt to demonstrate without further learning and which ones would need to be developed. Then each decided on the way he or she would learn, the timeline of the learning experience, and when he or she would arrange to be tested on the given objective(s). Testing, in general, occurred on demand.

Each week, then, each trainee functioned both in a junior position as a bank operations manager and as a learner completing the learning plan. Each trainee consulted regularly with the existing operations manager, who then consulted with the corporate LCI training manager, giving regular reports on progress and solving problems that occurred.

In reviewing this case against the LCI Model, one sees that a *naive performer* is presented with the following:

- A trigger for learning (the objectives)
- A variety of means for learning and demonstrating that learning (including the ongoing bank resources and personnel)
- An existing performance environment (a real bank)
- Immediate access to performance assessment at a time and place selected by the trainee

The assessment, commensurate with the action terms of the performance objective, could be conducted through demonstration of skills, written exam, oral exam, running meetings, or feedback from reports on long-term projects. All elements of learning were thus learner controlled.

As a result, the LCI Model not only reduces training time (from one year to less than three months), but also produces a performer (that is, an operations officer) who learns the important skills of planning, guiding, and executing work within the learning environment. In the case study, not only did each performer learn the bank operations, but the LCI program itself served as a means of discovering which learners were incapable of managing their own learning and would, therefore, not be likely to be able to manage a bank's operations.

Resources and References

Also see the intervention titled "Accelerated Learning" in this volume.

Clement, F. J. (1992). Accelerated learning systems. In H. D. Stolovitch & E. J. Keeps (Eds.), *Handbook of human performance technology: A comprehensive guide for analyzing and solving performance problems in organizations* (pp. 528–548). San Francisco: Jossey-Bass.

Fuller, R. B. (1981). *Critical path*. New York: St. Martin's Press. Discusses discovery learning.

Langdon, D. G. (Series Ed.), & Wydra, F. T. (Vol. Author). (1980). *The Instructional Design Library: Vol. 26. Learner controlled instruction*. Englewood Cliffs, NJ: Educational Technology.

Wydra, F. T. (1975, August). Learner controlled instruction. *Training*, pp. 53–55.

Intervention Authors

Frank T. Wydra
Principal
IRI Consultants to Management
440 E. Congress, Suite 330
Detroit, MI 48201
Phone: 313-965-0350
Fax: 313-965-7545
E-mail: iri@irisolutions.com

Monica M. McKenna
President
Learning Technologies
647 Andrus Pitch Road
Cornwall, VT 05753-9232
Phone: 802-462-2111
Fax: 802-462-2115
E-mail: mmckenna@sover.net

▪ ▪ ▪ ▪ ▪ ▪ LEVERAGING DIVERSITY

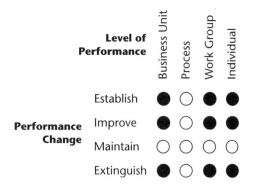

Level of Performance	Business Unit	Process	Work Group	Individual
Establish	●	○	●	●
Performance **Improve**	●	○	●	●
Change **Maintain**	○	○	○	○
Extinguish	●	○	●	●

Definition

Diversity conveys similarities, differences, or variety. *Leveraging*, or managing, diversity consists of a series of interventions with the common goal of changing an organization so that the workforce, the marketplace, and its internal structures are improved.

Description

It is important to use a generally accepted definition of diversity in order to understand leveraging diversity as an intervention. Loden (1996), in *Implementing Diversity*, establishes the following parameters:

> There are biological and environmental differences that separate and distinguish us as individuals and groups. It is this vast array of physical and cultural differences that constitute the spectrum of human diversity. . . . [A] workplace definition of diversity would minimally include:
>
> - Age
> - Ethnicity
> - Gender

- Mental/physical abilities and characteristics
- Race
- Sexual orientation

These six differences are termed core dimensions of diversity because they exert an important impact on our early socialization and a powerful, sustained impact throughout every stage of life. These dimensions represent properties and characteristics that constitute the core of our diverse identities. At the core of each of us, there are these six.

. . . [T]here are many secondary dimensions that play an important role in shaping our values, expectations, and experiences as well. These include:

- Communication style
- Education
- Family status
- Military experience
- Organizational role and level
- Religion
- First language
- Geographic location
- Income
- Work experience
- Work style

These secondary dimensions share certain characteristics. Generally, they are more mutable, less visible to those around us, and more variable in the degree of influence they exert on our individual lives.

A graphic depiction of the primary and secondary dimensions of diversity appears in Figure 1.

Leveraging diversity can be pictured by visualizing three intersecting circles (a vector diagram), with the circles representing the workforce, the marketplace, and the organization's structures (see Figure 2).

Most organizations focus on workforce diversity, which consists of the differences and similarities between individuals in the current and future workforce.

Marketplace diversity, which frequently excites management and can give impetus to an intervention, involves organizational opportunities related to the following elements:

- Market segmentation
- Variety of products offered to market segments

FIGURE 1. PRIMARY AND SECONDARY DIMENSIONS OF DIVERSITY.

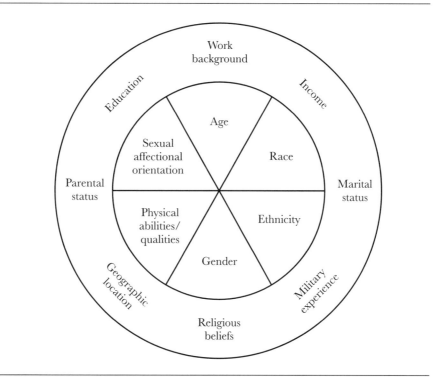

FIGURE 2. BUSINESS DIVERSITY.

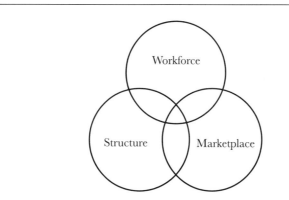

- Specialized customer service
- Global marketing
- Customs and cultures in doing business

Structural diversity, which is not often included in diversity work, involves the following kinds of differences and similarities within the organization:

- Across functions
- Across levels
- Between units
- Between parents and subsidiaries
- Between newly merged organizations or units
- Between work teams

For the performance technologist, the initial task is to understand the ways in which differences in the primary and secondary dimensions or in the organization's structure negatively affect the performance of individuals or work groups. The organization's ability to compete in the marketplace may be related to its inability to deal with diversity; this can also be a trigger for a series of diversity interventions.

A number of activities and interventions can be integrated in order to meet a need for increased diversity within the workforce. For example, many organizations conduct diversity-awareness sessions or courses in managing diversity, sometimes calling such activities *diversity training*. Also, policies may be developed to ensure that affirmative action and/or equal employment opportunity laws or guidelines are upheld. In addition, programs may be developed to ensure that glass ceilings are eliminated, that networking opportunities are offered equally to all populations, and that native speakers of different languages are identified and accessible to customers. The human resource department or function may develop initiatives involving recruiting, quality of work life, and career development in order to support a more diverse workforce. Systems within the organization may be examined for their negative impact on certain groups of individuals (such as women or parents) and revised so that they are fair to all employees.

In the marketplace, diversity can be increased by using any of the following strategies:

- Segmenting the market into ethnic markets
- Altering the variety of products that are offered
- Offering specialized customer service (including using different languages)
- Targeting global markets

- Learning and following the customs in different cultures for doing business and recognizing the power of competitive pressures

An organization may want to build diversity interventions in response to any number of business needs. The business goal may be to attract and retain the best employees; to increase creativity, quality, teamwork, or innovation; to contain costs; to gain a marketing advantage and serve customers better; or to demonstrate leadership and enhance the organization's image.

What to Strive for

Interventions for leveraging diversity should include data collection and analysis to create a vision; the objectives to be achieved; and a plan with action steps, activities to be used, and timelines. In addition, the best interventions share the following characteristics:

- *Visible leadership:* There is a sincere and knowledgeable demonstration by those at the top of the organization that leveraging diversity is not only a business imperative, but also the right thing to do.
- *Clear tie to the organization's mission and vision:* A strategic connection is made between the various activities and the organization's goals.
- *Accountability and measurement:* The organization incorporates the leveraging of diversity into its accountability process instead of just adding it as a side interest.
- *Integrated actions, not random activities:* The organization creates a strategic plan of action that makes it clear why various activities are being used.
- *Continual learning:* Interventions aimed at leveraging diversity constitute a long-term change process that requires continual learning.
- *Variety of methods:* A variety of methods are used to maintain momentum and to ensure that performers have the tools they need to perform as desired.
- *Inclusive, effective structure:* Both staff and line are important: diverse department members often serve as the resident experts in diversity; members of cross-level, cross-functional teams serve as advisers and implementers in various business units.

What to Avoid

Some pitfalls to be avoided in leveraging diversity are as follows:

- Engaging in activities that would bring about the opposites of the previously listed positive characteristics

- Failing to leverage diversity expertise in the organization (diverse employees have their own competencies and skills, which should not be underrated; an external consultant may be used as needed, but should not substitute for internal expertise)
- Approaching a diversity intervention with a single focus (for example, conducting training without evidence that training is truly needed)
- Moving too quickly, before the key players in the organization have committed to the effort
- Not providing adequate resources for a high-quality intervention
- Not involving all levels of employees in the planning process

When to Use

Leveraging diversity should be considered appropriate in situations such as the following:

- When a merger or acquisition is in progress: mergers and acquisitions blend cultures. Many of the processes used in leveraging diversity apply equally well to blending the cultures of two or more organizations or units.
- When performance falls below expectations: sometimes the barriers to performance include stereotyping, prejudice, or harassment. For example, a gay or lesbian person who feels it is unsafe to reveal that orientation might expend significant energy in being cautious about what he or she says. That energy could be used more productively in performing well on the job. Also, someone who is homophobic might expend energy trying to figure out how to avoid working with a gay or lesbian, thereby decreasing the energy available for work.
- When employees complain of disparate treatment
- When marketplace goals are not being met
- When innovation, creativity, and teamwork need to be enhanced to meet organizational goals: the key to increasing creativity and innovation is to encourage employees to demonstrate respect for one another while working together with candor. Leveraging diversity can help employees to build such skills.

Case Study

In late 1993 the Royal Bank of Canada (which has 56,000 employees in 1,700 locations in Canada and thirty other countries) began noticing that its employees apparently had problems related to gender diversity, including some missed marketplace opportunities. Data collection and analysis identified thirteen areas of need, each of which was supported with employee comments. Following are three examples of the needs identified:

- There was a lack of visible role models for women because of inequitable representation of women at senior levels.
- Men and women continued to perpetuate myths and misinformation about each other and made value judgments based on gender.
- Many staff members either lacked access to mentors or received inconsistent mentoring, thus decreasing their chances of career advancement.

A business case was built to communicate excitement and commitment regarding needs and opportunities. The business case defined the gender gap and identified needs for change based on the bank's changing customers as well as its changing workforce. The business case then listed the desired outcomes of a diversity intervention. The five objectives (to be achieved by October 31, 1999) were as follows:

- To provide an environment in which employees can manage their work, family, and life needs
- To become an organization that others wish to emulate with regard to gender equity
- To eliminate gender-related biases and assumptions so that systems, policies, and practices are equitable and fair (note that this objective is phrased in the style of a *stretch* goal; as there is recognition that bias cannot be totally eliminated, the objective will be considered to be met at an 85 percent level)
- To have a more equitable representation of women and men in all positions: men in entry-level positions and women in more senior roles
- To attract and retain both women and men who best meet the bank's business requirements

For each goal, a number of specific objectives were also developed. Finally, the bank developed a methodology that included twenty-five different actions to be taken, some of which were as follows:

- Senior management will add the goal of "closing the gender gap" to its strategic plans.
- Gender equity will be facilitated in the call centers (which were full of entry-level employees who answered customer phone requests).

- Management will set up a formal mentoring program with concrete account-abilities and measurement devices.
- The ability to relocate will be removed as a measure of promotability.

The results, three years after the initiative began, include hard data, soft data, testimonials, and progress toward goals. In addition to receiving several merit awards and participating in *best-practices* surveys, the Royal Bank also took the following actions:

- It offered to rectify a pension situation that had negatively affected 1,800 women.
- It removed mobility from the job-posting process.
- It stopped supporting events that discriminate based on gender, race, age, and so forth.
- It increased the number of women represented in management (from 15.7 percent in 1994 to 25.0 percent in 1996).

Resources and References

Baytos, L. M. (1995). *Designing and implementing successful diversity programs.* Upper Saddle River, NJ: Prentice Hall.

Gardenswartz, L., & Rowe, A. (1993). *Managing diversity: A complete desk reference and planning guide.* Burr Ridge, IL: Business One Irwin.

Hayles, R., & Mendez R. A. (1997). *The diversity directive: Why some initiatives fail & what to do about it.* Burr Ridge, IL: Irwin.

Jamieson, D., & O'Mara, J. (1991). *Managing workforce 2000: Gaining the diversity advantage.* San Francisco: Jossey-Bass.

Loden, M. (1996). *Implementing diversity.* Burr Ridge, IL: Irwin.

O'Mara, J. (1994). *Diversity activities and training designs.* San Francisco: Jossey-Bass/Pfeiffer.

Thiederman, S. (1991). *Bridging cultural barriers for corporate success: How to manage the multicultural work force.* Lexington, MA: Heath.

Thiederman, S. (1991). *Profiting in America's multicultural marketplace: How to do business across cultural lines.* Lexington, MA: Heath.

Thomas, R., Jr. (1991). *Beyond race and gender: Unleashing the power of your total work force by managing diversity.* New York: AMACOM.

Intervention Author

Julie O'Mara
President
O'Mara and Associates
5979 Greenridge Road
Castro Valley, CA 94552
Phone: 510-582-7744
Fax: 510-582-4826
E-mail: omaraassoc@aol.com

■ ■ ■ ■ ■ ■ MENTORING/COACHING

	Level of Performance	Business Unit	Process	Work Group	Individual
	Establish	○	○	○	●
Performance Change	Improve	○	○	○	●
	Maintain	○	○	○	●
	Extinguish	○	○	○	●

Alternative Names

Advising
Counseling
Tutoring

Definition of Mentoring

Mentoring is a process that deliberately pairs a person who is more skilled or experienced with one who is less skilled or experienced in order to transfer skills and experience in a focused, effective, and efficient manner. The skills transferred may be job specific, technical or professional, generic, or enabling. The experience transfer is intended to shorten the learning time and to avoid costly trial-and-error approaches.

The mentoring process includes the following elements:

- Determining which goals, needs, and opportunities of the organization will be supported by increased skills and experience
- Developing strategies for pairing people in a mentoring relationship on the basis of skill deficits in one person and the presence of those skills in another

- Establishing an agreement for each pair that defines the roles, focus, and duration of the mentoring relationship

The person designated as the *mentor* is the one who transfers skills and experience, and the person who receives these benefits is known as the *protégé*. The mentor carries out various tasks such as teaching, tutoring, coaching, modeling, serving as a sounding board, demonstrating, listening, reflecting what the other person says, giving feedback, warning, counseling, guiding, and so on. The skills that a mentor needs parallel the tasks that he or she performs in interaction with the protégé. Mentors have come to be known "as those who gently guide and nurture the growth of others during various stages of their development" (Al Huang & Lynch, 1995, p. xi).

Definition of Coaching

Coaching is a process in which an individual interacts with another to teach, model, and provide feedback on technical, professional, and interpersonal skills and behaviors in a future-focused, constructive way. A coach often interacts with another person in *real time* by participating in team or committee activities with that individual. The coach provides insight, feedback, and opportunities for the other person to rehearse or practice before dealing with a similar situation again.

Description

As organizations become more concerned about the cost-effectiveness of skill development, they are increasingly looking to one-to-one coaching in a mentoring process in order to transfer needed skills and experience within the organization. The recent emphasis on improving human performance through a wide range of strategies has illustrated the limitations of looking only to training as the solution to a performance problem. Facilitated mentoring processes have proven to be an effective strategy for creating a multiskilled, flexible workforce. These processes facilitate the organization's efforts to meet the demands of changing goals, competition, and doing more with less by forging a winning team focused on the organization's real goals. As Jackson (1995, p. 5) explained, "working with the Bulls [a great professional basketball team with a multiyear winning record] I've learned that the most effective way to forge a winning team is to call on the players' need to connect with something larger than themselves."

With the increasing popularity of mentoring processes, there has been some confusion about what is involved in mentoring. In a book titled *Beyond the Myths and Magic of Mentoring*, Murray (1991, p. xiv) defines mentoring as "a deliberate pairing of a more skilled or experienced person with a lesser skilled or experienced one, with the agreed-upon goal of having the lesser skilled person grow and develop specific competencies." Notice that this definition says nothing about the relative age of the partners, the organizational levels they represent, or their seniority.

Throughout history master performers have practiced modeling and mentoring as key elements in the continuity of art, craft, and commerce. In the arts and crafts guilds, a young person was often apprenticed to a master who was considered to be a highly skilled practitioner in the trade or profession (Murray, 1991). The master taught, coached, and guided the development of the necessary skills. To become a master, the apprentice's skills were judged from a work sample, such as a piece of silverware, a painting, or even a horseshoe. The word *masterpiece* originated from this sample of skillful work, which was used as the criterion for advancement to master.

In many organizations informal mentoring has long been a means of preparing people for leadership roles. However, there is a downside to such informal pairings: mentors often choose people very much like themselves and continue to impress their own styles on their protégés, in effect creating clones. When many people in an organization think alike, solve problems with the same strategies, and seek opportunities in the same way, the organization becomes progressively weaker. Strength comes from diversity of thought, approach, and work style. Furthermore, many people with significant growth potential may be left out of these informal, mentor-selected relationships because they are "different." Obtaining a mentor is likely to be a function of personality and luck. As a result, the organization is deprived of the potential talent of its less assertive employees.

A more systematic approach, known as *facilitated mentoring*, makes the mentoring process available to any individual who (1) perceives that he or she has growth potential and (2) is willing to take greater responsibility for contributing to the results of the organization and for his or her own growth and development. Facilitated mentoring is described as "a structure and series of processes designed to create effective mentoring relationships, guide the desired behavior change of those involved, and evaluate the results for the protégés, the mentors, and the organization" (Murray, 1991, p. 5).

When to Use

Creating a mentoring process is an appropriate alternative in the following situations.

When New Skills Are Needed

Organizations with rapidly changing goals often find that their current employees do not have the skills required to meet future needs. Teaching and coaching in a mentoring relationship can develop those skills. For example, when computer salespeople truly seek to provide customer-oriented solutions, mentors can teach them the missing and relevant customer service skills, thus broadening the capabilities of the salesforce.

When Traditional Training Would Not Be Efficient

Traditional classroom courses are aimed at a mythical *average* learner. When entry-level employees have widely varying skills and knowledge, as little as 15 percent of the content of a traditional course may be relevant to any individual student. In a mentoring relationship, however, the coaching and feedback are precisely targeted to the protégé's individual needs. With this specific focus, both effectiveness and efficiency are improved.

When Traditional Training Would Not Be Fast Enough

Courses and training workshops designed for groups of learners must be scheduled on the basis of demand for larger numbers of people; individuals must wait until a desired course is scheduled, often floundering on the job in the meantime. When an employee needs help in order to perform, a mentor with appropriate skills, experience, and willingness can transfer those skills in a timely fashion.

When Admitting Deficiency to One's Supervisor Is Not Advisable

Sometimes it is politically inappropriate to acknowledge a skill deficiency or lack of experience to one's direct supervisor. People often are understandably reluctant to admit weaknesses when talking to those who make decisions about their salary treatment and advancement. Consequently, their growth and development may be delayed or inhibited. An individual is much more likely to describe specific skill or growth needs to a mentor than to his or her supervisor, as the mentor is viewed as a caring and objective advocate for success.

Case Studies

The following two case studies illustrate both approaches to mentoring and reactions of participants.

Developing Leaders

"The objective of our mentoring program," states a manager in one organization's human resource unit, "is to provide a communication process whereby an employee and a manager work together to develop a mutual understanding of a leader's role and to identify opportunities and create action plans for the employee's leadership development. This process is a tool that we propose to offer to employees who are interested in developing their leadership abilities."

This organization is in a highly competitive industry, competing not only for customers but also for the best and brightest people to employ and retain. Goals for growth in market share create a demand for a workforce with exceptional technical and professional skills as well as excellent leadership skills. The mentor-protégé pairing matches an individual with a high level of skill in a defined area with an employee who desires to develop that skill. Although the establishment of a mentoring relationship is not a replacement for the traditional role that managers play in the development of their employees, the organization hopes that its mentoring program will help employees to build their skills and increase their contributions to the organization.

For example, one individual who participated in this program commented, "I requested a mentor in part to develop my computer skills to increase my effectiveness in my assignment as a human resource division manager." This protégé was matched with the company's education and technology manager, who had exemplary skills in computers and information systems. The mentor said, "I volunteered to be a mentor because in my earlier years an informal mentor had a positive impact on me."

Another individual noted how "Larry, my current mentor, seemed to be a natural match for me. He has technical experience in the discipline that I'm interested in, and his career path has been one to which I aspire."

Building Opportunities to Network

At a conference arranged to discuss a bank's gender gap at the higher levels of management, staff members decided that coaching was a great idea. The issue was how to give all employees an equal opportunity to network. The selected strategy was a formal mentoring process for men and women in a number of different functions in the bank.

Pairs were matched on the basis of each protégé's specific skills needs and each mentor's ability to transfer those skills. In addition to creating a network accessible to all employees who wished to enhance their development by interacting regularly with mentors, the managers hoped to develop a multiskilled and flexible workforce. The network that was subsequently created provides a variety of options in placing people in order to achieve the greatest effectiveness and efficiency for the bank as well as greater worker satisfaction.

For example, Paul, a manager in personal banking, considered himself a good leader but said, "I'd like to improve, though. The best way to pick up the less tangible skills I need is to draw on the insights of people with years of experience." He and his mentor entered into an agreement that included regular and frank discussions, job shadowing, and observing the mentor at work. "I was able to borrow her techniques and adapt them for my own people and style," Paul reported. The mutual exchange of knowledge and skills contributed to the growth of both partners and supported the bank's goal to develop leaders who could assume greater responsibility as the organization grew.

Resources and References

Al Huang, C., & Lynch, J. (1995). *Mentoring: The TAO of giving and receiving wisdom.* San Francisco: HarperCollins.

Freedman, M. (1993). *The kindness of strangers: Adult mentors, urban youth, and the new voluntarism.* San Francisco: Jossey-Bass.

Jackson, P. (1995). *Sacred hoops: Spiritual lessons of a hardwood warrior.* New York: Hyperion.

Murray, M. (1991). *Beyond the myths and magic of mentoring: How to facilitate an effective mentoring program.* San Francisco: Jossey-Bass.

Murray, M. (1995, Spring). Upgrade core competencies with mentoring: Downsizing doesn't mean drop your skills. *Beta Gamma Sigma News,* pp. 1–5.

Intervention Author

Margo Murray
President and Chief Operating Officer
MMHA The Managers' Mentors, Inc.
2317 Mastlands Drive, Suite A
Oakland, CA 94611
Phone: 510-531-9453
E-mail: MMHA@mentors-mmha.com
Web site: http://www.mentors-mmha.com

Description

The study of work motivation was more or less ineffective until the 1970s. Its slow development may have been caused in part by the fact that motivation is very close to people's basic human values and beliefs. Until recently, motivation specialists focused only on external events at work in their efforts to understand commitment and persistence. As a result, the only motivational tools available to performance specialists were vague suggestions to "reinforce" good work with "incentives" and to "ignore" negative or ineffective behavior. This approach left a number of questions:

- What was a reinforcer?
- Why did many people not respond positively, no matter what reinforcement was provided?
- Why did some reinforcers backfire and cause motivational problems?

In the 1970s a new group of cognitive researchers asked important questions about the effects of people's beliefs, values, and expectations on their commitment to work goals. One of these early motivational researchers was John Keller at Florida State University. Keller developed an approach to building motivation into training based on the research of Albert Bandura and other psychologists; he calls it the ARCS (attention, relevance, confidence, and satisfaction) model.

Now a great deal is known about how to influence the mental processes that enhance motivation. For example, we now know how to match the values and expectations of different types of people with the requirements of work goals and tasks. This intervention describes a practical approach to motivation that has been derived from these more recent efforts at cognitive research.

A motivational intervention is a way to establish or increase the level of commitment, enthusiasm, and active pursuit of work goals. Such interventions help people turn their intentions into actions and their passive resistance to work goals into active and enthusiastic acceptance. They foster this important performance enhancement by suggesting specific, cost-effective ways to describe the benefit of a goal to different individuals and teams and also ways to encourage people's belief in themselves. The new generation of motivation interventions also shows how to diagnose and solve problems in motivation.

Research on motivation (Bandura, 1997) indicates that a person avoids commitment due to a belief that he or she will be less effective or seem less effective to others if he or she attempts the goal or task. People will commit only to goals that pay off for them in increased effectiveness. The effectiveness motivator is assumed to be paramount in all human commitments, regardless of cultural background or individual differences. Yet there are many individual and cultural differences in beliefs about exactly what makes people effective and successful. Three primary factors have been found in research and practice to increase or decrease effectiveness beliefs and, therefore, commitment to work goals: people's assessment of the task, their emotional state, and the value placed on the task.

Task Assessment Problems

Everyone asks two questions when confronted with a challenge: Can I do it? And if so, Will I be permitted to do it? When people think they have the ability to accomplish the goal and they will be permitted to accomplish it, their commitment increases. However, if they doubt their ability or the organization's willingness to let them use their skills, their commitment decreases.

Solving task assessment problems requires people to be convinced that they can do a job and that existing barriers to their performance will be removed. One way to do this is by pointing out familiar past examples of successful job performance that are similar to the new task. It also helps to break big goals into smaller, specific tasks with short timelines and clear performance requirements. In addition, job aids can bolster people's confidence. The key element here is to persuade or empower people to believe that they have the ability and environmental conditions necessary to succeed at the task they are avoiding.

Emotional Problems

Positive feelings about a goal facilitate commitment to that goal, whereas negative feelings discourage commitment. This is why angry or depressed people find it nearly impossible to make a commitment to new work goals.

Solutions that have been found to change people's emotional states include listening to positive music; writing or telling about a positive, emotion-related experience; and watching a movie or listening to a story that emphasizes positive emotion. A great deal of research indicates that positive emotions and commitment to work goals are enhanced by trusted, enthusiastic, positive, energetic managers as well as by positive, coping but not perfect, coworker *models* (Bandura, 1997; Locke & Latham, 1990).

Value Problems

The third and final factor that influences the strength of goal commitment is the extent to which the person values the goal. When people expect that achieving a goal will result in learning important skills or being perceived as competent by others whom they respect, their level of commitment to that work goal is maximized. The reverse is also true: few people give high priority to tasks that they sincerely believe will lead them to failure or to being seen as incompetent.

The following three types of *effectiveness values* have been found to be important:

- *Utility value:* One does not like or value the task at hand but may highly value some desired condition or result of successfully completing the task. Many college students, for example, suffer through uninteresting college courses because they want to earn degrees.
- *Interest value:* One is curious about or simply likes the pursuit of a particular goal. A consultant friend of mine, for example, takes any job in San Francisco simply because she is interested in the history of the city.
- *Importance value:* One recognizes that a specific task represents one's strengths and personal goals. People who think of themselves as having ability in art, for example, could be expected to commit easily to tasks involving decorating the office or selecting styles of office furniture.

Suggesting new value for a work goal is often the best way to increase commitment. People will not do what they believe will make them less effective or less successful, and many people are suspicious of change simply because they feel that they will be perceived as less effective under new or uncertain conditions. They must be convinced that if they commit themselves to the avoided task(s) they will become significantly more effective or successful. The specific solution that accomplishes this goal may be quite different for different individuals and work cultures.

Studies have found that value attached to a work goal is enhanced when the following conditions exist:

- The person who assigns the goal is perceived as a legitimate, trusted authority with an *inspiring vision* that reflects a *convincing rationale* for the goal (importance value).
- The person who assigns the goal expresses an expectation of outstanding performance (importance value).
- The individuals and teams that must complete tasks associated with the goal feel *ownership* of those tasks (interest value).
- The person who assigns the goal expresses confidence in both individual and team capabilities (interest value).
- The person who assigns the goal provides feedback on progress that includes recognition for success as well as supportive suggestions for correcting mistakes (utility value).

When to Use

The best indicator of a commitment problem is avoidance or delay of important tasks. Tasks can include routine events such as getting to work on time or novel challenges such as the need to solve a complex problem. People with commitment problems may avoid a task altogether or argue that it is less important than some other tasks. They may attempt to hand off resisted tasks to someone else or to blame others for their own failure to perform.

In addition, people who lack adequate commitment to important work goals tend to be more easily distracted by tasks that are less important. They sometimes convince themselves that their managers are wrong, arbitrary, undependable, or ignorant and therefore not able to assign adequate priorities to tasks. When people resist commitment to a work goal, they also find it easy to convince themselves that they do not have the time or resources to achieve the goal.

Consequently, the use of motivation systems is most appropriate when people demonstrate a lack of commitment by avoiding tasks.

If people or groups are avoiding a task by procrastinating, arguing about task importance, trying to shift the assigned task to others, or simply doing less important things to avoid the task, consider using the job aid presented in Figure 1. Interview people; form focus groups; and adopt a supportive, empathic manner in asking the questions listed on the job aid.

Case Study

After learning that more than 65 percent of its customers were either "unhappy" or "very unhappy" with service on purchased equipment, the executive vice president of "XYZ Corporation" mandated a new service policy. The new approach, developed over a weekend at his vacation retreat, allowed customer service representatives (CSRs) to bend and change service policies to handle complaints and required "empathy training" for all CSRs to allow them to handle angry customers more effectively. A new, computerized call-monitoring system was installed so that line managers could monitor CSRs, collect systematic information about service transactions, and limit the time spent on calls so that efficiency could be increased.

After the new system had been in use for three months, a new customer study found that customer dissatisfaction had actually increased 12 percent. An analysis of the problem revealed a number of important motivational issues.

FIGURE 1. SOLUTIONS TO COMMITMENT PROBLEMS.

Questions

Ask the person or group with the commitment problem to answer the following questions.

Task Assessment

- Do you think you can do this task? (Ability)
- Do you think you will be permitted to do this task? (Context)

Emotion

- How do you feel about doing this task? (Emotion, mood)

Value

- In the future will you value being able to do this task? (Utility)
- Are you curious about the task? (Interest)
- Does the task fit with your current values? (Importance)

If the person or group with the commitment problem answers any of these questions with "no" or "maybe," solve the problem with one or more of the approaches suggested under the heading "Solutions." Remember to see the problem and the solution from the viewpoint of the person or group with the problem. Do not assume that what will motivate that person or group will be the same things that motivate you. Instead, tailor the solution so that it has maximum meaning and value for the person or group with commitment difficulties.

If the person or group answers "yes" to all the questions, either there is no commitment problem or people feel threatened and therefore are concealing the truth. Eliminate any threat and ask the questions again.

Solutions

The solutions shown on the following wheel can be applied to the commitment problem after it has been identified as a problem of *task assessment, mood or emotion,* or *task value.*

The Problems

First, although the CSRs knew how to use the new empathy technique, a majority of them were not using it with customers (a commitment problem). They disliked it and either believed that it made them look "stupid" and it did not work (a utility issue) or that they could not use it effectively (a task assessment and importance value issue). Another complicating factor was the fact that line managers were not using the new call-monitoring system or giving needed feedback to the CSRs (a commitment problem). The line managers felt that they had no time to monitor calls (a utility issue).

FIGURE 1. SOLUTIONS TO COMMITMENT PROBLEMS (CONTINUED).

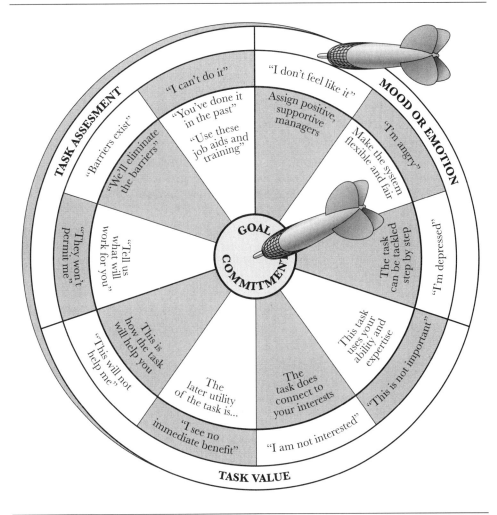

Source: Adapted from an original figure by Patrick Moffitt, artist. Used with permission.

Second, line managers were deeply resentful, and many were angry that the new system invaded their turf and allowed the CSRs to make decisions that clearly conflicted with policy. They had not participated in creating or implementing the new system, and they believed that they were losing effective control over their areas (a commitment problem). They were sending informal signals to the CSRs that bending policy to accommodate customers would be punished. These informal signals were clearly received by the CSRs and further discouraged their commitment to the new system. The CSRs realized that their calls were not being monitored and thus felt free to ignore the new system.

Third, customers who were interviewed in depth reported that the CSRs seemed uncertain about how far they could go to solve a problem and gave customers the impression that they were in a hurry to get rid of them.

This situation had caused a chain of motivation problems. The managers did not value the new approach. They let the CSRs know their feelings, and that caused a motivation problem for the CSRs. (As the managers wrote the CSRs' performance evaluations, the CSRs felt pressure not to use the approach). The CSRs were uncertain about how to handle customers and so tried to "get rid of them" in a hurry without using the new approach, which would upset their managers. Customers, in turn, who felt that they were being treated poorly, complained about the service and took their business elsewhere.

Motivational problems were being experienced by three groups: the line managers, the CSRs, and the customers. The executive vice president who had mandated the new service policy requested increased training for the line managers and the CSRs. He was willing to consider a motivational analysis before a new training exercise was attempted.

The Solution

The solution to this problem required task assessment and value interventions for CSRs and value interventions for line managers. First, the executive vice president asked a highly respected and very enthusiastic line manager to work with her colleagues to find a solution to the turf problems that would be acceptable to as many stakeholders as possible. The line managers were allowed to solve the problem in any way that reduced the negative customer evaluations without increasing costs above an agreed-on target or causing serious problems in other areas. Because this new approach was under their control and because they perceived it as enhancing their effectiveness, their commitment to it was increased.

Second, the line managers were asked to give "active support" to the revised policy and procedures in all interactions with the CSRs. Active support was interpreted as follows:

- Consistently monitoring CSR phone contacts with customers
- Convincing the CSRs that they could effectively use the empathy technique with angry customers (by making positive comments such as "you can do it," "this will work," and "we'll help you make it work")
- Giving clear, corrective feedback to the CSRs about their performance.

This active support created critical utility and importance value for the CSRs' use of the new approach. It also helped to increase the CSRs' confidence (task assessment) in their ability to use the new techniques.

Third, to create additional value for both line managers and CSRs for the revised approach, customer satisfaction was added to everyone's performance evaluation. This ensured that the result of the motivation intervention focused directly on the organization's business goals.

After another three months, a customer satisfaction study found that almost 80 percent of customers were now either "satisfied" or "very satisfied" with the service they received. Moreover, an internal study found that 90 percent of the line managers strongly supported the revised plan that they had helped to create. Only 55 percent of the CSRs were "confident" or "very confident" about the new system. However, the evidence from the computerized tracking system suggested that the CSRs' use of the new system, including the empathic approach, was almost 100 percent and the cost was 22 percent below expectations. It was hoped that the CSRs' confidence would grow as the benefits and accomplishments of the new system were publicized.

Resources and References

Bandura, A. (1997). *Self-efficacy: The exercise of control.* New York: Freeman.

Clark, R. E. (1998). Motivating Performance. *Performance Improvement 37*(8), 39–47.

Clark, R. E. (in press). The CANE model of motivation to learn and to work: A two-stage process of goal commitment and effort. In Lowyck, J. (Ed.). *Trends in corporate training.* Leuven, Belgium: University of Leuven Press.

Ford, M. E. (1992). *Motivating humans: Goals, emotions and personal agency beliefs.* Thousand Oaks, CA: Sage.

Keller, J. M. (1987). Development and use of the ARCS model of instructional design. *Journal of Instructional Development, 10*(3), 2–10.

Locke, E. A., & Latham, G. P. (1990). *A theory of goal setting and task performance.* Upper Saddle River, NJ: Prentice Hall.

Intervention Author

Richard E. Clark
CEO
Atlantic Training Inc.
3664 Hightide Drive
Rancho Palos Verdes, CA 90275-6135
Phone: 310-377-7220
Fax: 310-544-1161
E-mail: clark@usc.edu

■ ■ ı ı ı ı NEEDS ASSESSMENT

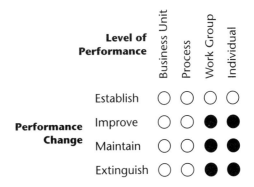

	Business Unit	Process	Work Group	Individual
Level of Performance				
Establish	○	○	○	○
Performance Change Improve	○	○	●	●
Maintain	○	○	●	●
Extinguish	○	○	●	●

Alternative Names

Gap analysis
Problem identification

Definition

Needs assessment is a tool for (1) identifying the gaps between current results and required results and (2) prioritizing the gaps according to the difference between the cost of closing them and that of ignoring them (Kaufman, 1998).

Description

Performance improvement specialists and trainers sometimes disagree on what organizational needs should be addressed. At such times what is needed is a results-focused needs assessment process that identifies gaps between the current and desired results. The practical identification of needs (gaps between the current and desired states) is best done at three levels (Kaufman, 1998):

- Needs at the *mega* level, which are gaps in *societal* results
- Needs at the *macro* level, which are gaps in *organizational* results
- Needs at the *micro* level, which are gaps in *individual or small-group* results

A needs assessment uses two parallel processes: one that identifies the desired results through strategic planning and visioning and another that identifies the current status of results through the collection of hard and soft data. (Hard data are independently verifiable, whereas soft data are perception based and, therefore, not independently verifiable.) The two processes are interdependent, and both are essential to the pragmatic determination and prioritization of needs.

Many conventional needs assessment processes focus only on the methods for collecting data concerning the current situation. These processes often center on surveys that too often turn into wish lists concerning an intervention (for example, training), a process (for example, quality management), or resources (for example, computers and money). Other so-called needs assessments focus only on demands—what people want in terms of services or support—and not on the gaps in results being observed. But by defining the desired results at all three levels (mega or societal, macro or organizational, and micro or individual/small group) and collecting data at all three levels, an individual or organization can identify and prioritize gaps in results, thereby determining *needs*.

Figure 1 offers an introductory *map* (algorithm or flow diagram) that describes the major steps in conducting a needs assessment. The clouds in the figure contain additional topics and questions that should be addressed during each step of the process.

When to Use

Needs assessment is appropriate under the following circumstances:

- When you want to know the extent to which your performance is successful and the extent to which it is not
- When there is a perceived or actual performance problem and you want to identify possible ways to close the performance gap based on performance data
- When you must demonstrate that the cost of meeting needs is less than that of ignoring them (when you have to demonstrate return on investment for what you are now doing and delivering or for what you recommend doing and delivering)
- When you want to ensure that your organization—what it uses, does, produces, and delivers—will add value to the organization itself, to external clients, and to society

FIGURE 1. SCAN QUESTIONS.

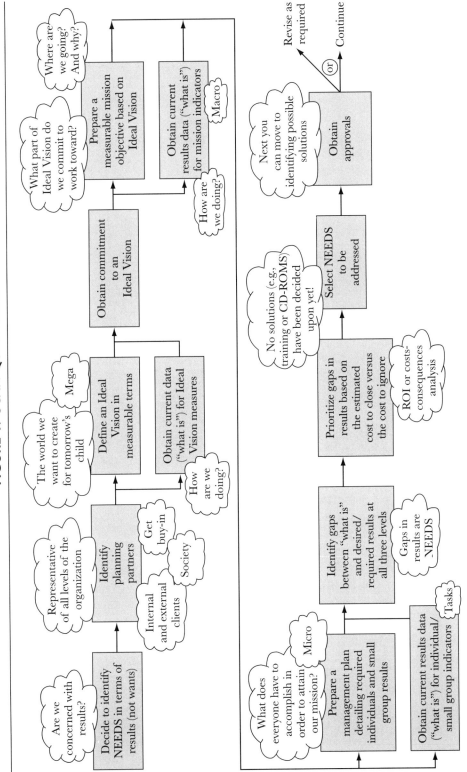

- When the organization is experiencing massive changes and wants to be responsive and responsible to both the current obvious realities and any underlying realities
- When employee morale or performance is low, according to hard or soft data
- When new equipment, new processes, or new procedures are to be implemented and you want to ensure that employees will be competent in performing the operations required
- When large numbers of new employees will be entering the organization and their competent performance is essential if the organization is to add value to the external world

Case Study

A needs assessment consultant ("Consultant") was called by a representative of a very large technological organization ("Organization"). The conversation went something like this:

Organization: We have completed a needs assessment of our entire professional staff worldwide. We have had our employees list "actuals" and "optimals" in our annual two-page company survey. And we still can't make any sense of our data.

Consultant: Let me guess—you sent out a questionnaire and asked people what they "needed."

Organization: How did you know?

Consultant: Well, that's where most conventional needs assessments start and end, with a long survey, or wish list, of favorite solutions.

Organization: Yes, that's our company policy. Each year we ask our employees what they want or "need." But isn't that important for internal customer satisfaction?

Consultant: Yes and no. It's good to know what results your employees envision themselves as achieving and what results they actually are achieving, but asking them to provide the solution often removes the opportunity for identifying and analyzing other possible solutions.

Organization: Hmm. Please continue.

Consultant: When you can't make sense out of such data, it is almost always because the questions and responses were focused on means and resources—the things people often mistakenly say they "need" rather than the results that will be of value to internal and external clients. Even "actuals" and "optimals" frequently end up being spoken of in terms of means rather than ends. And without clear gaps in results, you can't make sense of your data; you can't prioritize the data on the basis of how much it will cost to close the gaps versus how much it will cost to ignore those gaps.

Organization: That's exactly what we did . . . and how our people responded. How can we fix it?

Consultant: There are several easy steps in developing a needs assessment process that will ensure that your organization achieves success in terms of two bottom lines: financial (the conventional bottom line) and societal (the new paradigm of the bottom line). The first step is to develop the organizational context for the assessment, which requires that you bring together several organizational groups as planning partners: the strategic planning team, the quality people, the marketing group, and others that have traditionally functioned separately. Through this partnership your people can identify gaps between current and desired results at three levels: (1) the societal or mega level, (2) the organizational or macro level, and (3) the individual/small-group or micro level. The process of identifying gaps may require that the organization try viewing itself differently—from a societal perspective.

When gaps in results have been identified, they need to be prioritized based on the cost of closing the gaps versus the cost of ignoring the gaps (a rough estimate of return on investment). Only after gaps have been identified and prioritized are they analyzed—broken down into component parts and root causes. Then solutions can be selected. Waiting until this stage of the assessment to select solutions ensures that your organization is not applying solutions to "nonproblems."

Unfortunately, the management of the organization did not want to spend any more money on another needs assessment, and today business continues as usual. A few training courses have been conducted; however, they are not working well because their objectives were not about ends and performance but rather about means and *knowing about*. Continuing cuts in funding are being felt each year. Although the organization's budgets have not fallen enough to threaten organizational failure, the organization is merely giving lip service to needs assessment without being committed to doing it well. The result is more than disappointing.

Resources and References

Kaufman, R. (1998). *Strategic thinking: A guide to identifying and solving problems* (Rev. ed.). Arlington, VA: American Society for Training and Development (ASTD).

Kaufman, R., Rojas, A. M., & Mayer, H. (1993). *Needs assessment: A user's guide.* Englewood Cliffs, NJ: Educational Technology.

Mager, R. F., & Pipe, P. (1997). *Analyzing performance problems* (3rd ed.). Atlanta, GA: Center for Effective Performance.

Robinson, D. G., & Robinson, J. C. (1995). *Performance consulting: Moving beyond training.* San Francisco: Berrett-Koehler.

Rossett, A. (1987). *Training needs assessment.* Englewood Cliffs, NJ: Educational Technology.

Triner, D., Greenberry, A., & Watkins, R. (1996). Training needs assessment: A contradiction in terms. *Educational Technology, 36*(6), 51–55.

Intervention Authors

Roger Kaufman, Ph.D.
Professor and Director
Office for Needs Assessment and Planning
Florida State University
3500 University Center, Building C
Tallahassee, FL 32306
Phone: 850-644-6435
E-mail: rkaufman@onap.fsu.edu

Ryan Watkins, Ph.D.
Research Associate
Office for Needs Assessment and Planning
Florida State University
3500 University Center, Building C
Tallahassee, FL 32306
Phone: 850-644-6435
E-mail: rwatkins@onap.fsu.edu

▪ ▪ ▪ ▪ ▪ ▪ ON-THE-JOB TRAINING (OJT)

Level of Performance	Business Unit	Process	Work Group	Individual
Performance Change Establish	○	○	○	●
Improve	○	○	○	●
Maintain	○	○	○	●
Extinguish	○	○	○	●

Alternative Names

One-on-one training
Coaching
Just-in-time training (JIT)
Real-time training
Structured on-the-job training
Unstructured on-the-job training

Definition

On-the-job training (OJT) is (1) carried out at the work site, (2) delivered while the learner is engaged in performing work activities, and (3) conducted one-on-one between trainer and learner. It is usually distinguished from *off-the-job training* (delivered away from the work site) or *near-the-job training* (delivered close to the work site, for example, at a machine devoted to training and placed next to one used in actual production.) In common usage, the term *coaching* is often substituted for OJT when the learners are supervisors, middle managers, or executives, and OJT is the term preferred for other targeted learner groups.

Description

On-the-job training is a very old form of training. Apprenticeship programs featuring an early form of OJT flourished in the European guilds of the Middle Ages and the Renaissance.

Modern thinking about on-the-job training dates from the work of Charles R. "Skipper" Allen during World War I. Tasked with the need to train a large number of people in a short time to meet the needs of the war effort, Allen decided that the training should be performed during the work and should be delivered by supervisors. He then invented a new approach to OJT, based on cutting-edge psychological principles of the period. This approach involved using a four-step method—*show, tell, do,* and *check*—to guide OJT.

Allen's approach proved to be so effective that it was revived and refined in World War II to become the immensely popular Job Instruction Training (JIT) program. Some defense contractors of the time were so impressed with the results of the JIT program that they retained it after the war, and a descendant of that World War II program can still be found in some manufacturing firms to this day.

Allen's innovation and its later refinements led to a distinction between two kinds of OJT: (1) unstructured or unplanned and (2) structured or planned. *Unstructured OJT* is carried out with no instructional plan. Perhaps the most familiar example is the practice of pairing an inexperienced worker with an experienced worker. The experienced worker is admonished to "show the ropes to the newcomer," and the inexperienced worker is told to "follow Joe around the plant" or "sit by Jane" to learn. The inexperienced worker is expected to learn simply by watching—what some call "learning by soaking it up."

Unstructured OJT is generally ineffective for two reasons. The first is that people cannot learn to perform simply by watching others. The second is that unstructured OJT is not organized around what a learner needs but rather around the chaotic workplace demands confronting the experienced workers who serve as trainers. Learners who watch activities with which they are unfamiliar have no way to make sense of them and see how they fit together or why they are important.

Structured OJT, in contrast, is a planned approach that is based on a thorough work analysis of what successful performers do. In the structured OJT process, the trainer uses the results of the work analysis and shows the new workers what to do, tells them what it is and why it is worth doing, lets them do it under his or her own watchful eye, and then checks the newcomers' performance and offers feedback on how well they performed and what they should do to improve. Although based on a work analysis, structured OJT is organized around what the learner needs to know and do to perform successfully.

To understand the difference between unstructured and structured OJT, consider how each would be applied to train a worker in operating a machine. In unstructured OJT the learner would merely watch an experienced operator in action—but might not understand what that operator was doing with the machine, why it was worth doing, or how to do it. In structured OJT, however, the learner would most likely receive a safety orientation on the machine to minimize chances of injury and would then receive step-by-step instructions on how to operate the machine, why those steps are important, how to troubleshoot problems, and so forth.

Many companies could realize substantial savings and increased productivity if they would substitute structured for unstructured OJT. But doing that requires a company structure to support it (Rothwell & Kazanas, 1994). Much attention has been devoted to OJT in recent years, however, which may indicate that interest in this low-tech—and often low-cost—performance improvement intervention has been on the increase (see Jacobs & Jones, 1995).

Two major developments have recently affected OJT practice. The first is that experienced workers rather than supervisors are now doing most OJT, because many organizations vest much decision making in empowered worker teams. Often the experienced workers need training on effective approaches to structured OJT if they are to be effective on-the-job trainers (see Rothwell, 1989), as knowing how to train others does not come naturally.

The second development is that many organizations are placing more emphasis on the learner's role in OJT. As many organizations are lean staffed, one-on-one training is sometimes impossible. One way to deal with that problem is to train newcomers in how to *pull* the information they need to perform out of experienced coworkers, instead of expecting trainers to *push* that information. For this reason, some writers now discuss planned and unplanned on-the-job learning (OJL). Planned OJL, a modification of structured OJT, places primary responsibility on the learner rather than the trainer. Instead of having a trainer apply Allen's classic OJT steps of *showing, telling, doing,* and *checking,* planned OJL has the learner *watching, asking, doing,* and *soliciting feedback* (Rothwell, 1996b). On-the-job learning is consistent with efforts to create learning organizations.

When to Use

The following conditions are conducive to the use of structured OJT:

- *When the performance requires immediate application rather than information:* on-the-job training can be used to show people how to do their jobs while they are in those jobs and in the work setting in which they are expected to perform. It reduces the transfer-of-training problem that occurs when people are trained off the job. In OJT the training is conducted where the performers do the work and often by the people who will hold them accountable for their subsequent work performance.

- *When time is critical:* on-the-job training can be used when there is no time to plan or organize time-effective, off-the-job instruction. In fact, structured OJT is sometimes called just-in-time training (Rothwell, 1996a) or real-time training.
- *When workers enter their jobs one at a time rather than in cohort groups:* structured OJT can be used to slash the unproductive breaking-in period of newcomers who are hired one at a time to fill vacancies.

When Not to Use

Circumstances under which structured OJT may not be appropriate are as follows:

- When OJT might pose a health or safety threat to the learner, trainer, or other workers (for example, training someone in how to use a forklift on the plant floor when an inexperienced performer at the wheel might pose a safety hazard to others)
- When OJT might undercut the learner's credibility with customers (for example, giving an emergency room doctor OJT while he or she is working with a patient in urgent need of medical care)
- When groups of learners share a common training need that it would make more economic sense to meet in a group and off the job rather than individually and on the job.

Case Study

A manufacturing firm was experiencing explosive growth. New plants and new capacity could not be added quickly enough to meet domestic product demand, let alone international demand. Product orders were backed up for a year, and all production employees were working maximum overtime every week. Demand was so great for new products that they were being introduced into production even as final engineering specifications were prepared.

"We are hiring constantly, often several people daily for different jobs," said the plant's human resource manager, "and it's not unusual for us to hire at least twelve people off the street on Friday every week and have them on different assembly lines on Saturday morning. We don't give them an orientation. We hire so many so fast that some of them fall through the cracks and don't even know where they are to supposed to show up for work, what they will be doing, or whom to see to start work."

In analyzing the performance need, the consultant concluded that (1) the company was in a highly time-sensitive mode, (2) a major part of the workforce was inexperienced, (3) the work process was highly unstable, (4) inexperienced workers were hired one at a time for different work, and (5) management placed great emphasis on "getting workers on the line." Not surprisingly, the company was not deriving much benefit from the new hires, who were placed on the assembly line with no preparation. Also, coworkers and supervisors were so busy that they did not know how to organize or carry out OJT. In fact, harried and experienced company employees, when questioned, complained that many new hires "stood around and didn't do anything" or "visited the restroom or watercooler for long periods of time."

Structured OJT was identified as one of several performance improvement interventions targeted for implementation in the company. The company managers were highly supportive of improving performance, as they could see for themselves that new workers who lacked training were unproductive and that their inactivity only demoralized the experienced, productive workers. The goal of the structured OJT effort was to slash the unproductive breaking-in period of newcomers, to improve the quality of the work they did (in order to avoid rework), and to ensure that the new workers received essential safety training in the work context.

As it was decided that structured OJT could not be implemented throughout the entire plant at once, the consultant asked the client (represented by the company's human resource manager and the plant manager) to identify the one assembly line where structured OJT would be likely to have the greatest positive impact on production, quality, and safety. Accordingly, one line was selected. The consultant then asked the client to select the best performers from each shift on that line to meet off-site for one-half day. The client rented a local motel conference room (because the plant was bursting at the seams) and the workers met off-site.

The consultant chose a variation of the DACUM (Developing a Curriculum) method as the means to analyze the work of the assembly line and to plan OJT (Norton, 1995). Developing a Curriculum is a form of structured brainstorming in which experienced performers identify what they do and then categorize it and critique it. To conduct this modified form of the DACUM process, the consultant suggested that the company do the following:

1. Target one group perceived to be of great strategic or performance importance to the organization to serve as a pilot test group.
2. Select a panel of exemplary (star) performers from the group, an exemplary shift supervisor of the group, and "internal customers" of the assembly line.
3. Invite the panel to a session to determine the sequence of training events for new hires.
4. Validate the panel's data.
5. Provide training on how to conduct structured OJT.
6. Implement a structured OJT program.

The company accepted the consultant's suggestions, and thirty-five exemplary workers from three shifts on one line were assembled in the motel conference room to go through the modified DACUM process. They were joined by an individual selected by the company to learn the modified DACUM process that the consultant would use, the consultant, two assistant facilitators, one of the three shift supervisors from the line (the exemplary supervisor), and internal customer observers of the assembly line (including a representative from the engineering department). The group then worked through a brainstorming and refining process (see Exhibit 1). By the end of an intense morning session, the consultant and his colleagues had a completed DACUM chart that depicted the entire work flow of the assembly line and a sequence of training events for new hires that was recommended by the line's top performers and by key internal customers.

The chart was reviewed by the workers, by management, and by engineers at a one-hour validation meeting held one week later. Minor modifications were made to the chart after the workers had time to reflect on it. The consultant then prepared a checklist to guide structured OJT based on the exemplary workers' recommendations. The exemplary workers were called back to a third meeting a few weeks later to receive training on how to conduct structured OJT using the checklist developed from the chart.

This approach—which involved several other important steps not fully described here—was highly effective and was *owned* by the exemplary performers, who also served as on-the-job trainers. Unexpected side benefits also resulted from this process. First, it was decided that all employees would be given a safety briefing at the start of training on *each* work process. Second, the modified DACUM process uncovered different approaches to the manufacturing process on each shift, which unnecessarily complicated intershift transfers and intershift OJT. As a result of the work analysis, those differences could be discussed, analyzed, and resolved by the workers and by the members of the engineering department. In addition, inconsistencies in the manufacturing process itself were uncovered from

EXHIBIT 1. EXAMPLE OF THE DACUM PROCESS.

In this example of a brainstorming and refining process to identify important training events for newcomers, the consultant (group facilitator) and two assistant facilitators led the group through the following steps:

1. The facilitators began the process by briefing the participants on the purpose of the modified DACUM and on job challenges facing the participants in the future.

2. The participants were asked to list duties, responsibilities, and tasks they performed in their jobs.

3. The facilitators wrote the statements on sheets of flip-chart paper and taped them to the wall.

4. The process continued until participants could no longer think of any duties, responsibilities, or tasks.

5. The facilitators called a break, during which they created *categories* in which to group the duties, responsibilities, and tasks.

6. After the participants returned from the break, the facilitators worked with them to verify and modify the categories so that every duty, responsibility, and task could be applied to a category.

7. The participants examined each duty, responsibility, or task listed to ensure that it was placed under the proper category and to ensure that it should not be revised or deleted (because other responsibilities overlapped with it). They also checked to see whether other responsibilities should be added (because they had been initially forgotten).

8. The facilitators led a brief discussion about the participants' thoughts on the best way to train a new employee in all of the categories.

9. Another break was called, during which the facilitators sequenced the work activities according to the participants' recommendations about how to train a newcomer.

10. The participants came back from their break and were asked to verify or modify the sequencing.

11. The meeting was adjourned.

12. The facilitators removed the chart from the wall and had it reproduced on a single sheet of paper.

13. Copies of the chart were then circulated, and the participants (as well as others) suggested modifications.

Source: Based on Norton, 1995.

the work analysis; resolving these inconsistencies led to improved communication between the workers who assembled the products and the engineers who designed them.

Resources and References

Jacobs, R., & Jones, M. (1995). *Structured on-the-job training: Unleashing employee expertise in the workplace.* San Francisco: Berrett-Koehler.

Norton, R. (1995). *The DACUM Handbook.* Columbus, OH: The Ohio State University, National Center for Research in Vocational Education.

Rothwell, W. (1989). *The structured on-the-job training workshop* (2 Vols.). Amherst, MA: HRD Press.

Rothwell, W. (1996a). *The Just-in-Time Training Assessment Instrument: Data collection instrument.* Amherst, MA: HRD Press.

Rothwell, W. (1996b). *The self-directed on-the-job learning workshop.* Amherst, MA: HRD Press.

Rothwell, W., & Kazanas, H. (1994). *Improving on-the-job training: How to establish and operate a comprehensive OJT program.* San Francisco: Jossey-Bass.

Intervention Author

William J. Rothwell
Professor
Human Resource Development
The Pennsylvania State University
305C Keller Building
University Park, PA 16802-3202
Phone: 814-863-2581
Fax: 814-863-7532
E-mail: wjr9@psu.edu

▪ ▪ ▮ ▮ ▮ ORGANIZATIONAL DEVELOPMENT

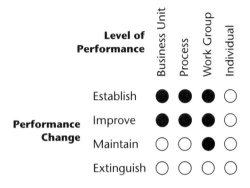

Level of Performance	Business Unit	Process	Work Group	Individual
Performance Change Establish	●	●	●	○
Improve	●	●	●	○
Maintain	○	○	●	○
Extinguish	○	○	○	○

Definition

Organizational development (OD) is a top management–supported, long-range effort to improve an organization's problem-solving and renewal process, particularly through a more effective and collaborative diagnosis and management of organizational culture (French & Bell, 1995).

Description

Organizational development is a unique improvement strategy that emerged in the late 1940s and early 1950s. One of the first fairly comprehensive change and evaluation studies was done in 1948 by Coch and French, who examined factors that influenced resistance to change. They reported that such resistance could be minimized by communicating the need for change and allowing the people affected by that change to participate in planning it. The late 1940s also saw the development of the laboratory training movement, which focused on improving interpersonal relations, increasing self-awareness, and making managers more aware of team dynamics.

Since these early works, the field has evolved into an integrated framework of theories and practices that are useful in solving important problems that confront the human side of an organization. Organizational development is about planned change—how to get people (individuals, teams, and cross-functional groups) as well as systems (human resources, production, research and development) to function more effectively. Planned change involves common sense, hard work, time, goals, and the use of valid knowledge and information about the organization and how to change it.

The field of OD has expanded from these early beginnings to include a number of intervention strategies designed to improve the effectiveness of the following:

- Individuals (for example, career planning, performance coaching, and training)
- Teams (for example, team building, role negotiation, and self-managed work teams)
- Intergroup relations (for example, process consultation, partnering, and third-party negotiation)
- The total organization (for example, sociotechnical systems, strategy planning and visioning, continual improvement, total quality management, and leadership development)

Although there are numerous tools in an OD change agent's tool kit, it is the values and assumptions that separate OD change agents from typical organizational consultants. These assumptions include the following:

- Individuals have the capacity for growth.
- Individuals desire to grow, achieve, and use their capabilities.
- Individual and organizational goals can be compatible.
- Collaboration is preferable to competition.

Some key values that OD change agents espouse include freedom, responsibility, self-control, justice, human potential and empowerment, dignity, respect, integrity, work, authenticity, openness, and an acceptance of diversity.

When to Use

A key component to the success of an OD intervention is to determine the readiness of the organization for change. The groundwork for a successful OD effort revolves around three key issues: (1) viewing the organization from a systems perspective, (2) involving people in the change process, and (3) emphasizing learning and adaptation.

Taking a Systems Perspective

Systems theory pervades all of the theory and practice of OD. It involves the assumption that all parts of the organization are connected, related, and interdependent. An organizational system can be characterized as a continual cycle of input, transformation, output, and feedback, whereby one element of experience influences the next. Some consequences of viewing organizations from this perspective are as follows:

- Issues, events, forces, and incidents are not viewed as isolated phenomena but are seen in relation to other issues, events, and forces.
- Every event is analyzed in terms of multiple causation rather than a single causation.
- Organizational activity is governed by the realization that one cannot change any part of a system without influencing the other parts.

Systems theory takes into account two fundamental concepts: stakeholder interests and organizational levels.

Stakeholder Interests. In addressing an organizational issue with a systems perspective, one maintains a focus on stakeholders—those who have interests relevant to that issue. Such a perspective attempts to understand the points of view of each interested party. In particular, one must understand and acknowledge that there is a possibility of both conflicting as well as common interests among stakeholders. Thus the systems framework forces one to consider to what extent and in what ways the interests of the various stakeholders are involved in decision making and in what ways attempts are made to foster common rather than competing interests.

Organizational Levels. The second fundamental concept that systems theory takes into account is that of organizational *levels*. The levels perspective posits that organizational events should be viewed within their larger contexts. This means that activities at one organizational level cannot be considered in isolation from influences at other levels within the organization. For example, strategic policy concerning the purchase of new technology cannot stop with activities related to purchasing equipment; it must also address a variety of related personnel issues concerning the safe and effective use of that equipment. Consequently, a systems approach recognizes that there is unique information available at all levels of the organization and that sharing that information is essential to planning and implementing effective programs. With a systems perspective, the organization can be prepared to deal with the complexities underlying organizational development, rather than taking a piecemeal approach to change.

Involving People in the Change Process

Organizational development specialists believe in people's potential to grow and develop. Not surprisingly, then, many OD change efforts are based on the assumption that those who will be affected by the change need to be involved in that change. Without this involvement, most change efforts are doomed to failure.

The kind of participation and involvement that is required extends beyond management. Research and practice have shown that increased involvement is desired by most people, has the ability to energize performance, produces better solutions to problems, and greatly enhances the acceptance of decisions. Some rules of thumb for involvement include the following:

- Involve everyone who is part of the problem or part of the solution.
- Treat those closest to the problem as experts on the subject.
- Provide the support and power needed by those closest to the problem in order to make decisions.

A number of positive outcomes can arise from involving employees in resolving organizational issues and problems: increased trust and confidence between supervisors and employees, increased communication and information flow, more effective decision-making processes, increased self-control, enhanced problem solving, and higher performance and quality goals. However, these results can occur only if employees are involved in all stages of an OD effort: the initial diagnosis of the organizational system and problem, the development of action plans for improvement, the evaluation of the effectiveness of the action plans, and the determination of what new actions or interventions are needed to continually improve organizational effectiveness.

Emphasizing Learning and Adaptation

A third cornerstone to effective OD is an orientation toward continual learning and improvement. This is a process of learning that can be conceptualized as a *learning cycle*. The learning process begins with the collection of data, which may include statistical process control charts, results from attitude surveys, everyday perceptions, and countless other types of information that summarize or reflect organizational operations. Data represent the point of departure in the learning process—the more focused and targeted the data, the more focused and targeted the learning.

Data, in and of themselves, are not knowledge, however. They must be interpreted. It is the interpretation of data that leads to hypotheses and theories that might account for the patterns or trends observed. When it is possible to make sense of the data, knowledge about organizational operations has been generated. Knowledge—not data—is power.

But knowledge alone is not enough to achieve continual learning. First, the knowledge must be shared among people. Second, action is required if the power is to be tapped. Such action might include experiments, pilot tests, policy changes, redeployment of resources, or other tangible moves.

Once taken, action calls for a new round of data collection in the form of feedback, monitoring, evaluation, and follow-through. The new data, in turn, then call for additional interpretation and adjustments to the knowledge base, thereby generating and guiding further action. Continual learning is achieved through a never-ending cycle of action steps, guided by knowledge and rooted in data. This orientation is necessary if OD efforts are to take hold and, over time, be sustained and improved.

Case Study

Since 1989 the intervention author has been involved with a small manufacturing company in Jackson, Michigan. The company has totally reinvented itself over the past eight years, from an assembly-line system to cellular manufacturing. The cellular manufacturing philosophy involves the development of a team-based work system in which employees are owners of a manufacturing process that leads to a finished product.

This OD effort began with the creation of the overall vision and underlying values that the organization wanted to pursue and create. The vision and values were generated by a team of employees and management. The vision included the following components:

"To remain competitive, we must continually improve quality, productivity, and profitability."

"Everyone in the company will have access to business knowledge, will understand the company's financial performance, and will share in the long-term success."

"The focus must be on meeting and exceeding customer needs and maintaining long-term relationships with valued customers."

The underlying values by which the vision would be accomplished were identified as follows:

"The operative principle is one of teamwork, involvement, empowerment, and responsibility among organizational members."

"Interactions among members will embody a climate of trust, mutual respect, and open communication."

"We will be characterized by continual learning that integrates problem solving, technical updating, and people skills."

A number of interventions were undertaken to move the organization toward its vision and values. The first intervention was to use *group technology* to achieve high quality standards in product planning and design. Group technology involves grouping similar problems to exploit similarities in product and processes in efforts to simplify and control the quality of work. The second intervention involved reorganizing the manufacturing function around *manufacturing cells* that operated as discrete, focused factories within the company. All aspects of cell operation, production, and quality were established to be controlled by the teams of people who operate and set them up. The third intervention involved building and designing "quality at the source." The primary responsibility for quality was to reside with the operators and cell-team members. In order to do things right the first time, the operator was given the resources, responsibilities, and tools to do the job.

The move to group technology, manufacturing cells, and quality at the source was accomplished through the shared efforts of management and line workers. Companywide teams were created to operationalize the vision by developing a prototype for the plant, evaluating its success, and developing procedures for generalizing from the pilot program to the development of other manufacturing cells. Cross-cell teams were formed to develop guidelines for safety procedures, quality, machine maintenance, and tooling. Other teams were formed to develop a standardized set of procedures on how to operate the various machines (hobs, lathes, drills, broaching) in the factory. Within each cell team, weekly meetings were established to review quality and safety concerns and to consider ways to keep improving cell processes.

In addition, workers were given extensive information on the company's financial situation so that they could see the big picture of the change effort. A great deal of effort and resources were also devoted to employee training. External consultants conducted training in areas such as working in teams, running effective meetings, improving internal and external customer relations, enhancing problem solving, and seeking root causes to problems in order to effect continual improvement. Consultants also trained technical experts within the company in training skills so that they could share with others how to work effectively in manufacturing cells. In addition, internal programs were created and used to improve skills in areas such as statistical process control, group technology, quality at the source, print reading, gauge usage, and geometric tolerance.

This OD change effort was based on the principles of systems thinking, participation, and learning. Each of the manufacturing cells became a minisystem within the larger system, in charge of its own inputs (determining what jobs to run), transformation (turning raw materials into products), outputs (preparing products for shipping to customers), and feedback (checking the quality of its own work). The cell members were empowered to set up the machines in their cell in whatever way made sense to them and to calculate their own cycle times for getting the work done. Eventually, the cells were able to schedule their own work, do their own maintenance, make purchases to improve their operations, and alter daily operations in ways that they saw fit. One key component of this transformation was standardizing work procedures. Another was training the cell members in areas such as statistical process control, blueprint reading, advanced machine processes, machine setup, basic maintenance, problem solving, team building, running meetings, and internal and external customer relations.

It has taken a number of years for this OD effort to unfold. It took time for people to see that management was serious about taking a systems perspective (rather than blaming individuals for problems), empowering others, and developing an orientation toward continual learning. Through sustained leadership and the efforts of many employees, this company has moved from the brink of collapse to a state of success characterized by profit, growth, and learning.

Resources and References

The annual series. (1972–1998). San Francisco: Jossey-Bass/Pfeiffer.

French, W. L., & Bell, C. H. (1995). *Organizational development* (5th ed.). Upper Saddle River, NJ: Prentice Hall.

Porras, J. I., & Robertson, P. J. (1992). Organizational development: Theory, practice, and research. In M. Dunnette & L. M. Hough (Eds.), *Handbook of industrial and organizational psychology* (2nd ed.) (pp. 760–797). Palo Alto, CA: Consulting Psychologists Press.

Price Waterhouse. (1995). *Better change: Best practices for transforming your organization.* Burr Ridge, IL: Irwin.

Rothwell, W. J., McLean, G. N., & Sullivan, R. (1995). *Practicing organizational development: A guide for consultants.* San Francisco: Jossey-Bass.

Senge, P. (1994). *Moving forward, thinking strategically about building learning organizations: The fifth discipline fieldbook.* New York: Doubleday/Currency.

Intervention Author

J. Kevin Ford
Professor of Psychology
Michigan State University
Department of Psychology
129 Psychology Research Building
East Lansing, MI 48824-1117
Phone: 517-353-5006
Fax: 517-353-4873
E-mail: fordjk@pilot.msu.edu

■ ■ ■ ■ ■ ■ ORGANIZATIONAL SCAN

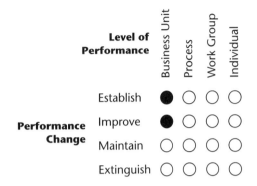

Level of Performance	Business Unit	Process	Work Group	Individual
Establish	●	○	○	○
Performance Change — Improve	●	○	○	○
Maintain	○	○	○	○
Extinguish	○	○	○	○

Alternative Name

Organizational performance analysis

Definition

An *organizational scan* consists of a framework and a general process for analyzing influences on *large-scale* performance—that is, performance that involves the efforts of many groups and individuals throughout an organization.

Description

The organizational scan builds on the work of a number of pioneers in performance technology—including Thomas Gilbert, Geary Rummler, Robert Mager, and Joe Harless—and reflects their emphasis on performance as a system, with results that are influenced by many factors.

The best of the early work in performance technology is characterized by precise definition of individual or *small-scale* performance; by careful, detailed, and comprehensive analysis of the influences on that performance; and by placement of the primary responsibility for performance improvement on the technologist rather than the performer. That foundation has served the technology well; it has contributed to the creation of a disciplined approach to performance that is based on solid, systematic models.

The organizational scan is designed for use with large-scale efforts (1) when it is not possible or cost-effective to conduct detailed, in-depth analysis of all performance influences and (2) when it is important to place primary responsibility for change on performers rather than technologists. In a strict sense, the organizational scan is not so much an intervention as an analytical approach to selecting and/or supporting large-scale interventions. When the scan framework is used by members of the organization, the analytical process itself becomes an intervention that increases people's knowledge about performance influences, provides them with a basis for taking action to address those influences in their own organization, and builds commitment to change.

Figure 1 is a summary description of the organizational scan framework.

All three components of the performance system—(1) the conditions under which people work, (2) the processes they follow, and (3) the outcomes (and resulting consequences and feedback) that are produced—can be influenced in ways that help or hinder performance. In addition, the following three kinds of factors can influence performance:

- *Organizational factors,* which tend to influence the performance of the whole organization and/or most of the people in it. These factors are related to such things as organizational structure, centrally controlled systems, corporate strategies, key policies, and organizational values and culture.
- *People factors,* which operate primarily for individuals or groups. These factors are related to such things as the climate in which the individuals or groups work, the nature of the demands on them, their skills and knowledge, and the feedback and rewards they receive.
- *Work factors,* which primarily influence a particular job category or set of job categories. These factors are related to such things as the typical work environment, the resources and information available, the work process, and the nature of the products and services produced.

The key to the success of an organizational scan is taking full advantage of the knowledge and abilities of employees, working with them as partners. The scan model is used to generate questions framed to reflect the nature of the performance improvement or change effort. Those questions then become the base for a review by representative members of the organization. Typically, the analytical review is conducted in small groups representing a cross-section of those who will be affected by the change and/or involved in implementing it.

FIGURE 1. ORGANIZATIONAL SCAN FRAMEWORK.

	Conditions	Processes	Outcomes
Organization Level	*Strategy, Structure* Mission, strategy External business drivers Functional grouping Budget/decision authority	*Systems* Degree of centralization Consistency of operations Flexibility	*Organizational Results* Satisfaction of investors Satisfaction of societal stakeholders Measures of success Goal alignment with mission
People Level	*Climate, Practices* Company values, individual values Management/leadership practices Team norms Ethics, integrity	*Performance Requirements* Skills, knowledge Job aids/references Selection Confidence	*Motivation, Feedback* Satisfaction of employees Frequency, timing, form Rewards and recognition Expectations
Work Level	*Environment, Resources* Physical environment Tools, materials, information Support personnel/services Accessibility of resources Work load, demands	*Methods* Allocation of functions Processes, procedures Work flow Duplication/gaps	*Products, Services* Satisfaction of customers Productivity levels Standards/criteria Quality of product delivery

Outcomes of a scan may include the following:

- A recommendation to consult other technologists with special expertise in a given area
- Identification of areas in which further analysis is needed
- Information that can be used to make sure a planned intervention will mesh well with the organization.

Often the scan will identify actions that can be taken immediately to improve performance.

When to Use

Although the organizational scan lends itself to a wide range of analysis situations, it is likely to be most useful under the following circumstances:

- *When a large-scale project is involved:* The organizational scan is particularly useful with very large-scale projects affecting many people, job roles, departments, or even a whole organization. Scanning is helpful when it is important to get a broad, comprehensive analysis of all performance influences, but virtually impossible to conduct an in-depth analysis of all.
- *When employee ownership is important:* The organizational scan works well when it is important to get widespread buy-in from members of the organization. The scanning process allows for active involvement of organizational members and is particularly valuable when their support is critical to implementation or to gaining support for further analysis.
- *When time, money, and resources are limited:* An organizational scan can quickly yield a broad picture of organizational influences and can help in setting priorities for further investigation.

Case Study

A transportation organization was experiencing serious problems with the quality of its service, and its productivity was deemed unacceptable. Inefficient and wasteful work processes had already been identified as a key factor, and the organization had created cross-functional work teams consisting of employees and external consultants to redesign processes. The project crossed many boundaries and would affect large numbers of people in quite a few departments.

In this instance the purpose of the organizational scan was to examine organizational influences in the light of the proposed work process changes. The scan framework was used to generate a series of questions, which were given to each work team. Team members first assigned a rating to each question to reflect the nature and severity of the factor's impact on their project goals. Then they discussed their ratings and the rationale for them and subsequently arrived at consensus. They divided the performance influences into the following categories:

- Those that were already being addressed effectively through their project
- Those that would support their efforts (or at least not hinder them)
- Those that would or might hinder the success of their efforts

The use of the scan uncovered several areas that the team members had not originally planned to address but that could have seriously limited the success of their efforts. For example, the scan revealed that the information system they had used and relied on did not actually provide information in a form that was usable to the people who needed it.

Figure 2 presents some of the questions developed using the scan framework. These questions are structured to help determine how well a proposed change effort is aligned with a current organizational system. Other situations may call for a different kind of structure.

FIGURE 2. SCAN QUESTIONS.

Conditions: **organizational factors** Strategy, structure	• Is the change compatible with the organization's mission and strategic direction? If so, is that clear to the people who will carry out the change? • Will people have the budget or decision-making authority they need to implement the change and meet their goals and responsibilities?
Conditions: **people factors** Climate, practices	• Do current management and leadership practices support the change? • Do current team norms about work behavior support the change?
Conditions: **work factors** Environment, resources	• Does the current physical environment support the change? • Are the resources that people will need to implement the change easily accessible to them?
Process: **organizational factors** Systems	• Are the current systems (information, rewards, and so on) centralized (or decentralized) in a way that supports the change? • Do the organizational systems currently have the degree of flexibility required to support the change?
Process: **people factors** Performance requirements	• Do the people who will implement the change have the skill, knowledge, and experience to make it work? • Are on-the-job references or job aids available to support the change, if needed?
Process: **work factors** Methods	• Is the current assignment of job functions or tasks appropriate to support the change? • Is the way that work is currently designed generally free of duplications of effort or gaps that could interfere with the change?
Outcomes: **organizational factors** Organizational results	• Are the goals of the units involved in or affected by the change consistent and compatible with the requirements of the change and the results expected? • Are there organizational measurements in place that will allow people to determine the success of the change? Are those measurements clearly tied to organizational success?
Outcomes: **people factors** Motivation, feedback	• Is the way in which people now receive feedback about their work compatible with the change? Are they frequent enough, timed appropriately, in usable form? • Are people currently rewarded and recognized for behavior that is compatible with or supports the change?
Outcomes: **work factors** Products, services	• Are current work standards or criteria compatible with those required by the change? • Is the predictability of the workload compatible with the requirements of the change?

Resources and References

Gilbert, T. F. (1978). *Human competence: Engineering worthy performance.* New York: McGraw-Hill.

Rummler, G. A., & Brache, A. P. (1990). *Improving performance: How to manage the white space on the organization chart.* San Francisco: Jossey-Bass.

Tosti, D. T., & Jackson, S. F. (1997). The organizational scan. Performance Improvement, *36*(10), 22–27.

Intervention Authors

Stephanie Jackson
Senior Partner
Vanguard Consulting, Inc.
P.O. Box 1685
Sausalito, CA 94966-1685
Phone: 415-332-7888
Fax: 415-332-8560
E-mail: Change111@aol.com

Donald Tosti
Senior Partner
Vanguard Consulting, Inc.
P.O. Box 1685
Sausalito, CA 94966-1685
Phone: 415-332-7888
Fax: 415-332-8560
E-mail: Change111@aol.com

OUTPLACEMENT

Level of Performance

	Business Unit	Process	Work Group	Individual
Performance Change Establish	○	○	○	○
Improve	○	○	○	○
Maintain	○	○	○	○
Extinguish	○	○	○	●

Alternative Name

Career transitioning

Definition

Outplacement is the process of teaching departing employees the skills they need to find new employment or entrepreneurial opportunities. Those administering this process strive to complete it quickly and efficiently, with the least amount of emotional wear and tear possible and with the best possible chances for professional and personal fulfillment.

Description

Employers frequently find that some of their employees do not possess the skills, abilities, or knowledge needed to achieve their assigned goals. As a result, employers often need to hire new people with the needed skills and abilities and to simultaneously lay off capable people who no longer fit. This delicate people-changing process must be planned and implemented humanely and with an eye toward limiting litigation exposure, controlling costs, and helping departing employees to land on their feet.

When faced with planning such departures, organizations frequently turn to outplacement firms for assistance. The selected firm (see Figure 1 at the end of this chapter) typically provides consultation to management, facilitation of meetings with departing employees, and the design and delivery of programs for departing employees.

Consultation to Management

The management consultation provided by an outplacement firm consists of meetings with the organization's management. During these meetings the consultants help the managers to plan appropriate communications, schedules, and procedures associated with the separation process. Another important topic addressed is how to maintain the productivity and morale of the remaining workforce.

Meetings with Departing Employees

On a date designated by the organization, representatives from the outplacement firm may hold orientation meetings with all personnel designated as eligible for outplacement assistance. The meeting agenda generally includes the following:

- The fact that career transition services will be offered to departing personnel
- The introduction of the selected outplacement firm as the provider of the services
- Introduction of the outplacement firm's designated facilitator
- An overview of the career transition process
- A series of suggestions on what the departing employees should and should not do as they prepare themselves for their upcoming job searches
- A schedule of the facilitator's availability for individual meetings to discuss feelings about job loss, a schedule for launching a successful job search, and the commencement of the transition process

Design and Delivery of Programs

The outplacement firm assists the client organization in identifying what programs it would like to sponsor for departing employees, what concerns it has about such programs, what objectives it wants to accomplish in offering the programs, and what its expectations are regarding costs. A strategy is then developed to meet the organization's objectives, and programs are created. Most outplacement firms provide several types of programs, including a senior executive full-service program, a professional program, a group program, and tailor-made programs.

Senior Executive Full-Service Program. The senior executive full-service program includes the following elements:

- Unlimited one-on-one career counseling
- Financial counseling
- Personal assessment with a trained professional specializing in the identification of marketable assets and career options
- Assistance in identifying job targets
- Private office space along with full support services
- Resume development and preparation
- Networking and marketing techniques and strategies
- Communication skills, video interviews, and telephone techniques
- Entrepreneurial business counseling, including assistance in developing business plans
- Career search management
- Online and printed job search research materials

Professional Program. This type of program is designed for professional and mid-level management personnel who require individual job search counseling and office access. The program usually includes the following elements:

- One-on-one counseling
- Self-assessment and analysis of values, interests, and marketable skills
- Job targeting
- Office support with access to personal computers
- Printed resumes and letterhead stationery
- Networking and marketing techniques and strategies
- Communication skills, video interview rehearsals, and phone use
- Career search management
- Access to computerized and printed job search research materials

Group Program. The typical group program consists of classroom sessions that focus on career transition training on job search strategies. Each program is custom designed to meet the organization's budgetary and time requirements as well as the individual needs of the program participants. The sessions are designed to provide participants with all the tools necessary to organize and implement an effective job search campaign. The subjects covered are as follows:

- Dealing with the frustration and anger often associated with job loss
- Becoming familiar with the job search process
- Identifying the correct job market
- Identifying marketable assets
- Constructing and using a resume
- Networking, prospecting, and developing leads
- Communicating and interviewing effectively
- Managing a job search

Tailor-Made Programs. Frequently a departing employee has been through outplacement programs previously or for other reasons already knows how to update a resume, how to network, how to interview, and so on. If this is the situation, the outplacement firm can design a tailor-made program that meets the needs of such an individual as well as the cost requirements of the organization. The employee and the outplacement consultant jointly determine specific outplacement services from the following selections:

- Individual, one-on-one counseling and support
- Office use and administrative support
- Application and interpretation of aptitude and interests and/or personality measurements
- Multimedia self-study materials

When to Use

Outplacement can be used whenever the organization chooses to assist individuals in making career transitions. This happens most often in the following situations:

- When there are reductions in the workforce
- When the organization is realigned
- When there are changes in the organizational direction
- When there are individual performance deficiencies

Case Study

Mr. "N." spent twenty-five years with a large, privately held supplier of industrial cutting tools. He held a series of progressively more responsible positions, including systems analyst, plant controller, international controller, assistant corporate treasurer, director of business planning, and chief information officer. In the course of his career with this organization, Mr. N. became a workaholic, which led to a divorce and estrangement from his children.

When he was laid off due to a merger with a publicly held organization, he was provided with a senior executive outplacement program. He approached the job search process in the same go-for-broke manner that he had successfully used throughout his career. He chose not to complete any self-examinations designed to help outplacement participants determine what might be the most satisfying kind of work to pursue. Mr. N. saw himself as a financial executive and was not interested in looking into any other career fields.

Shortly after completing the core training, Mr. N. became a finalist for a position as chief financial officer with a local, privately held firm. He informed his outplacement counselor of the fact that he expected an offer within a week and that he would probably accept the position. He also expressed some misgivings about reentering the "rat race," fearing that his workaholic tendencies would cause problems with his new wife.

The outplacement counselor implored Mr. N. to go through the introspective assessments and gain a better understanding of who he was and what he really wanted to do for the rest of his career. Mr. N. again passed up the opportunity. His outplacement counselor asked him to at least answer the following questions:

- Is this really where you want to work? Geographically? Organizationally? In terms of type, size, product?
- Are these truly the duties and responsibilities you want to perform?
- Is this the industry in which you want to work?
- Are the pay and benefits (both financial and mental) likely to remain suitable and acceptable?
- Are the supervisory and peer relationships likely to be mutually rewarding and satisfying?

As usual, Mr. N. essentially dismissed the questions. However, in deference to his counselor, he did write them down to discuss with his new wife. Over the course of the ensuing weekend, Mr. N. and his wife had several conversations about what their lives would be like when and if he took the probable job offer.

On Sunday of that weekend, a friend invited him to attend a franchise exhibit. At the show Mr. N. found himself attracted to a printshop booth. His father had owned a printing business, and Mr. N. had worked his way through college by helping his dad in the business. He had decided many years ago that he never again wanted to work that hard.

At the exhibit he also learned that he could go into his own business with a relatively small investment and that the hours required were not as formidable as he assumed. He remained intrigued with the prospect of being his own boss, and while he was awaiting the job offer he investigated the franchise opportunity further. By Thursday of the following week, he was enamored of the prospect of buying a printshop franchise. When he received a call offering him the job he expected, he said he would respond in a week.

He then held a series of conversations with his outplacement counselor and reluctantly agreed to complete the self-assessment instruments previously offered, one of which included an entrepreneurial quotient. In so doing, he got to know and understand himself better. He learned more about the things he did best as well as the things he most enjoyed doing. He also found out that he wanted to set his own priorities and not have them imposed externally.

When Mr. N. and his spouse reviewed these findings and the job opportunity against the franchise opportunity, the die was cast. He turned down the

FIGURE 1. WHAT TO LOOK FOR IN AN OUTPLACEMENT FIRM.

Criteria	Measurement
Good track record	90 percent placement within six months
Absence of litigation	Lawsuit-free for people taking advantage of program
Humane approach	Mission statement and principal's behavior judged to be humane
Cost-effective	Per-person cost is consistent with usual and customary charges
Strong client base	Experienced with all functions and industries as well as profit and nonprofit sectors
Good references	Participants and firms speak highly of firm and staff
Service orientation	Extent, type, and duration sufficient to meet clients' needs
Location of staff	Near enough to avoid excessive transportation expenses
Facility	Mail, phone, clerical, and other support services sufficient to meet needs of probable participants
Materials (training tools)	Present useful information in a high-quality, professional format
Staff	Have the qualifications, experience, and mien needed to meet all participants' needs
Training ability	Demonstrates knowledge and experience to train all levels of employees in job-seeking skills

employment opportunity and spent his remaining separation money on purchasing the franchise.

Today—four years later—Mr. N. owns two franchised printshops. He works an average of forty-five hours per week, very little on the weekends. In addition, his work brings him a great deal of satisfaction and he makes more money than he ever did as an employee.

Resources and References

Bolles, R. N. (1997). *The 1998 what color is your parachute: A practical manual for job hunters and career changers.* Berkeley, CA: Ten Speed Press. Richard Bolles's Web site, with the *Washington Post*, has links to many other on-line job-hunting sources: http://www.washingtonpost.com/wp-adv/classified/careerpost/parachute/front.htm#book

Morin, W. J., & Cabrera, J. C. (1991). *Parting company: How to survive the loss of a job and find another successfully.* Orlando: Harcourt Brace.

Intervention Author

Richard Robinson
Senior Consultant
Hugh Anderson Associates, Inc.
755 West Big Beaver, Suite 1210
Troy, MI 48084
Phone: 248-362-2050
Fax: 248-362-3743
E-mail: robin919@mail.idt.net

▪ ▪ ▪ ▪ ▪ ▪ PARTNERING AGREEMENTS

Level of Performance	Business Unit	Process	Work Group	Individual
Establish	○	○	●	●
Improve	○	○	●	●
Maintain	○	○	●	●
Extinguish	○	○	●	●

Performance Change labels the rows Establish, Improve, Maintain, Extinguish.

Definition

A *partnering agreement* states the roles, responsibilities, and actions to be assumed by two or more parties who have agreed to work together to create a product or process.

Description

Partnering agreements capture the commitments made by two or more parties who will create a product or process together. The partners may be from different levels within the organization or may be a combination of internal and external people. Often the partners have diverse skills and talents.

A successful partnership consists of the activities described in the following paragraphs.

Identifying Results

Successful partners determine the desired outcomes of their venture and put them in writing. The outcomes should be specific and challenging, yet attainable. Because these outcomes determine the direction of the partnering effort, the written plan should include whatever is required to move the partnership forward. All partners must be focused in the same direction, with their efforts supporting one another.

Clarifying Roles

The partners clarify the roles, responsibilities, and authority of each partner with regard to the creation of the product or process.

Sharing Information

The partners share information related to creating the product or process. The sharing of frequent, accurate, and timely information is a must.

Using Skills

Each partner contributes skills to the effort and possibly develops new skills as a result of the partnering relationship.

Sharing Resources

The partners share resources and actively seek any additional resources needed in order to enhance the product or process.

Recognizing Achievements

The partners acknowledge their success in terms of both the desired results and the partnering effort itself.

Making Corrections

Effective partners develop a relationship that allows for mistakes and encourages learning from them. The partners analyze their errors so that they can move ahead more effectively, avoiding similar mistakes in the future.

Encouraging Creativity and Risk Taking

The partners are open to new ideas and outside-the-box thinking. This openness often involves taking some risks along the way.

Challenging and Coaching Each Other

The partners challenge each other to think of ways to make work more productive and interesting. When they collaborate, they make each other's contributions count, and they give credit where it is due.

Evaluating Results

The partners evaluate and monitor the effectiveness of their working relationship as well as the results of their efforts.

Contracting

Working solely from a verbal contract can lead to confusion about responsibilities and expectations. Working from a written contract, however, facilitates discussion and decision making, helps each partner to develop understanding, and leads to clarity on everyone's part. Although the format of the written contract varies with the nature of the project and people involved, the document always includes the following information:

- Desired outcome
- Partners involved
- Primary roles and responsibilities of each partner
- Action plan or timeline
- Evaluation methods

When to Use

Partnering agreements are appropriate under the following circumstances:

- *When time is available for the collaborative approach:* Initiating and building partnering agreements takes time and effort at the beginning of the partnership. Once the partnership has been formed, however, it enables the people involved to work more effectively, thereby saving time in the long run.
- *When the product or process is important enough to warrant the use of multiple talent:* When diverse talents are brought together, partnering behaviors are very helpful. The individuals involved in a partnership generally see the product or process differently, according to their own experiences, background, and inclinations.

Forming a partnership allows them to bring all of their talents to bear, making best use of those talents and determining which responsibilities and deliverables are most appropriate for each person.

- *When attempting to empower people:* Partnering agreements not only necessitate the sharing of information, resources, and authority, but also foster skill development. Therefore, they naturally lead to the empowerment of those involved.
- *When current working practices inhibit quality production:* Partnering agreements can be used to enhance working relationships, which in turn can lead to improvement in the quality of the work to be produced.

Case Study

A senior manager at B&E Manufacturing decided to develop a performance management system and asked other managers in the organization to partner with him to create it. The partners developed a plan for fulfilling the organization's needs that included the following:

- Suggestions for creating a performance management system
- Project outlines with appropriate approaches and resources
- Internal and external staffing requirements
- Costs for the project

The partners and an external consultant met with upper management to explain the project and to seek approval for using the services of an outside consulting firm. The partners then identified expected outcomes and clarified roles and responsibilities. As both they and the organization's upper management desired a more participative culture, they brainstormed ways to involve employees actively in the process. The partners outlined a tentative time frame for the project and decided on methods for evaluating their work. They later shared the goals of the project with the full employee group.

The consultant gathered information by interviewing upper-level managers and other employees, some individually and others in groups. Then the partners reviewed previously established policies, past attempts at conducting performance appraisals, and content from previous performance appraisal training programs. The partners visited employee work sites to observe work being done and to interview employees about problems they encountered.

The partners identified eleven major problem areas related to performance, most of which they believed could be resolved by involving employees in developing the following products and processes:

- A manual of policies and procedures
- Current position descriptions
- A performance planning system
- A means for performance feedback and evaluation

The partners completed these products and processes within a year. While they worked, they continually monitored their own roles, responsibilities, and deadlines. As each phase was completed, the results were evaluated. Employees were involved at every step, from the development of the manual of policies and procedures to the implementation of a system for performance planning, feedback, and evaluation. As a result, a more participative culture evolved. Long-term evaluation systems were put into place to ensure that the new culture and the new tools that were developed continued to serve managers and employees.

Exhibit 1 is the partnering agreement that these partners constructed.

EXHIBIT 1. PARTNERING AGREEMENT.

Desired Outcome

Create a performance management system that evaluates and develops individuals in the organization

Partners Involved

Carl Fernandez, senior manager and project initiator
Pat Winston, project manager, with direct reporting relationship to C. Fernandez
Chris Reed, consultant
Dale Pulaski, manager
Lynn Swartz, manager

Roles and Responsibilities

- Pat Winston, internal project manager, will be one of two primary contributors. The project manager will schedule all meeting of the partners, will arrange all site visits and interviews, and will gather all existing materials in the organization that will facilitate the partners' work.

- Chris Reed, consultant, will serve as the other primary contributor.

- The remaining partners will meet no less often than monthly to review progress and make decisions.

Action Plan

- Interview randomly selected managers and employees to identify performance-management needs.

  Coordinator: Pat Winston
  Interviewer: Chris Reed
  Timeline: 30 days

- Review current policy and procedures manual, existing and previously used performance-appraisal systems, and previous performance-appraisal training.

  Coordinator: Pat Winston
  Reviewer: all partners
  Timeline: 60 days

- Conduct work-site visits and gather information.

  Site visitors: all partners. (Each visit will be made by Chris Reed and one other partner.)

Evaluation

After the accomplishment of each primary task outlined under the heading "Action Plan," the partners will review their progress and how well they are working together. The will adjust roles, responsibilities, and assignments as necessary.

Resources and References

Covey, S. R. (1989). *The 7 habits of highly effective people.* New York: Simon & Schuster.

Gardenswartz, L., & Rowe, A. (1994). Group process: Human engineering to keep the team on track. In *Diverse teams at work: Capitalizing on the power of diversity* (pp. 145–187). Burr Ridge, IL: Irwin.

Katzenbach, J. R., & Smith, D. K. (1993). "Moving up the curve: From individual to team performance. "*The wisdom of teams: Creating the high performance organization* (pp. 109–129). Boston: Harvard Business School Press.

Kouzes, J. M., & Posner, B. Z. (1995). *The leadership challenge.* San Francisco: Jossey-Bass.

Sujansky, J. G. (1991). *The power of partnering: Vision, commitment, and action.* San Francisco: Jossey-Bass/Pfeiffer.

Intervention Author

Joanne G. Sujansky, Ph.D.
President
Training Connection®
1800 St. Claire Plaza
1121 Boyce Road
Pittsburgh, PA 15241
Phone: 724-942-7900
Fax: 724-942-4648
E-mail: trngconn@aol.com

PERFORMANCE ANALYSIS

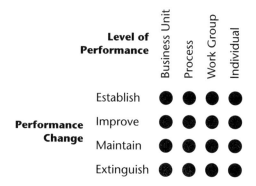

Level of Performance	Business Unit	Process	Work Group	Individual
Performance Change Establish	●	●	●	●
Improve	●	●	●	●
Maintain	●	●	●	●
Extinguish	●	●	●	●

Alternative Names

Front-end analysis
Needs assessment

Definition

Performance analysis is the process of aligning business results, performance processes and products, and performance support.

Description

Performance analysis has been a fundamental part of human performance technology for more than thirty years. Performance analysis is often called *front-end analysis,* a term probably invented by Joe Harless (cited in Dean & Ripley, 1997, p. 94), who defined it as "all those smart questions a trainer or manager or consultant asks before doing anything." Early research on the effectiveness of programmed learning showed that part of that effectiveness came from the analysis and part from the program. Intellectual leaders in the field of human performance technology have emphasized performance analysis from the beginning (Dean & Ripley, 1997).

In most modern workplaces performance analysis occurs every day. Managers analyze the performance of product lines, of production lines, of competitors, and of direct reports. Instructional designers and human performance technologists analyze to identify existing performance gaps or to specify the performance that will be needed to implement a new strategy, operate new equipment, service new customers, or initiate new procedures.

Much of the analysis is quite good—but much of it is seriously flawed. Practical managers have two bad habits in conducting performance analysis: jumping to solutions and using quick fixes that leave the underlying causes intact to bring about further problems. Instructional designers and human performance technologists have two equally bad habits: experiencing *analysis paralysis* and making recommendations that are disconnected from the practical realities of the workplace. The bad habits are the fruits of natural forces at work in today's workplaces. Competitiveness, globalization, movements toward niche marketing, technological innovation, changes in workforce competencies and motivations, and organizational restructuring and downsizing make workplace reality hard to pin down. Priorities, goals, personnel, and internal politics keep changing rapidly, making it hard for managers, instructional designers, and performance technologists to learn better ways of conducting performance analysis.

Fortunately, many of the specific techniques of modern performance analysis can be practiced in today's workplaces. Modern performance analysis uses techniques that are well known and commonly taught in educational institutions, leadership institutes, management workshops, and off-the-shelf training programs. Specific sets of analysis techniques such as Pareto analysis, fishbone analysis, or force-field analysis can be found in many good training programs associated with quality initiatives. Group problem-solving techniques have been described in many packages, including cooperative learning, guided design, and guided group interaction. The tools are not mysterious but they are, unfortunately, easy to misuse by defining problems too narrowly or too broadly, attempting to solve complex technical problems with common sense, or attempting to solve commonsense problems with complex technology.

Proper uses of performance analysis techniques achieve two things:

- They focus on important workplace performance, which can be measured in terms of timeliness, quality, and cost.
- They focus on a complete set of key workplace variables, which include performance standards, feedback, incentives, goals, guidance, instructions, tools,

materials, and the knowledge and skills of the workers. Furthermore, the analyses should not focus on only one or two subsets of those variables.

A number of people have provided effective performance analysis techniques: Brethower and Smalley (1998); Gilbert (1978); Kaufman, Thiagarajan, and MacGillis (1997); Langdon (1995); Mager and Pipe (1997); and Rummler and Brache (1995). In addition, it has been argued that performance analysis techniques should be integrated into performance improvement projects rather than used before beginning a project (Brethower, 1997). (Refer to the case studies later in this chapter for examples of an integrated approach.)

When to Use

Performance analysis is appropriate under the following circumstances:

- When there is a suspected performance gap (that is, a mismatch between the existing level of performance and the desired level of performance)
- When a performance gap has been verified, but the causes have not been identified
- When suspected causes of a performance gap have been identified but not verified
- When some causes of a performance gap have been verified, but the full set of performance support variables (performance standards, feedback, incentives, goals, guidance, instructions, tools, materials, and worker knowledge and skills) has not been examined

Case Studies

The following two case studies illustrate the many areas on which performance analysis focuses.

Technical Writers

The manager of a technical writing group was concerned about the quality of his group's output (product specifications, technical manuals, procedure updates, and a variety of other documents). Errors in some of the manuals had the potential to create costly equipment failures, unclear procedures, increased training costs, and workplace mistakes. The manager was also concerned about the amount of time spent in correcting the errors found in manuals.

A performance analyst discussed the situation with the manager and, within a few minutes, discovered several kinds of problems:

- *Guidance problems:* The writers were good at the mechanics of sentence and paragraph construction. However, there were no clear standards—and no models of good and poor writing—available to them.
- *Work process problems:* Because of the manager's concern for quality, he reviewed nearly everything written by the writers. That created a bottleneck so that there was no time to return work products to the writers; instead, the manager frequently worked far into the night rewriting.
- *Feedback problems:* The manager frequently complained about quality problems in staff meetings, in one-on-one meetings, and in memoranda. However, the complaints were general and unsystematic rather than suggestions for specific, remedial action. Most feedback to the writers, then, was delayed, general, and negative. Occasional positive comments were also delayed and general. Most customer complaints came directly to the manager.
- *Motivation problems:* The manager claimed that the writers were lazy and that they believed they were better writers than he was. Consequently, they ignored feedback from him.
- *Incentive problems:* The manager believed that the writers did not particularly enjoy technical writing and wanted to be journalists or novelists instead.

The rationale for the manager's jumping to conclusions in this way was that the recommended changes would probably improve performance and would, at the same time, provide better data to verify and correct any errors in the performance analysis (see Brethower, 1997). The analyst decided to bypass further analysis and to work with the manager to make several changes. The analyst recommended making "before" and "after" exhibits from several manuscripts that the manager had rewritten and discussing these exhibits in a series of staff meetings (a training solution). The analyst also recommended that whenever possible the manager mark corrections on manuscripts and return them to the original writers to make the corrections indicated (a change in work process that provided better feedback to the writers). The analyst volunteered to help the manager keep track of the number of manuscripts that had to be rewritten, the amount of time the manager spent rewriting, the number of recurring errors, the number of manuscripts that went out on time, and so on, so that the manager could tell if the procedures were improving the performance of the writing group (an improvement in feedback to the manager). In addition, the manager posted examples of "best writing" done by writers each week (which the manager and the performance analyst hoped would provide an incentive for writers to improve).

It took several meetings with the manager to recycle recommendations and do further analysis for the purpose of checking out assumptions. The performance analyst and the manager were, in effect, combining the knowledge and information that each had in order to analyze the problem and identify solutions that made sense to the manager.

According to the manager and the data collected by the analyst, these changes resulted in significant improvements in writing quality, significant reductions in the number of manuscripts that went out late, and significant reductions in manager time. The analyst, the manager, and the writers reviewed and refined the procedures further, based on data collected and feedback obtained.

Concession Stand Operators

The manager of a movie theater was concerned that concession stand operators were doing a poor job of cleaning the stand at the end of the day. The stand frequently had to be cleaned by the manager before she left for the day or cleaned the next day, making it difficult to get the stand ready to operate.

After discussing the situation with the performance analyst, the manager believed that part of the problem was poor standards. She had assumed the concession stand operators knew what "cleaning the stand" meant and that it did not mean leaving the stand with disorganized shelves, greasy fingerprints on the glass, and displays left in disarray. She also felt that the operators did not care much about the threats she had made to fire them; the pay for the job was low and they could easily get other jobs elsewhere.

The intervention began with further performance analysis. The analyst talked to the stand operators, who confirmed that the manager occasionally "pitched a fit" about cleanup. They attributed these fits to bad moods, saying that the stand did not seem to be any worse than usual on those days. The analyst and the manager developed a checklist for stand cleanliness and then collected and reviewed data. The data collection enabled them to ensure that the checklist in fact captured the manager's standards. It also verified the manager's view that end-of-shift cleanup was quite poor.

The next step was to train the operators to use the checklist to monitor their own performance. The operators reported cleaning almost everything all the time; they told the analyst that they filled out the checklist as the last item of work and just checked off everything unless they remembered deciding not to do something. The checklist focused on the results of cleaning, not the process of cleaning, enabling the analyst and the manager to monitor performance without being there to see the work as it was being done or not being done. There was a slight improvement in the actual performance.

The next step involved feedback on accuracy. At the beginning of each shift, the manager went over the checklists with the operators, noting areas of agreement and pointing to items that were "good enough" according to the operators and "not good enough" according to the manager. The analyst persuaded the manager, with difficulty, to treat this phase as analysis. To the manager that meant that she could comment on specific agreements and disagreements between what she saw and what the operators checked on the checklist, but that she could not yell at the operators for things they did not clean. (The analyst argued that consequences could be added later, but it was not fair to do so until it was clear that the operators knew what was expected of them.) This phase of the analysis showed that the operators correctly reported that they left anywhere from 0 percent to 20 percent of the items uncleaned and that they incorrectly reported cleaning many items that were not cleaned according to the manager's standards.

This phase of training in standards and analyzing performance continued for several days, during which accuracy improved. The accuracy showed that the manager and operators were now agreeing about what the standards incorporated into the checklists meant. The manager—but not the performance analyst—was surprised to discover that the performance also improved. Operators began reporting that they cleaned more than 90 percent of the items and did so in contrast to the 60 percent they had been cleaning. In effect, they claimed to have reasonably high standards and then improved their performance to match the standards they claimed.

In the next phase, the intervention, the manager set a standard at 95 percent of the items. Performance stabilized near the standard, with operators typically missing only a few items that both the manager and the operators agreed were not very important. The analyst recommended either changing the checklist to remove those items or using a combination of work redesign and incentives to attain 100 percent, but the manager was satisfied with the result as it was.

Resources and References

Brethower, D. M. (1997, November). Rapid analysis: Matching solutions to changing situations. *Performance Improvement*, pp. 16–21.

Brethower, D. M., & Smalley, K. A. (1998). *Performance-based instruction: Linking training to business results.* San Francisco: Pfeiffer/Jossey-Bass.

Dean, P. J., & Ripley, D. E. (1997). *Performance improvement pathfinders: Models for organizational learning systems.* Washington, DC: International Society for Performance Improvement (ISPI).

Gilbert, T. F. (1978). *Human competence: Engineering worthy performance.* New York: McGraw-Hill.

Kaufman, R., Thiagarajan, S., & MacGillis, P. (Eds.). (1997). *The guidebook for performance improvement: Working with individuals and organizations.* San Francisco: Jossey-Bass/Pfeiffer.

Langdon, D. G. (1995). *The new language of work.* Amherst, MA: HRD Press.

Mager, R. F., & Pipe, P. (1997). *Analyzing performance problems* (3rd ed.). Atlanta, GA: Center for Effective Performance.

Rummler, G. A., & Brache, A. P. (1995). *Improving performance: How to manage the white space on the organization chart* (2nd ed.). San Francisco: Jossey-Bass.

Intervention Author

Dale M. Brethower, Ph.D.
Professor of Psychology
Western Michigan University
8190 Two Mile Road N.E.
Ada, MI 49301-9518
Phone: 616-676-3485
E-mail: dalebrethower@compuserve.com

Case Study Author

The second case example is based on R. D. Bennett (1988), Improving performance without training: A three-step approach, in *Performance Improvement Quarterly, 1*(1), 58–68.

▪ ▪ ▪ ı ı ı   PERFORMANCE APPRAISAL

	Level of Performance	Business Unit	Process	Work Group	Individual
	Establish	○	○	○	●
Performance Change	Improve	○	○	○	●
	Maintain	○	○	○	●
	Extinguish	○	○	○	●

Alternative Name

Performance evaluation

Definition

Performance appraisal is the process of determining how well employees do their jobs according to a set of standards and of communicating that information to the employees.

Note that performance technologists are involved in identifying the need for performance appraisals. They might develop a form or a process. But the real intervention should be designed and used by the employee's manager, as described below.

Description

The performance appraisal may be the most versatile intervention available to a manager to improve employee performance. The process of appraising performance forces the manager to define the employee's performance requirements as an individual contributor and answer the question, What level of performance is needed from this individual in order for the organization to meet its goals? The appraisal process requires the manager to observe what the employee actually has contributed toward organizational goals over a sustained period of time. These two action steps in the appraisal process allow the manager to do a comparison between what is needed and what is being received. This comparison allows the manager to determine whether the performance and product received by the organization are above, below, or at the level of the expectations in terms of meeting organizational goals. Those identified as falling short can then receive focused attention aimed at determining the cause of the shortcoming. The performance appraisal also collects all this information and communicates it directly to the performer so that improvement actions can begin.

Each of these steps is described in the following paragraphs.

Defining Performance Requirements

To be able to appraise performance, that performance must be measured against a standard, a goal, or a need. The manager must organize the performance requirements so that individual contributions support the goals of the organization. The performance appraisal should help the manager to create an alignment between organizational goals, departmental abilities, and individual contribution.

Following are some examples of errors that managers may make when determining performance requirements:

- Measuring employee attributes against global norms created outside the organization rather than against performance requirements driven by organizational need
- Measuring one employee's performance against the performance of another employee in a forced ranking (although this method may reveal who is doing more, it does not reveal if what is being performed is actually needed by the organization)
- Beginning with broad or vague annual objectives that do not provide enough direction to guide the performance toward the level desired
- Failing to accommodate changes during the course of the year (if the organization is dynamic and changing, then a performance requirement is that the employee must be dynamic and have the ability to change focus as needed; a manager can observe an employee's skill at responding to changing priorities)
- Softening the findings in order to "be gentle" on the employee
- Excusing lack of results by blaming circumstances that affected the individual

Observing Employee Performance

To be able to appraise performance, the manager must observe that performance. The effective manager knows that individual performance must be reviewed by observing either the results of the effort or the process used during the effort. When results can be observed, then actual measurement and comparison against performance requirements are cleaner. In some tasks, the results are harder to observe; they may be delayed, as in a long project, or they may be more cognitive, as with a plan. In these cases the process used to perform the work can be observed. In all cases it is important to observe the work or results and not the employee's personality.

An effective evaluation captures as cleanly as possible the true performance of the employee. Performance improvement strategies that result from the appraisal will be effective only if actual performance is truthfully defined. For example, assume that an employee has produced at maximum rate given the equipment available but has not met the standard. The resulting appraisal should indicate the deviation from the standard as well as the need to upgrade to better tools; both elements must be present to produce a truthful appraisal of the individual.

Comparing Employee Performance to Performance Requirements

The result of any comparison can be one of only three conclusions: the observed behavior exceeds the performance requirements, meets those requirements, or falls short. Some appraisals separate these three to a greater extent by adding an element of frequency to each—that is, *consistently* exceeds or *occasionally* falls short.

The comparison allows the manager to locate those areas of performance that fall short of the requirements. Cause analysis can be conducted on the negative deviations. This analysis reinforces the fact that objective observation is critical to effective management of performance. The manager's goal is to improve the employee's performance so that the organization's requirements can be realized; the goal is not to punish the employee. Therefore, when locating negative deviations, the manager must plan to analyze these areas further so that everything that may be affecting the performance is considered.

Analyzing Performance Deficiencies

Performance deficiencies tend to fall into one of three categories:

- The employee does not have the ability to perform at the required level
- The employee has the ability but is being prevented from performing at the required level

Resources and References

Mathis, R. L., & Jackson, J. H. (1991). *Personnel/human resource management.* San Francisco: West.

Walker, J. W. (1980). *Human resource planning.* New York: McGraw-Hill.

Intervention Author

Brian M. Desautels
President
The DunnRowen Group
10717 NE 197th Street
Bothell, WA 98011
Phone: 425-483-1748
E-mail: Madison4@GTE.net

PERFORMANCE MANAGEMENT

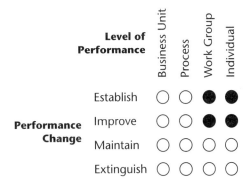

Level of Performance	Business Unit	Process	Work Group	Individual
Performance Change Establish	○	○	●	●
Improve	○	○	●	●
Maintain	○	○	○	○
Extinguish	○	○	○	○

Alternative Name

Applied behavioral analysis

Definition

Performance management is a systematic, data-oriented process of managing people to achieve a high and steady rate of performance. It involves the application of behavioral analysis, including pinpointing desired results and tasks, measuring performance, giving feedback, and providing positive reinforcement.

Description

Performance management is a term that has been widely used in business circles for more than three decades. Most frequently it is applied to a system of performance appraisal or evaluation in which a worker and his or her manager agree on performance expectations for the coming year, discuss progress against those expectations on some regularly scheduled basis, and finally have an appraisal event. Frequently this approach to performance management is used to justify a salary or wage increase. Although very popular, this type of performance management most often becomes an administrative duty with little or no relevance to actual on-the-job performance.

Performance management as described here is very different. It is the business application of *applied behavioral analysis*, the science of behavior developed by John B. Watson and popularized by B.F. Skinner. Applied behavioral analysis was introduced to business and industry by Aubrey Daniels in the early 1970s and termed performance management because of the stigma attached to the word *behavior* as well as some mistaken associations with *behavior modification*.

Performance management is a process for influencing behavior with the purpose of helping people at all levels and in all functions to perform better on the job. It is more than an evaluative process. It is a data-based system for identifying, measuring, and accelerating performance on the job.

The basis for the performance management process is found in the ABC Model, in which behavior (B) is influenced by some stimulus, or antecedent (A), but is sustained, accelerated, or extinguished by the consequence (C) that follows it. Understanding how behavior is influenced by events that precede it and follow it can significantly change how people are managed on the job.

The performance management process is derived from a problem-solving model based on behavioral analysis. It is this systemic model that allows performance management to be used in a practical way in business applications. The five-step model involves the following:

- Precise pinpointing of results and behavior
- Measurement
- Feedback
- Changing behavioral consequences (in particular, adding reinforcement)
- Monitoring the results

Step 1: Pinpointing Results and Behavior

Most organizations measure results. Few measure the behaviors necessary to achieve the results. Performance management requires measuring both. It also requires precision when pinpointing behaviors. The behavior in question must be measurable, observable, reliable, under the control of the performer, and active.

Step 2: Measuring

The measurement requirement involves counting and judging behaviors. Typically, measurement in business is used to identify problem performers. Therefore, it often results in negative feedback to or negative action taken against the performer to get the problem corrected. In contrast, measurement in performance management is used to enable employees to do better by increasing the frequency of positive reinforcement for desirable behaviors.

Step 3: Receiving Feedback

Feedback, as it is used in a performance management system, allows the performer to have information about his or her own performance in a complete and timely manner. Feedback information used in this way actually allows performers to use the information to change their own behavior.

Step 4: Receiving Positive Reinforcement

Positive reinforcement is an acknowledgment that the performance is to some degree correct and that it is recognized and appreciated in a timely fashion. Appropriate reinforcement must be added at the right time and at the right frequency. For example, a clerk who processes more that the usual number of pieces of paperwork with high accuracy should be given a reinforcer, perhaps verbal praise from his or her manager, while in the act of doing the paperwork. Similarly, a machinist who does a quality check before sending work to the next station might get a thumbs-up sign from the supervisor who witnesses the inspection.

All consequences—positive reinforcement, negative reinforcement, punishment, and extinction of the behavior—are appropriate given the right circumstances. However, performance management has shown that only positive reinforcement is capable of capturing discretionary effort, which is the level of effort people could give if they wanted to but which is beyond what is required.

Step 5: Monitoring

Because we are measuring both behavior and results, we can monitor and add more reinforcement or remove something from the environment as necessary to maximize gains. Monitoring allows us to correlate whether particular events are yielding gains in desired results and to adjust management behavior accordingly.

Frequently, performance management is used as an administrative tool to allow an organization to justify changes in compensation. One of the distinct advantages of having a true performance management system is that it allows the organization to use compensation effectively, rewarding good performers and differentiating levels of performance among employees.

When to Use

Performance management is a serious undertaking that requires a significant investment of energy and time on the part of the organization. It should therefore be applied when a change is determined to be of significant business advantage.

The following are situations in which the application of performance management would be advantageous:

- When the organization is contemplating or has initiated a strategic business change that requires significant changes in employee behavior
- When the organization is implementing tactical initiatives that depend on changing individual behavior—such as new work management systems, the introduction of new technology, or a shift in focus from sales to service
- When numerous tactical initiatives are under way, are experiencing varying degrees of success, and are requiring ever-increasing expenditures of time and money without providing a satisfactory return
- When the linkage between organizational goals and individual performance is unclear
- When employee performance is not satisfactory even within the status quo
- When money is being spent on incentives or other reward systems and little or no performance improvement is apparent
- When training programs are failing to produce acceptable levels of performance
- When safety systems have been installed, but the safety-related outcomes are not acceptable

Case Study

Like many companies today, the Washington Public Power Supply System, operator of electrical generating facilities in the Pacific Northwest, has experienced uneasy times. Demands for change have been drastic in the prevailing do-more-with-less corporate culture. With the impending deregulation of the electric utility industry, the supply system must reduce the power cost of its commercial nuclear power plant and improve the performance of its twelve hundred employees while maintaining the highest of safety standards.

Traditionally, the nuclear power industry has been characterized by a strong regulatory process coupled with a heavy dose of negative reinforcement and punishment as a baseline management style. Policies, procedures, and deadlines are simply a way of life. Yet old management strategies for doing business as usual eventually result in performance burnout. At the supply system, it became clear to the executive staff that although the company had to be "leaner" to survive, its leaders also had to adopt more effective management practices. In fact, traditional management techniques were determined to be part of the problem. Vic Parrish, supply system CEO, explained the situation this way:

> Achieving success in our industry has never been more vital to the future of our organization. Yet, we also recognized that the manner in which we went about accomplishing our top goals would greatly impact our employees and work environment, and, frankly, we haven't always selected the best approaches to implementing change. Performance management provides the measurement methods for achieving results and, equally important, fosters a creative and positive environment for meeting our business needs.

To succeed to the required level of excellence, the supply system needed a new corporate culture—a culture capable of (1) analyzing what consequences are directly connected to the various behaviors important to the organization, (2) developing new ways of measuring the critical factors needed to drive the strategic results of the company, and (3) creating core values that use performance management principles to foster change and growth.

Given the importance of these changes, the supply system undertook a comprehensive, companywide, two-year implementation.

Implementation Strategy

The implementation strategy consisted of five steps.

Step 1: Training and Consultation. The supply system provided advanced performance management training (APMT) for all its managers and supervisors (approximately 240 people). In addition, each participant received three follow-up consultations. The outcome from the training and consultations was the installation of a common problem-solving language and method throughout the company. Also, each participant developed a performance improvement plan (PIP) aligned with the CEO's targeted strategic results. A sample PIP is provided in Exhibit 1.

Step 2: Sponsorship and Champions. The CEO and the vice presidents are the key sponsors of the performance management effort. They not only verbally endorse performance management but also model the process. Each member of the

EXHIBIT 1. SAMPLE PERFORMANCE IMPROVEMENT PLAN.

Results Pinpointing

Measurable result _Increase in percentage scored on departmental matrix_

Who is the performer? _Managers_

Which business objective does this result support? _Decrease human error_

Result Data

How will you measure the result?

Percentage scored on matrix

How will you gather the data?
- ☐ Existing reports
- ☐ New report
- ☐ Observation/counting
- ☐ BARS
- ☐ Checklist
- ☐ Self-monitoring

How often? _____

Result Feedback

Sketch graph with legends, baseline data, and goal levels (if known).

☐ *Individual author* and/or ☐ *Group*

Updated by: How often: Location:

Result Reward/Celebration Plan

Performance subgoals
and final goal:

How we will celebrate:

Subgoal 1 _90_   _Pocket knife_

Subgoal 2 _95_   _Department manager brings in VP_

Subgoal 3 _98_   _Pizza lunch on department manager_

Final goal _____

Antecedent/Kickoff Plan

Communications meeting plan: _Gather managers to review measurement tool, get input_

Materials/supplies needed: _____

Anything else I can do? _Discuss linkage to significant results_

Additional training: _Practice observations_

Obstacles I can remove: _____

EXHIBIT 1. (CONTINUED).

Behavior Pinpointing

List the key behaviors that the performer(s)
need(s) to do that will significantly affect the results.

Meet with direct reports weekly to
discuss matrix issues
Maintain current data
Collect and compute baseline

Complete assigned number of individual and
joint observations weekly
Establish subgoal and baseline

Behavior Data

How will you measure the behavior?

Behaviorally Anchored
Rating Scale (BARS)
Observation Sheet

How will you gather the data?
☐ Existing reports
☐ New report
☐ Observation/counting
☐ BARS
☐ Checklist
☐ Self-monitoring

How often? _____

Behavior Feedback

Sketch graph with legends, baseline
data, and goal levels (if known).

Baseline

Average Score on BARS

☐ *Individual author*   *and/or*   ☐ *Group*

Updated by: *How often:*   *Location:*
_____   _____   _____

How often will you discuss this verbally
with the performer(s)?

_____

Reinforcement Plan for the Key Behaviors

How will you make the positive reinforcment immediate?

Key Behaviors:
_____
_____
_____
_____
_____
_____

Reinforcer:
Social reinforcement; coffee break with
department manager
_____
_____
_____
_____

Theme for behavior/result? (Optional)_____
_____
_____

executive staff has an individual set of PIPs, and performance management projects are discussed at each of the CEO's staff meetings. A proactive attempt is made to visit APMT graduates, to discuss their PIPs, and to attend celebrations. A record of active PIP advancements is maintained and reviewed continually. In addition, a board of performance management champions (approximately thirty people from various departments) has been established to help fuel the process, and review and recognition meetings are held regularly throughout the organization.

Step 3: Orientation.   A sitewide performance management orientation with an emphasis on safety was held for all employees. A comprehensive performance management safety program that is being launched this year will provide a prominent performance improvement project for the entire company.

Step 4: Executive Coaching.   A senior consultant observed members of the executive staff as they interacted in a variety of settings, including staff and individual meetings. The consultant observed each executive's ratio of positive reinforcement to punishment, body language, recurring patterns that interfered with communication, pinpointing skills, inadvertent forms of punishment (interruptions and extinction), and strategic linkage capability. Personal PIPs were then developed to enhance each executive's performance management skill base.

Step 5: Systems Analysis.   The Behavioral Systems Compatibility (BSC) survey was conducted eighteen months into the implementation. Each organizational system (such as employee development, rewards and awards systems, and business plans) designed to influence human performance was evaluated against a BSC scorecard. This scorecard examined various dimensions of reinforcement and behavior: focus, frequency, timeliness, and significance.

Results

Currently the supply system has more than one hundred active business performance improvement plans (PIPs). Return on investment (ROI) is threefold. The supply system's most recent ratings from the Nuclear Regulatory Commission and the industry's Institute of Nuclear Power Operations (INPO) reflect marked improvement. Also, the intangible ROI is evidenced by the teamwork throughout the organization. Greg Smith, the nuclear power plant's general manager, said, "At one time there was a lot of finger pointing across departments, but today people are working together. They take ownership and help others. Operations, engineering, and maintenance are responsive to the needs of one another. The PIPs are helping us to cross departmental lines."

Teamwork within and across departments has greatly affected the schedule effectiveness of the plant. Historically, schedule effectiveness was about 60 percent. With the aid of performance management, schedule effectiveness has improved to more than 85 percent.

The tangible ROI continues to build. In the following months, each APMT graduate will assess the estimated cost savings of his or her PIPs, which include a variety of projects. The projects represent a range in savings—some small, some large—but each contributes to the overall goal.

"Our cost-reduction teams are using PIPs with subgoals that have produced cost savings of $2.6 million in the first six months of PIP activity," said Paul Bemis, vice president of nuclear operations. "We predict $12.8 million per year over the next three years in additional reductions, and we attribute much of that to the power of positive reinforcement."

While the supply system has shown a remarkably high and steady rate of incorporating performance management into the corporate culture, this is only the beginning of a new way to do business. The organization now has in place an understanding of the common denominator in any initiative—an understanding of behavior.

Resources and References

Boyett, J. H., & Conn, H. P. (1994). *Maximum performance management: How to manage and compensate people to meet world competition.* Lakewood, CO: Glenbridge.

Daniels, A. C. (1989). *Performance management: Improving quality productivity through positive reinforcement* (3rd ed., rev.). Tucker, GA: Performance Management.

Daniels, A. C. (1994). *Bringing out the best in people: How to apply the astonishing power of positive reinforcement.* New York: McGraw-Hill.

Hurst, P. W. (1997, Summer). The energetic pace of the Washington Public Power Supply System. *Performance Management Magazine,* pp. 16–24.

Skinner, B. F. (1976). *About behaviorism.* New York: Vintage Books.

Weiss, T. B., & Hartle, F. (1997). *Reengineering performance management: Breakthroughs in achieving strategy through people.* Delray Beach, FL: St. Lucie Press.

Intervention Author

Takatsugu Amano
Consultant
Aubrey Daniels and Associates, Inc.
3531 Habersham at Northlake
Tucker, GA 30084
Phone: 770-493-5080
Fax: 770-493-5095
E-Mail: amano@mindspring.com

Case Study Author

Philip W. Hurst
Senior Consultant
Aubrey Daniels and Associates, Inc.
3531 Habersham at Northlake
Tucker, GA 30084
Phone: 770-493-5080
Fax: 770-493-5095

POLICIES AND PROCEDURES

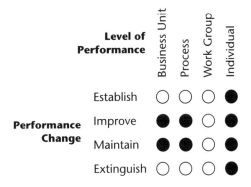

Performance Change	Level of Performance	Business Unit	Process	Work Group	Individual
	Establish	○	○	○	●
	Improve	●	●	○	●
	Maintain	●	●	○	●
	Extinguish	○	○	○	●

Definition

Policies are statements about the decisions an organization will follow. They reflect the values and assumptions of the management of the organization. They are broad statements, written to cover the widest range of possible occurrences. *Procedures* are detailed statements about how to follow or execute the policies. As an intervention, policies and procedures can include developing and installing new policies, revising old policies, or installing a new level of compliance to current policies.

Description

Policies are often assumed to be in place in organizations. Few books on management or organizational behavior deal with policies as a vehicle for performance change. However, developing policies can be a useful intervention to establish, improve, maintain, and even extinguish performance.

- The establishment of performance can occur when a new policy allows or mandates a certain behavior that was not permitted previously.
- Improvement in performance can occur because the policy becomes a standard of performance, requiring certain behaviors.

- Maintenance of behavior can occur when policies are written that codify or in-stitutionalize behaviors that are currently part of informal practice.
- The extinguishing of performance can occur when the consequences for non-compliance with newly stated policies are so great that people are deterred from behaving in ways in which they formerly did. For example, consider a situation in which there is a change in policy regarding the level of approval needed to authorize payments of certain amounts. Dependence on higher management can be extinguished by allowing junior-level employees to approve higher pay-ments or write-offs. The reverse is also true.

For the performance technologist, the initial task is to identify the role that policies play in the organization. In start-ups, there may be none. In older com-panies, policies may exist, but they may have no impact or a negative impact on employees and customers. When measuring the gap between the actual and desired states, examining the role that policies and procedures play in the or-ganization can help to identify an important but often neglected intervention.

When examining the culture, one may find that asking probing questions such as the following is helpful:

- Is this a rule-run company?
- Are there many mavericks in this company?
- Are old policies retarding growth?

Policies reflect the culture of the organization in a number of ways. For ex-ample, the presence or absence of policies often reflects the level of centralization in the organization. Sophisticated organizations that have been in business for a long time are likely to have more policies in place than young, small, or entre-preneurial organizations. Ichak Adizes (1988) notes in *Corporate Lifecycles* that as baby organizations grow and develop they have a greater need for policies and bureaucratic mechanisms. Some large, older organizations, however, wishing to prevent the hardening of the arteries that can result from bureaucracies, eschew policies for fear of squelching the creative spirit among employees. The desire of such organizations to maintain a decentralized philosophy is illustrated in the lan-guage of their policies. The authority levels are widely distributed, the methods of obtaining exceptions are liberal, and consequences for noncompliance are minimal.

One can tell a great deal about an organization by determining whether it views information as abundant and available to all or as power and available only to a few. An organization's philosophy of information is reflected in its practices concerning policies. Some organizations do not make policies available to ordi-nary employees or those who carry out those policies.

One company, for example, currently has only one policy manual per office. This practice reflects its disregard for the corporate office; every regional office feels that it has the right to "do its own thing." Other organizations disseminate their policies widely, expecting everyone to follow them.

An organization's theory of compliance can be detected in its approach to policies. Companies that expect managers and employees to follow certain policies will support the implementation of those policies with communication and training on how to use the policies. In contrast, organizations that expect managers to "think for themselves" have few policies in place.

Understanding the architecture of an organization's policies contributes to the understanding of its culture. One way in which a performance technologist develops an understanding of an organization is to pay particular attention to the structure and unstated purpose of those policies and to compare the statements that employees have made about the organization to the kinds of policies that exist.

- Are benefits more or less generous than the industry standard?
- How do employees talk about the company as a place to work? Its benefits? Its policies and practices?
- Are the comments consistent with what has been observed?

A performance technologist also talks with nonmanagerial and managerial employees to determine how the mission and vision of the company are reflected, if at all, in the policies. Both activities—reading policies and having discussions with employees—are very revealing.

Sometimes companies use policies and procedures to protect themselves from lawsuits. They write and communicate policies on topics that are often litigated. For example, employment policies, which delineate the causes and steps that must be pursued before termination, can be used to protect an organization from wrongful termination lawsuits. The presence of other policies, on sexual harassment or immigration status, for example, can offer some protection to an organization, even if individual employees do not comply.

Other organizations find that there are financial consequences to having written policies. Sometimes lending institutions will not require escrow payments if their corporate clients have written financial policies to guide them. The policies will cover employee action in investigating credit risk, granting credit, pursuing nonpayment, and doing write-offs within specific guidelines. For these organizations, having financial policies in place indicates only a desire to meet the needs of external parties; employees' needs for information are not as important to such groups.

Having examined the policies in order to determine what can be learned about the culture from them, one then turns to the procedures. Procedures are the step-by-step descriptions needed to perform the duties outlined in the policies. In some cases the procedures might best be written in the form of a job aid or a flowchart rather than a prose description.

Procedures can also be a way to *localize* actions in multicompany organizations. For example, the headquarters or corporate office may write policies on a number of topics. These policies may specify that the president of each division is responsible for ensuring that procedures are written to meet the specifics of policies in the local unit. This approach is consistent with the concept "think globally, act locally."

Policies need to include the following:

- Topic
- Policy statement
- Roles and responsibilities
- Date of implementation

See Exhibit 1 for a sample policy.

It may be useful to add information about who may make exceptions to the policy. Other topics might be needed as well, depending on the needs of the organization. Procedures may or may not be included within the policy manual.

In designing policies as a performance change intervention, one should develop strategies for the approval process, the revision process, and communication with affected parties. Frank Wydra (1988), a master at using policies to change organizations, notes, "If you cannot explain the policy to employees to their satisfaction, you may want to consider revising the policy." This proves to be a good rule of thumb.

When to Use

Policies and procedures should be considered as a performance change intervention in situations such as the following:

- *When a merger or acquisition has just taken place:* Implementing policies and procedures can help to achieve some consistency between the two previously separate entities.
- *When performance falls below expectations:* For example, when lack of good purchasing policies causes overspending or poor business practices, the development of policies can improve organizational performance.
- *When employees complain of disparate treatment:* For example, when employees do not believe that their pay is determined in a consistent way, it is a good idea to consider creating compensation policies.

EXHIBIT 1. SAMPLE POLICY.

Name: Financial Services Policy

Objectives

- To provide a consistent method of doing business
- To ensure best business practices
- To ensure timely approval and communication of policies

Policy Statement

The M Group's Financial Services policies support the execution of the company policies that can be found in *The M Group's Reseller Handbook.* They are all designed to support sales while mitigating risk for The M Group, thereby ensuring The M Group's profitability and viability.

Effective Date

January 1, 1998

Responsibilities

Each associate is responsible for following the policies in this manual. When the associate has followed the policy as well as every step of the appropriate procedure and still has been unable to meet The M Group's goal, the associate should refer the problem or situation to the team leader or supervisor.

Each associate is responsible for following the levels-of-authority matrix provided in Appendix A.

Procedures

None required

- *When the law changes or other companies are sued for actions that were not governed by policy:* Sexual harassment policies were developed after the law changed on this topic. Recently many organizations have implemented policies on intellectual property, copyright infringement, and the privacy of electronic communications, largely because lawsuits on these issues have been levied against other organizations.

Case Study

A construction company with revenues of $3 billion a year consisted of six separate companies that had been merged over a period of several years. When a new corporate president was hired, he was surprised at the size and number of lawsuits that occurred after construction jobs were completed. These lawsuits arose out of differences of opinion regarding the cost to make changes in the original contract. After reviewing the content and particulars of several typical cases, he came to the conclusion that poor contract administration was a significant factor contributing to the organization's poor profitability. His response was to demand that a training program on contract administration be devised, and contract administration became his theme for a year. This focus led to the development of the organization's internal Council on Contract Administration.

The council consisted of representatives from each of the six divisions. Their first activity was to develop a strategic plan, outlining everything that would be necessary in order for good contract administration practices to occur in the company.

Research showed that only two of the six companies had policies in place regarding contract administration, and in those companies the policies were difficult to find. Project managers felt that their primary duty was to get the buildings built, not to worry about paperwork. Corporate officers were responsible for finding the paperwork to defend against litigation; the project managers exacted no consequences for sloppy record keeping (also known as poor contract administration) because they were transient and moved quickly to the next project. Collecting fees and defending against short payment was someone else's work.

It became clear that although training was needed, it was only a partial answer. The council's strategic plan identified a significant threat to the organization to be lack of uniformity among the divisions in terms of contract administration. This lack of uniformity, which came from a lack of policy, was deemed an important deterrent to good contract administration practice. Consequently, the council took on the task of developing policies in contract administration.

This process of drafting policies included the use of an internationally known external expert in contract administration in the company's industry. The input of this expert was critical for two reasons:

- It imbued the policies with credibility and gave the project managers the power to control costs.
- It served as a wake-up call that the topic was of such importance that a leader in the field was needed to help the company.

The council members worked with the expert to draft policies that were based on the principles of good contract administration. They also designed a process for policy approval as a part of chartering the council. This process required that policies be approved by all of the division presidents, after their input and commitment were obtained. Once approved, policies were sent to the executive team (consisting of the corporate president, the treasurer, the human resource vice president, and the legal counsel) for final approval. The council would then be charged with implementing the policies. Once implementation began, it became clear that providing training in the policies and procedures was needed to support good contract administration.

Having a council that wrote policies and oversaw implementation meant that the training was targeted to the appropriate audiences. The highest-level people received training on the policies from the expert in the field. All employees were trained in the elements of the policies that had been converted into flowcharts, checklists, and other learning aids. (No one—but no one—can tolerate being trained on policies by just reading them.) These learning aids supported the training in the practical aspects of good contract administration.

Results are still coming in from this project. What is predicted is that the project managers' performance will be improved in terms of ensuring that paperwork is completed in a more timely fashion and that systems are set up to document changes in the project. Office personnel are expected to perform better because of direction from the top and the expectations of the project managers. The presence of policies and job aids will increase their ability to perform, ask questions, and conduct follow-up. In addition, the policy now requires that a full-time contract administration person be assigned to every project over a certain dollar value. Making this a policy requirement ensures that budget proposals will include the funding of this position and that project managers will assign a full-time contract administrator when required.

Resources and References

Adizes, I. (1988). *Corporate lifecycles.* Upper Saddle River, NJ: Prentice Hall.

Levesesque, J. D. (n.d.). *People in organizations: Managing policy, behavior and performance problems.* Sacramento, CA: California Chamber of Commerce (phone: 800-331-8877).

Wydra, F. (1988). *Policies change organizations.* Unpublished manuscript. Detroit, MI.

Intervention Author

Kathleen S. Whiteside
Partner
Performance International
1330 Stanford, Suite D
Santa Monica, CA 90404
Phone: 310-829-7006
Fax: 310-829-3457
E-mail: KatPerform@aol.com

PROCESS MAPPING

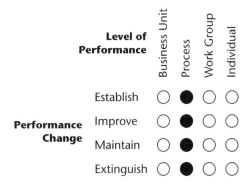

	Level of Performance	Business Unit	Process	Work Group	Individual
	Establish	◯	●	◯	◯
Performance Change	Improve	◯	●	◯	◯
	Maintain	◯	●	◯	◯
	Extinguish	◯	●	◯	◯

Alternative Names

Process analysis
Process diagrams

Definition

Process mapping consists of developing a map that depicts the process (work activities) used to create organizational outputs.

Description

A *process map* illustrates how the process in question meets customer needs. A variety of elements may be incorporated into the map. These generally include (1) inputs, (2) steps to be taken to achieve outputs, and (3) the outputs themselves. Process maps may also include some suppliers' needs, although this is not necessary. As Hammer and Champy (1993) suggest, the creation of a process map begins with the customer's requirements, not with the role of suppliers.

Process mapping has been described in a number of different ways. Rummler and Brache (1990, p. 49) define a process map as that which "documents, in sequence, the steps that the department goes through to convert inputs to outputs." A more generic but equally useful definition offered by Hammer and Champy (1993) characterizes a process map as giving "a picture of how work flows through the company."

The following three questions need to be answered before a process is mapped:

- What will the process map focus on?
- What will the map consist of?
- What level of detail will be required in order to understand, improve, reengineer, or align the business?

When constructed well, a process map guides the articulation of jobs so that those jobs can be aligned to carry out the process. A process map can also be used to determine how a team organizes itself to achieve its work.

What Will the Process Map Focus on?

The focus is actually on the entity that the process map is to serve—the customer. This may mean the external customer or client who buys the organization's services and products or the internal customer who shares certain steps of the process. (Employees sometimes think of this relationship as "my output is your input.")

To address customer needs, the process map should begin at the end—the point at which the customer receives the deliverable—and then work back to the beginning (the input, suppliers), filling in the intermediate steps. The in-between steps can focus exclusively on the actual steps of the process, or they can show the steps carried out by functional groups (departments) sequentially or concurrently. If the work groups are known, then the steps of the process may show who does what. If the work groups have yet to be defined, then the process should be defined first; subsequently, the individual jobs can be defined, and finally, the work group can be designed to achieve communication and to facilitate the work of the group.

Hammer and Champy (1993) offer a useful guideline on how to establish the span for process mapping. They suggest naming the process that gets done between two points, *start* and *finish*. For example, in a product development process map the focus might be from the time the product is named a *concept* to the time it is a *prototype*. Another focus might begin with the prototype and end with the *working model*.

Another approach to the span, suggested by Langdon (1995), is to begin the mapping at the business-unit level, proceed to the process level, and then proceed to the individual and work group levels. Thus the business unit (which represents the organization's purpose in terms of its customers) would be defined first. This establishes the outputs and consequences that the business desires to achieve. Process maps would then be defined to illustrate how these desires are achieved. In turn, individuals and work groups would define their maps, based on the business units and process maps.

What Will the Process Map Consist Of?

Various authors suggest different important elements that should be included in a typical process map. All agree on the need to define *inputs* and *outputs*, with *process steps* to link the inputs to outputs. Other elements (conditions, feedback, tasks, and so on) can be added to these models for more inclusive work definitions as needed.

What Level of Detail Will Be Required?

Determining the level of detail required for a process map may be a very difficult task. Most authors on the subject agree on not defining the process too finely. Too much detail prevents understanding of the data displayed and, therefore, makes the map less useful for reengineering, reorganization, loading jobs, or any other purpose that the mapping is intended to achieve. A good rule of thumb is, *define only to the level of detail needed to achieve consensus on the process components.*

When to Use

Process mapping is appropriate under the following circumstances.

When Employees Cannot Describe the Process

Process mapping is appropriate when the employees involved in a process do not know that process definitively and cannot describe or discuss its improvement with one another or other work groups. As Hammer and Champy (1993, p. 118) noted, "Processes are invisible and unnamed because people think about the individual departments, not about the processes with which all of them are involved." In instances in which group members can describe what their department does, but cannot adequately agree on how to accomplish their outputs, process mapping is useful in providing clarity and making improvements.

When Employees Have Individually Defined the Process

When the workers and managers individually define how the work will be accomplished and their efforts are not driven by a defined process, process mapping is useful. It is not unusual in any organization to find that individuals are hired to perform jobs that they define for themselves. In such cases there is no clear idea of the connection between the job(s) and the process; the individuals create the processes they use. This is mainly because the processes themselves have not been articulated. This situation calls for process mapping to clarify the process used to achieve what the organization desires for its customers and to describe how employees will help in meeting the organization's objective. Completing the process will also result in greater work efficiency and/or effectiveness.

When Work Groups Have Been Restructured but Jobs and Processes Have Not

Sometimes organizations attempt reorganization by restructuring work groups without improving either jobs or processes. One of the most common errors that executives make is to reorganize work groups rather than to improve processes and the jobs that support those processes. Process mapping should always occur before reorganization. As Langdon (1995) notes, the correct order of analysis and definition is (1) business unit, (2) processes, (3) individual jobs, and (4) work groups. However, if reorganization has already occurred, process mapping can help to determine how the work flow can be improved within the new structure.

Case Study

A high-tech company established a system to repair its several hundred component pieces of hardware—hard drives, printers, scanners, and so on. The company had recently been experiencing a problem in the collection of data from service calls and repairs. The service representatives had not been reporting the exact nature of the repair, which prevented design engineers from making changes in new products that could avoid or minimize the recurring problems. The service representatives were good at repairing the equipment, but the information they recorded about the repairs was untimely and incomplete.

Process mapping was undertaken as an intervention to resolve the need for complete repair data. The starting point of the process map was determined to be receiving the repair order; the process then moved through repair completion and ended with documentation. Figure 1 presents the completed process map.

FIGURE 1. PROCESS MAP: FROM SERVICE REQUEST TO INVOICE.

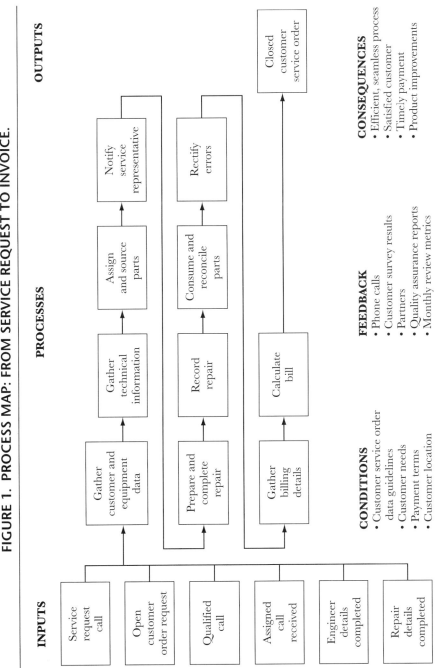

In this case the map was completed by a performance consultant, stakeholders, and field customer representatives (exemplary performers).

This process map was completed in accordance with the Language of Work Model (Langdon, 1995). It identifies six elements of work: outputs, inputs, processes, conditions, consequences, and feedback. The first element to be defined is the key output: a closed service call. Then the needed inputs are listed, the conditions that will affect the service call are named, the consequences to be achieved are described, the process (steps) to be followed are listed, and the feedback that will aid in the process is defined. This process map gave all parties concerned a clear picture of the process.

Then they addressed the issue of what should be measured to assess whether the process was working. They asked if the outputs and related consequences were being achieved. From this question they identified problem areas (for example, the lack of detailed data) and analyzed these areas to determine whether the failure occurred in inputs, conditions, process steps, or feedback. They designed a new process that included motivating the service representative to complete the repair documentation and giving feedback about that documentation.

Resources and References

Damelio, R. (1996). *The basics of process mapping.* White Plains, NY: Quality Resources.

Hammer, M., & Champy, J. (1993). *Reengineering the corporation.* New York: HarperCollins.

Hung, D. V. (1996). *Process mapping: How to reengineer your business processes.* New York: Wiley.

Langdon, D. G. (1995). *The new language of work.* Amherst, MA: HRD Press.

Langdon, D. G. (in press). *Human performance: Leveraging the Language of Work Model in organizations.* San Francisco: Jossey-Bass/Pfeiffer.

Rummler, G. A., & Brache, A. P. (1990). *Improving performance: How to manage the white space on the organization chart.* San Francisco: Jossey-Bass.

Intervention Author

Danny G. Langdon
Partner
Performance International
1330 Stanford Street, Suite D
Santa Monica, CA 90404
Phone: 310-453-8440
E-mail: PerformI@aol.com

▪ ▪ ▪ ▪ ▪ ▪ RECOGNITION PROGRAMS

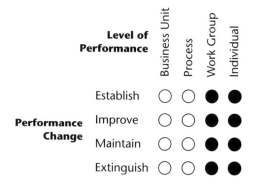

	Level of Performance	Business Unit	Process	Work Group	Individual
Performance Change	Establish	○	○	●	●
	Improve	○	○	●	●
	Maintain	○	○	●	●
	Extinguish	○	○	●	●

Alternative Name

Informal recognition programs and rewards

Definition

Recognition programs are incentive efforts to maintain or improve the work performance of individuals, departments, and teams. Forms of recognition include monetary payments, in-kind payments, or other means of highlighting desirable performance.

Description

Managers have long relied on the power of recognition programs to improve employee performance. However, despite the fact that many managers believe formal recognition programs to be the most motivating to employees, such is not the case. More and more organizations are learning that informal recognition and related programs are actually much more effective than formal ones.

The value of informal rewards—spontaneous, nonmonetary forms of recognition—as employee motivators is increasing today for two reasons. The first is that traditional rewards such as compensation and promotions—although still important—are becoming less and less effective in motivating employees to achieve high performance. The second reason is that informal rewards are effective and highly desired by today's employees.

Rosabeth Moss Kanter (1986) summarizes the problem and need for better incentives and recognition well: "In this time of corporate hierarchy shrinking and organizational layer removal, companies cannot afford the old-fashioned system in which promotion was the primary means of recognizing performance. Greater accessibility to rewards—at all levels—is a necessity when employees stay in place longer; and recognition is an important part of this."

Although they are given little or no attention in management literature and practice, informal rewards have proven to be effective. In a recent survey of U.S. workers, 63 percent of the respondents ranked "a pat on the back" as a meaningful incentive (Lovio-George, 1992). In another recent study of sixty-five potential incentives, four of the top five incentives ranked by employees as most motivating were initiated by their managers, were based on performance, and required little or no money (Graham & Unruh, 1990):

1. Manager personally congratulates employees who do a good job.
2. Manager writes personal notes for good performance.
3. Manager publicly recognizes employees for good performance.
4. Manager holds morale-building meetings to celebrate successes.

When the positive reinforcement is given by colleagues or members of an informal work group, the results can be even more significant. For example, the Office of Personnel Management in Washington, D.C., has what it calls the Wingspread Award. This beautiful engraved plaque was first given to the division's *special performer* by the department head. Later that person passed the award to another person who, he believed, truly deserved it. The award continued to be passed along and came to take on great value and prestige, because it came from one's peers. A recipient can keep it as long as he or she wants or until he or she discovers another special performer. When the award is to be passed on, a ceremony and lunch are held for the presentation.

Individuals tend to be more strongly motivated by the potential to earn rewards than by the fear of punishment, which suggests that management programs and activities should be reward oriented. For informal rewards to be effective, they must be linked to organizational goals, have clearly defined parameters, have employee commitment and support, obtain measurable results, and be linked to formal rewards programs.

Linkage to Organizational Goals

To be effective, informal rewards need to support behavior that leads to the attainment of organization goals. Good management is that which leads to the desired behavior on the part of organizational members. Management must see to it that the consequences of behavior are such as to increase the frequency of desired behaviors and decrease the frequency of undesired behaviors.

Individuals respond to many kinds of rewards—tangible and intangible, on the job and off the job. Tying these rewards to desired performance is not always simple. Insofar as flexibility permits, the granting of rewards should be clearly and explicitly related to desired performance in a timely and meaningful way.

Clearly Defined Parameters

Once the behavior to be reinforced is identified, the specifics of a reward system need to be defined. The rules for awarding incentives must be clear and understood by all. This is a less obvious feature that can make an incentive system powerful. It makes a clear connection between the level of desired performance and the awarding of the incentive.

Employee Commitment and Support

Once the mechanics of an informal reward system are clear, the program needs to be communicated to those who will use it. Usually this part of the program can be carried out in a group setting by presenting the program as a positive, enjoyable activity that will benefit all employees as well as the company. An even better approach is to elicit the help of employees in both planning and implementing the program.

Measurable Results

Any program is only as good as its implementation. Informal reward systems must be monitored to see whether they are being used and whether the desired results are being obtained. Even the best informal reward program will be apt to lose its effectiveness over time, because one of the defining characteristics of a reward is that it is special. Old programs often lose their "special" quality.

Linkage to Formal Rewards Programs

Management must ensure that informal rewards are in line with the formal reward structure. This outcome can most easily be achieved by making informal rewards a subset of larger, more formal reward programs that are in place. For example, a company award (a formal reward) could be given to the employee who receives the greatest number of praising letters (an informal reward) from customers over the course of a year.

When to Use

In general, studies indicate that informal recognition is more powerful than formal recognition because it is more personal and immediate. Informal recognition is appropriate under the following circumstances:

- When planning the implementation of a formal rewards program
- When it is desired to put a short-term focus (of ten to twelve weeks) on an important issue or behavior to call attention to a pressing need
- When it is desirable to increase a particular behavior on a daily basis, such as exceptional customer service (as opposed to an event-centered activity based on achieving a certain goal, such as obtaining a particular revenue sum, at the end of a quarter or fiscal year)

Once informal rewards are determined to be appropriate in an organization, some simple guidelines need to be followed. The following paragraphs describe suggested guidelines.

Must Directly Reinforce the Desired Behavior

The reward needs to be clearly given in response to the desired behavior.

Must Be Given Immediately

Informal rewards need to be given as soon as possible after the desired behavior occurs. As Walter Nord (1974) explains, "Most rapid conditioning results when the desired response is 'reinforced' immediately. In other words, the desired response is followed directly by some consequence. In simple terms, if the outcome is pleasing to the individual, the probability of his repeating the response is apt to be increased."

Must Be Delivered Personally

Part of the power of informal rewards derives from the way they are personally delivered. The fact that a manager is taking time—a limited, precious resource for everyone—to recognize or praise an employee underscores the importance of the activity to the employee. Time taken by a peer to recognize a colleague has an equal or greater effect in that it is both unexpected and not required of the colleague.

Must Be Valued by Recipients

A final guideline for making informal rewards effective is to be sure that they are valued and meaningful to the individuals who receive them. The rewards that are meaningful to a particular employee, however, depend on personal circumstances and tastes. The best way to find out what employees value in terms of rewards and recognition is to ask them.

Case Study

At Blanchard Training and Development, a management training and consulting company located in San Diego, California, the Eagle Award was established to recognize "raving fan service" to customers—one of the organization's strategic objectives. The program, which was initially announced and explained at a companywide meeting, was open to any employee. Any employee could submit the name of another employee who had gone out of his or her way to help satisfy a customer request. Typical examples included staying late to ship materials, helping a customer locate a lost order or resolve a billing problem, rearranging trainer schedules to deliver a last-minute training request by a customer, and so forth.

The employee's name was submitted with a brief description of the activity that was considered exceptional. The recommendations were reviewed by a committee, primarily to screen out items that were considered to be an expected part of someone's job. The Eagle Committee then surprised the winner with a visit to his or her work site and took a picture of the person holding the award—one of several eagle trophies that rotated around the company.

The photograph was displayed on a lobby bulletin board around a graphic of an eagle along with a brief description of the activity being recognized. The winner got to keep the eagle trophy on his or her desk until it was needed for a new recipient—typically a week or so. At the end of the year, one of the recipients was selected by employee vote to be Eagle of the Year. This person was presented an engraved clock at the company's annual holiday celebration.

One of several such efforts, this program was credited with making "raving fan service" an established part of the company's culture. It was implemented at virtually no cost. A few employees criticized the program, pointing out that it favored those individuals who dealt with customers on a daily basis, but that input was used when the program was revised after a year to expand the focus to include internal customer service as well.

Resources and References

Blanchard, K., & Bowles, S. (1992) Raving fans. New York: Morrow.

Graham, G. H., & Unruh, J. (1990). The motivational impact of nonfinancial employee appreciation practices on medical technologists. *Health Care Supervisor, 8*(3), 9–17.

Kanter, R. M. (1986, December). Kanter on management: Holiday gifts: Celebrating employee achievements. *Management Review*, pp. 19, 21.

Lovio-George, C. (1992, April). What motivates best? (Survey conducted by the Society of Incentive Travel Executives Foundation). *Sales & Marketing Management.*

Nelson, B. (1994). *1001 ways to reward employees.* New York: Workman.

Nelson, B. (1997). *1001 ways to energize employees.* New York: Workman.

Nelson, B. (1997). *Motivating today's employees.* Chicago: Successories.

Nord, W. R. (1974). Beyond the teaching machine: Operant conditioning in management. In H. L. Tosi and W. C. Hammer (Eds.), *Organizational behavior and management: A contingency approach.* Chicago: St. Clair Press.

Intervention Author

Bob Nelson
President & Founder
Nelson Motivation, Inc.
11848 Bernardo Plaza Court, #210B
San Diego, CA 92128
Phone: 619-673-0690
Fax: 619-673-9031
E-mail: BobRewards@aol.com
Web site: www.nelson-motivation.com

▪ ▪ ▪ ▪ ▪ ▪ REENGINEERING

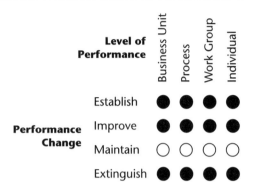

	Business Unit	Process	Work Group	Individual
Level of Performance				
Establish	●	●	●	●
Improve	●	●	●	●
Maintain	○	○	○	○
Extinguish	●	●	●	●

(Performance Change: Establish, Improve, Maintain, Extinguish)

Alternative Name

Transformation

Definition

Reengineering is a systematic approach used to dramatically change the processes, technology, structure, and infrastructure of an organization in order to eliminate non-value-added work and to improve delivery of quality products and services.

Description

In 1990, in the article "Reengineering Work: Don't Automate, Obliterate," Michael Hammer coined the term *reengineering* to describe a technology-enabled approach to reinventing the way in which organizations operate. He and others who followed him recognized the futility of attempting to gain significant improvements in productivity and quality by tinkering with outmoded processes, practices, and policies. His call to action led to the development of a methodology that forces organizations to rethink the fundamental assumptions and methods under which they operate. In their book, *Business Reengineering: The Survival Guide,* Andrews and Stalick (1994) further define business reengineering as a systematic, interdisciplinary approach that addresses all aspects of the organization, not just processes. Transforming an organization and achieving sustainable improvements requires changes to processes, technology, the organizational structure, the infrastructure, and the culture. Early reengineering projects were often limited in scope, focusing on one or two dimensions of operation, usually process and technology. As a result, those expecting radical changes were disappointed.

Business reengineering projects follow a clearly defined life cycle beginning with a definition of the vision and goals for the organization and ending with the transition to an environment of continuous improvement:

Business Reengineering Project Life Cycle

    Step 1. Frame the project

    Step 2. Create vision, values, and goals

    Step 3. Redesign the business operations

    Step 4. Conduct proof-of-concept

    Step 5. Plan the implementation

    Step 6. Obtain approval for implementation

    Step 7. Implement the redesign

    Step 8. Make transition to continuous improvement environment

Each step in the life cycle results in outcomes that are created by a reengineering team of organizational stakeholders during a series of disciplined, tightly planned, and facilitated events. These outcomes include a clearly defined project scope, an organizational or project vision, measurable goals, baseline measures, process and data models, technology architecture, management and performance measurement systems, reward and compensation systems, business policies and practices, an implementation plan, a business case for change, and the developed and installed changes.

Although the reengineering facilitator is responsible for designing and managing these events, the reengineering team makes all decisions that will affect the outcomes. The job of the facilitator is to create and manage the change process by deciding what outcomes must be created and when and how they will be created. The facilitator executes the reengineering methodology but does not determine the content of the work. The facilitator is accountable for ensuring that the work is completed on schedule with quality outcomes that meet or exceed expectations. Without strong facilitation to guide the reengineering team and accelerate the creativity and learning processes, the team members can easily suffer from their own resistance to change, become overwhelmed with the magnitude of change, and succumb to antichange pressures from within the organization.

Reengineering draws on proven tools and techniques from many different disciplines, such as organizational development, systems design, and Total Quality Management (TQM). These techniques include conflict management, consensus decision making, diagnosis and intervention techniques, team building, activity-based costing, state-transition diagraming, process-flow diagraming, and cause-and-effect diagraming. In addition, reengineering interventions demand a thorough understanding of the systemic and political nature of organizations.

When to Use

Reengineering is an appropriate intervention under the following circumstances (Andrews & Stalick, 1994):

- When significant improvements in productivity and quality are required to compete in the marketplace
- When the organization has recently undergone a significant change (for example, downsizing, merger, or acquisition)
- When the current technological infrastructure no longer supports the organization's needs
- When the organization's structure, policies, and practices impede its ability to respond rapidly to customer needs
- When the organization begins to lose business to its competitors due to a lack of responsiveness, poor product quality, or poor customer service
- When bottlenecks and non-value-added work add unnecessary time and costs to the delivery of products and services
- When organizational strategy changes

When Not to Use

Reengineering should not be used as an intervention when the following conditions exist:

- When there is little support from the organization's leaders
- When the organization has a history of short-term thinking

- When there is an unwillingness to commit the necessary time and resources
- When there is no incentive to change

Case Study

In 1996 the Energy Information Administration (EIA), the U.S. government agency authorized by Congress to collect and publish objective global energy information, was faced with the threat of drastic budget reductions—possibly even its elimination as an agency. The EIA's top executive leaders perceived this crisis situation as an opportunity to radically improve the agency's effectiveness and control its "downsized" future.

Like many agencies today, the EIA had *stovepipe* program offices with duplicate functions, roles, and technology led by people with many years in the job. Remembering the severe resistance and morale problems that occurred from a previous reduction-in-force (RIF) action and the fact that TQM efforts within the various program offices had failed, the two top executives knew that any large, cross–program office change effort would have to be different.

They chose an approach that required the involvement of many of their highly trained professionals and their program heads. They selected as their project director a seasoned assistant program head with a reputation for challenging the status quo. Once assigned, he reported directly to the two executive leaders; his normal work was distributed among his subordinates. The project team had a core group of seven people and included an external business process reengineering (BPR) consulting organization. Two people from each of the six program offices directly affected by the project scope were appointed champions. The scope of the project included 80 percent of the agency's business operations and seven major business processes.

In a series of eleven three- and four-day workshops over a period of six months, this team, with the help of more than fifty subject-matter experts from inside and outside the agency, created a radical blueprint for the EIA that fundamentally altered how it did business. All dimensions of the agency (process, technology, structure, infrastructure, and culture) were affected. The team members communicated with others in the agency in a variety of ways. They attended brown-bag lunches with the executive leaders on a regular basis; they held formal and informal discussions with their peers; they invited observers to attend the workshops. As a result of these involvement activities, the agency personnel developed a deeper understanding of the intentions of the project and less fear regarding its consequences.

To involve the program heads, the executive leaders appointed them members of the executive sponsor team. As expected, implementation approval from the program heads was not easy, as the redesigned operations radically changed their areas. Their program offices were replaced by integrated centers for operational excellence, supported by a single integrated technology services organization. The redesigned operations called for flexible, cross-functional teams that had end-to-end process responsibility for survey, product quality, and customer satisfaction. The creation of these teams eliminated a complete layer of management and replaced the traditional hierarchical, individual-based supervisory approach.

It took several months of discussion for the executive sponsor team to agree to move forward with the implementation. The budget, traditionally controlled at the program office level, was consolidated at the agency level so that any expenditure above basic operations had to be approved by the executive sponsor team and had to align with the blueprint recommendations. This prevented fragmentation of change efforts.

The implementation took place in phases. The first phase took six months and is now complete. The technology organization is in place, and technology teams are negotiating service agreements with key business units, restructuring the architecture, and implementing a new data structure to ensure cross-agency and customer information access. This phase also included the piloting of integrated survey operations, which quickly expanded to include most of survey operations. The second phase, the restructuring of the program offices, is now under way.

When asked whether this business transformation has been successful and what the EIA has learned from the experience, the project manager responded with these five points:

- Implementation is a time for diplomacy and tact. People's fears and concerns must be addressed. Misunderstanding can be avoided if major changes to the organization are summarized in a way that everyone will understand.
- Expectations must be managed throughout the project.
- Reengineering requires patience. It is worth remembering that it took years to get the organization where it is today and it will take years for it to change fully.
- The key to success is to *communicate*. Those who expressed the most concerns were the first- and second-line managers, who did not participate in the project or the many briefings that were held. These people are the link to the rest of the organization.
- Transformation goals must be incorporated into the performance objectives of the program heads.

Resources and References

Andrews, D., & Stalick. S. (1994). *Business reengineering: The survival guide.* Upper Saddle River, NJ: Prentice Hall.

Hammer, M. (1990, July–August). Reengineering work: Don't automate, obliterate. *Harvard Business Review,* pp. 104–111.

Hammer, M., & Champy, J. (1993). *Reengineering the corporation.* New York: Harper Business.

Intervention Author

Susan Stalick
President
Canal Bridge Consulting
6805 Canal Bridge Court
Potomac, MD 20854
Phone: 800-618-5699
E-mail: sstalick@canalbc.com
Web site: www.canalbc.com

Case Study Authors

Dorine Andrews
Susan Stalick

RESULTS-BASED MANAGEMENT

Level of Performance	Business Unit	Process	Work Group	Individual
Establish	●	●	●	●
Improve	●	●	●	●
Maintain	●	●	●	●
Extinguish	●	●	●	●

(Performance Change rows: Establish, Improve, Maintain, Extinguish)

Alternative Names

Balanced scorecard
Summative evaluation
Performance management

Definition

Results-based management is a process in which measures of organizational or program performance are compared to prescribed expectations for the purpose of identifying and acting on any meaningful differences.

Description

The heart of results-based management is measurement, which includes the following two steps:

1. The performance outcomes of an organizational action are measured and compared to explicit performance expectations that were originally set when the goals or objectives were established.

FIGURE 1. RESULTS-BASED MANAGEMENT.

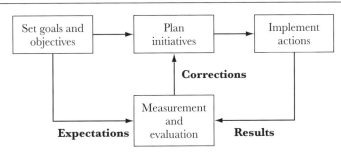

2. The difference, if any, between the expectations and the results is analyzed so that corrective action can be taken.

The process of results-based management has three component phases or activities (see Figure 1), which are explained in the following paragraphs.

Phase 1: Set Goals and Objectives

When a customer uses an organization's or program's product, the outcomes or results can be observed and measured. For example, suppose an organization introduces a new information system in order to improve the efficiency of its business processes. To assess this action, it might very well collect financial costs associated with the business process before and after the implementation of the new system. However, a single measure provides a perspective that is too narrow for results-based management.

For several years Robert Kaplan and David Norton of Harvard University have been discussing an approach to results-based management called the *balanced scorecard*. They say that organizations have too often focused on a single dimension—financial accounting measures or bottom-line results—to assess their performance. Although Kaplan and Norton do not discount the importance of financial measures, they believe that "reliance on summary financial performance measures were hindering organizations' abilities to create future economic value" (1996, p. vii).

Consequently, they defined three other types of measurement indicators that were needed along with financial measures in order to obtain a complete and balanced view of organizational performance: (1) customer, (2) internal business processes, and (3) learning and growth. Measures involving the customer element included indicators of satisfaction, market share, and the nature of the relationship with the customer. For example, one might ask, "Are users of the recently introduced information system satisfied with the new way of doing things?"

The internal dimension of the balanced scorecard relates to measures dealing with the quality of the products or services, the efficiency of the operations, and the extent of innovation demonstrated by the organization. For example, one might ask, "Has cycle time for the business process been significantly reduced by the new system?"

The last element of the scorecard, learning and growth, includes measures indicating the potential for the organization to continue to improve such elements as the competency of the staff, the capability of supporting technology, and the climate of the organization. One might ask, for example, "Does the new information system allow the organization to provide new types of services?" The four elements combine to provide a clear and complete view of performance results.

Phase 2: Plan Initiatives

Of course, measuring performance results is not enough. It is only one component of results-based management. Suppose that measurement shows that a data center averages 68.7 percent data-processing (DP) utilization during prime shift operations. Should action be taken to boost the demand on services? A question of this sort is very difficult to answer unless there is a meaningful expectation to which the measured results can be compared. On the one hand, if a DP utilization rate of 70 percent is deemed essential for prime shift operations, then the answer is yes and corrective action should be taken. On the other hand, if the expectation for DP utilization is 65 percent, then performance seems to be acceptable and no action other than ongoing monitoring is necessary.

Identifying the gap in performance is easy, provided that a clear-cut standard of performance is defined for comparison to the measured results. The hard part is to make these expectations meaningful and credible. For example, why should the DP utilization rate be 65 percent or 70 percent? Any or all of four types of performance expectations—benchmark, target, baseline, and threshold—may be used to give meaning and credibility to a standard.

Benchmark. To set this type of expectation, results using the same measurement process for either a comparable organization or an exemplary organization must be available. To be considered successful, the measured results must either exceed or attain a particular proportion of that benchmark: for example, "The best industry practice for DP utilization during prime shift operations is 93.7 percent, and our data center should continually strive to attain that value."

Target. This type of expectation represents a high level of performance that if achieved will virtually ensure the organization's success. The particular level is determined either by the judgment of senior management or by statistical analysis of past organizational performance: for example, "The executive committee at the data center determined by consensus that aggressive marketing efforts will continue until a 90 percent DP utilization rate is achieved."

Baseline. To set up this type of expectation, the organization must have previously collected data over time using the same measurement process. To be considered successful, the current results must exceed the results obtained during a comparable period earlier in time: for example, "The DP utilization rate was 79.2 percent for the previous quarter, and we should do better this quarter."

Threshold. For the organization to use this type of expectation, a particular value is derived analytically or intuitively that defines the minimally acceptable value of the measure that will enable the organization to be successful: for example, "A financial analysis reveals that the data center will 'break even' if DP utilization meets or exceeds 71.8 percent, so we must at least meet that level of performance."

Phase 3: Implement Actions/Measurement and Evaluation

There is one more critical phase in results-based management: closing the loop (detecting any gap in performance results, diagnosing its causes, and fixing the problem). It would not be unusual for an organization to track twenty or more measures to monitor the vital signs of organizational performance. Yet management needs to be highly sensitive to the emergence of gaps in performance so that corrective action can be taken as soon as possible.

A few approaches have evolved over recent years to aid this process. For example, technology has been introduced to ensure that any gap in any organizational vital signs is signaled vividly. Some organizations are developing executive information systems that include a display of vital performance indicators on the executive's desktop computer. The executive information system (EIS) receives the selected measures in real time as well as definitions of performance expectations for each measure. It graphically displays the measures and their relation to the performance expectations, sometimes in the form of an automobile dashboard. Depending on the size and direction of the performance gap, the measure may show up as red, amber, or green. In serious cases, the indicator may blink to draw attention.

Suppose that a set of performance scores for a particular organization or program reveals a very low score for customer satisfaction. Also assume that all of the other contributing scores are fair or better. How would program management go about using these results to improve performance? Other sources of information must be brought to bear on the problem. Some may be quantitative in nature, but most will probably be qualitative. A somewhat low score in budget, schedule, or technical performance might give a clue to the lack of customer satisfaction. Assuming that the overall customer satisfaction score was derived from the total score on a survey questionnaire, the responses to individual items and possibly written comments could detail particular issues of concern to customers. Other metrics collected as part of the process of ongoing organizational monitoring should also be considered to see if they shed light on the cause of the performance gap.

But it is most likely that fresh anecdotal information must be gathered. The people at the front lines of the organization could be queried for their observations and views on the potential causes of dissatisfaction. Have customers written letters of complaint or called in to grumble about problems they have experienced? Customers can be contacted individually or in groups to elicit their concerns. The idea, of course, is to use as much information as possible as soon as possible to unearth and overcome the real causes of any performance gaps. The process does not have to be scientific. If the diagnosis is right, the gap will begin closing soon after the correction is put into effect. If the diagnosis is wrong, the gap will remain or get worse and something else will have to be tried.

The thing to avoid is waiting until all the information is in before something is done. At that point it might be too late. Most managers are problem solvers at heart. As long as they are open to all of the information available to them and aggressively seek out the views of other key individuals, there is a good chance that they can quickly identify causes of poor results and implement appropriate corrections.

When to Use

In a theoretical sense, results-based management is a fundamental management practice used to monitor the performance of an organization. It ought to be used continually. However, in a practical sense, an organization cannot afford to define precise expectations and create a balanced scorecard consisting of valid and reliable measurements for each and every unit and program under its control. The use of results-based management is appropriate under the following conditions.

When the Executive Office Has Defined One or More Strategic Goals

A system of results-based management should be created for each of the organization's strategic goals. If the executive office has gone through a formal strategic planning process and has defined goals for the organization, explicit performance expectations and measures should also be established in order to track and make midcourse corrections to initiatives designed to achieve those goals. Otherwise, the strategic planning process is merely an academic exercise.

When Vital Information Is in Doubt

When information needed for a critical decision, such as a decision to outsource specific functions or select specific vendors, is in doubt, a one-time application of results-based management would be beneficial. A successful decision can be made based on expectations and corresponding measures obtained for each option being considered. The option whose measures best meet or exceed the stated expectations would be chosen.

When an Influential Stakeholder Needs to Be Convinced

All too often the survival of an organization or program depends heavily on the image it projects to its stakeholders. If they view the organization or program as effective, trustworthy, and innovative, they create an environment in which it can flourish and succeed. Conversely, if a negative view is held, funding dries up, political support is denied, and the viability of the organization or program becomes questionable. Results-based management is useful in providing convincing evidence to help persuade influential stakeholders of organizational efficacy. In this case the expectations and measures must specifically address the personal values of the stakeholders who are to be convinced.

Case Study

A major goal of the chief information officer (CIO) of a major telecommunications company was to improve delivery of existing automation to internal customers. Discussions with functional managers at the company indicated that *system availability* should be the most important product of the information technology department. To this end, the CIO instituted an *availability manager* program in which individuals were appointed to be responsible for the availability of key systems. These availability managers were paged as soon as a system outage occurred. They also made conference calls daily to key people so that they could assess the health and status of their assigned systems. The availability managers also set up a war room approach to work out strategies for upcoming new software releases of their systems.

FIGURE 2. DOWNTIME AND INCIDENT PER WEEK FOR TOP TWENTY INFORMATION SYSTEMS.

Quarter	Downtime Minutes/Week	Incidents/Week
4Q95	550	311
1Q96	379	204
2Q96	246	182
3Q96	105	138
4Q96	66	110
1Q97	44	81
2Q97	30	72

The CIO also established a results-based management requirement to track outages over time. He dictated that the target for downtime for the top twenty systems would be no more than 270 minutes per week, approximately half of the current 550 minutes of downtime per week being experienced during the fourth quarter of 1995.

Thereafter, the downtime results for the top twenty systems were published weekly. Also, monthly meetings were held to analyze the previous month's outages and to review the impact, root causes, and resolution of those outages. As a result, the measured downtime decreased steadily, as shown in Figure 2.

Resources and References

Austin, R. D. (1996). *Measuring and managing performance in organizations.* New York: Dorset House.

Holloway, J., Lewis, J., & Mallory, G. (1995). *Performance measurement and evaluation.* Thousand Oaks, CA: Sage.

Kaplan, R. S., & Norton D. P. (1996). *The balanced scorecard: Translating strategy into action.* Boston: Harvard Business School Press.

U.S. General Services Administration. Performance Pathways (Web site: http://www.itpolicy.gsa.gov/mkm/pathways/pathways.htm). An excellent source of information about performance measures.

Wholey, J. S., Hatry, H. P., & Newcomer, K. E. (1994). *Handbook of practical program evaluation.* San Francisco: Jossey-Bass.

Intervention Author

Jay Alden
Director of Distance Education
National Defense University
IRM College
300 5th Avenue, Marshall Hall
Fort McNair, DC 20319
Phone: 202-685-3890
E-mail: Alden@ndu.edu

SAFETY MANAGEMENT

	Business Unit	Process	Work Group	Individual
Level of Performance				
Establish	○	○	○	○
Performance Change Improve	○	○	○	●
Maintain	○	○	○	●
Extinguish	○	○	○	●

Alternative Names

Behavioral safety
Behavioral safety management
Behavioral accident prevention

Definition

Safety management is the process of ensuring ongoing reduction in at-risk behavior in the workplace. Concerns related to safety management include using protective equipment, following procedures, using work tools and equipment in a prescribed manner, and reducing facility-related hazards.

Description

In traditional safety management, the focus has been on final outcomes, in the form of numbers of injuries, injury rates, injury severity indices, or costs. If the outcomes are unacceptable, managers typically intervene with training or with consequences. Discipline is applied to those who violate safety rules. Conversely, with positive results come positive consequences, usually rewards of various kinds for individuals or groups who function for defined periods without injury. A problem with the traditional approach is that outcomes are often cyclical: results improve for a short time following an intervention; then they become worse. Gradually it was realized that the typical interventions did not adequately address the main factor in injuries—the behavior of the injured workers. It is commonly estimated that worker behavior is a factor in 80 percent of injuries.

Academically based psychologists such as Judy Komaki, Beth Sulzer-Azaroff, Scott Geller, and Bill Hopkins applied behavioral principles to influencing worker safety-related behavior. In controlled studies in work situations, they demonstrated that safe behaviors could be significantly increased and unsafe (or at-risk) behavior could be significantly decreased. The interventions in these studies typically consisted of providing workers with operational definitions of behaviors considered critical to avoiding injury, periodically observing them as they engaged in these behaviors, and giving them feedback.

The feedback was usually at the work group level and consisted of posted graphs that displayed ongoing percentages of observed behaviors that were recorded as safe. Usually either the supervisor or the experimenter discussed these graphs with the work group. Most of the early studies were relatively short (weeks or months), so that connections between changes in worker behavior and injury rates were not easy to demonstrate. It was also not clear that the interventions could be sustained for long periods. Later Tom Krause (1995, 1997) and his associates demonstrated that behavior-based interventions could be sustained effectively for years in a variety of work settings, with continuing declines in injury rates.

Behavior-based safety interventions vary in their details. However, to be effective, they need to address the following two classes of behavior:

- Behaviors that the worker could perform safely, but does not for some reason. An example is not wearing hearing protection in a noisy area, even though hearing protection is readily available.
- Behaviors that are difficult or impossible to perform safely without an environmental or system change. An example is working with ergonomically risky posture because the workstation cannot be adjusted to the worker's dimensions.

Both types of behaviors can be addressed using behavioral observation and feedback. The steps in the process are as follows:

1. Define the behaviors critical for avoiding injury.
2. Train a group of employees in observation techniques and interaction skills.

3. Have these employees regularly sample worker behavior, collecting data on safe and at-risk behaviors.
4. Have observers give immediate feedback to workers and converse with them to determine the causes for nonperformance of safe behaviors.
5. Use data from observations to identify and resolve systems issues.

When to Use

Behavior-based safety management is useful in situations in which a significant proportion of safety, health, or environmental exposures are associated with observable behaviors.

Case Study

Safety performance at a chemical plant of five hundred employees improved for several years as a result of an emphasis on engineering "fixes," but then it plateaued. The personnel at the plant discovered that worker behavior was one of the immediate causal factors in a high proportion of injuries. Management, with agreement from the union, decided to implement a behavioral safety process.

A steering committee of mostly hourly employees was put together, charged with designing, implementing, and overseeing the process. The committee analyzed injury reports from recent years and identified the behaviors critical to avoiding injury. The twenty-three resulting behaviors were grouped into five categories (for example, *personal protective equipment* and *body use and position*). Operational definitions were written for each behavior. For instance, "line of fire" was one behavior assigned to the category body use and position. The definition read in part: "Is the employee positioned so that if something discharges, sprays, falls, releases, or springs back, the employee will not be contacted?" The committee then trained fifty-five hourly employees on techniques for observing these behaviors and also on interaction skills. The committee also held information sessions for all plant employees.

Two to three times a week the observers spent fifteen to twenty minutes observing peers at work. Immediately after their observations, the observers shared what they had seen with their coworkers, tried to discover the root causes of any at-risk behaviors, and discussed ways of making the work safer. The observers recorded what they had seen and been told (data were anonymous) on a data sheet, which was then given to a steering committee member to enter into a database.

Once a month data summaries and graphs were prepared for work groups. The groups used this information in safety meetings. They identified the behaviors that gave them the greatest exposure to injury and developed action plans for addressing the root causes. Plans requiring significant expenditures were forwarded to management.

A year after observations started, the injury rate had dropped 40 percent. The committee stayed active, with gradual turnover of membership. New observers were trained and rotated into active participation. Four years after initiation of the behavioral safety process, the plant injury rate had decreased 65 percent.

Resources and References

Geller, E. S. (1996). *The psychology of safety: How to improve behaviors and attitudes on the job.* Radnor, PA: Chilton.

Komaki, J., Barwick, K. D., & Scott, L. R. (1978). A behavioral approach to occupational safety: Pinpointing and reinforcing safety performance in a food manufacturing plant. *Journal of Applied Psychology, 63,* 434–445.

Krause, T. R. (1995). *Employee-driven systems for safe behavior: Integrating behavioral and statistical methodologies.* New York: Van Nostrand Reinhold.

Krause, T. R. (1997). *The behavior-based safety process: Managing involvement for an injury-free culture* (2nd ed.). New York: Van Nostrand Reinhold.

McSween, T. (1995). *The values-based safety process: Improving your safety culture with a behavioral approach.* New York: Van Nostrand Reinhold.

Intervention Author

Kim C. M. Sloat, Ph.D.
Vice President-Development
Behavioral Science Technology, Inc.
417 Bryant Circle
Ojai, CA 93023
Phone: 800-646-4595, ext. 525
Fax: 714-951-7456
E-mail: KCSloat@bscitech.com
Web site: http://www.bscitech.com

▪ ▪ ▪ ▪ ▪ ▫ SIMULATION

	Level of Performance	Business Unit	Process	Work Group	Individual
	Establish	○	○	●	●
Performance	**Improve**	○	○	●	●
Change	**Maintain**	○	○	●	●
	Extinguish	○	○	●	●

Alternative Names

Simulation Game
Simulator
Laboratory Learning
Virtual Reality
Model

Definition

A *simulation* is a means of experiencing an event that is as close to the real experience as possible without being the real experience itself.

Description

People have used simulations (often in the form of mock battles and rituals) since prehistoric times. Ancient Chinese and Indians developed such games as chess and *chaturanga* to simulate war and politics. In relatively recent times, Germans and other Europeans have used war games to establish and improve the performance of officers and soldiers. For the past several decades, business schools have used simulations to teach complex concepts. Personal computers have brought complex simulations on such areas as space travel, politics, and urban planning within everyone's reach.

The concept of the *simulation* is related to the concept of the *model*. The globe, as a model of our planet, enables us to experience the astronaut's view from a space shuttle without leaving Earth. In contrast to the globe as a static model, most simulations are dynamic.

The definition of simulations implies that they are designed to reflect reality. A more precise definition would suggest that a simulation reflects the designer's model of reality. In addition, most simulations reflect only selected elements of reality.

There are different types of simulations. *High-fidelity* simulations incorporate a large number of factors and capture all relationships among them. The physical artifacts used in high-fidelity simulations exhibit a high degree of verisimilitude. In contrast, *low-fidelity* simulations incorporate only a few selected factors and use a simplified model of relationships among them. We can also divide simulations on the basis of the aspects of reality that they reflect. In a *mega* simulation, for example, you may play the role of GOD (Game Overall Director) and create universes and populate them with sentient beings. In a *macro* simulation, you may test the impact of a new team-based incentive system by playing a computer version that takes into account the relationships among several inputs, incentives, and outputs. In a *micro* simulation, you can replay, in extremely slow motion, the events and thoughts behind a sudden panic attack.

Although our focus is on the instructional use of simulations, they can be incorporated into a variety of interventions. A simulation can be used as a performance test for *assessment*. A simulated project (such as crossing a mine field) can be used for *team building*. During the Apollo 13 crisis, engineers in Houston simulated the space capsule to design and test alternative *problem-solving* approaches. Simulations can also be used in *counseling* and *therapy*. Snapping a rubber band on your wrist every time you crave a cigarette uses the immediate minor pain of the rubber band to simulate the delayed major pain of lung cancer.

When to Use

Using a simulation is appropriate under the following circumstances.

When Transfer of Training Is Desired

On-the-job training is obviously the best way to ensure effective application of new skills and knowledge. The next best way is training in a simulated situation.

For example, the best way to train a salesperson is through a special type of simulation called *behavior rehearsal* (or *role playing*) under authentic conditions.

When Repeated Practice Is Needed

Training in emergency procedures requires practice in making instant decisions in tense situations. For example, flight simulators can provide repeated practice in landing a fighter on a carrier deck without the risk of damaging expensive equipment or killing the pilot. Similarly, police officers practice making repeated decisions on whether or not to shoot to kill an armed assailant by working through an interactive videodisk simulation.

When Time Needs to Be Manipulated

Time is a critical factor in planning, analyzing, and decision making. For example, the impact of a strategic decision may become salient only after a decade. In a computerized business simulation, we can compress those ten years into ten seconds and present the decision maker with long-term consequences. In contrast, certain electronic activities take place in nanoseconds. We can use a simulation to slow down these activities for better understanding and analysis.

When Complex Interactions Need to Be Illustrated

In the real world, the link between inputs and outcomes is seldom linear. The decision to raise the price of a product, for example, may depend on hundreds of variables (such as global demand, production cost, competition, available alternatives, economic conditions, regulations, import-export factors, and production time). We can develop a series of increasingly complex simulations in which these variables are gradually introduced and experienced.

When Paradigm Shifts Need to Be Introduced

Most people are oblivious of the many assumptions they make in their daily lives. The first step in bringing about major changes in assumptions is to jolt people out of their comfort zones. Simple metaphorical simulations are best suited for achieving this instructional purpose.

Case Study

During the past decade, hundreds of thousands of employees have been trained in techniques for satisfying customers. In a majority of these situations, the transfer of the newly learned skills and knowledge is sparse and rapidly decreases. In response to this situation, we designed a simulation game called Triangles.

In Triangles the participants are not told the intent of the simulation. Instead, the activity is presented as an exercise in working under tight deadlines. The participants are divided into *planners, implementers, observers,* and *customers.* The planners are given instructions and materials for cutting *megatriangles* (printed on card stock) into nine smaller triangles and rearranging them into six different silhouettes called *trigrams.* The planners are given twenty minutes to master the procedure and to instruct the implementers. After twenty minutes the planners are not permitted to talk to the implementers. For the next fifteen minutes, the implementers follow the planners' instructions and produce as many trigrams (of one or more types) as possible. At the end of this time, the customers are brought in. They inspect the trigrams and award points according to their personal preferences among the different silhouettes. The points given range from 100 for the most preferred to 1 for the least preferred silhouette.

If the planners (or the implementers) talk to the customers, determine their preferences, and mass-produce the most preferred silhouette, it is possible for the participants to accumulate thousands of points. However, almost invariably, the participants ignore the customers and feel chagrined when they realize that their score depends on the customers' reactions. In addition, the planners ignore their internal customers (the implementers) until the last moment. Then they rush the implementers through the production procedure. On the other hand, the implementers passively wait for instructions from the planners rather than participating in the planning process.

The major aspects of workplace reality that are simulated in Triangles include the following:

1. Customer preferences and purchases determine the success of planning and manufacturing efforts.
2. Planners are usually higher than implementers in the organizational hierarchy. They rarely interact with the implementers.
3. During the debriefing discussion, the participants discover the following principles related to customer focus:

   When working under tight deadlines, most employees tend to ignore the customer.

   Although the planners and the implementers are members of the same team, there is an implicit competition between them.

   Finding customer needs and preferences should be the first step in any planning activity.

Lack of involvement in planning leaves the implementers frustrated and anxious.

The transition from the planners to the implementers tends to be abrupt.

When things go wrong, everyone blames the people rather than the processes.

More than seven thousand participants—including large groups of employees in a bank, in an automobile manufacturing plant, and in a public sector organization—have participated in the Triangles simulation. Performance data indicate that the simulation provides insights into factors that inhibit customer focus. These insights encourage the participants to remind themselves of the customer throughout all planning, manufacturing, and selling processes. In addition, Triangles provides a convenient metaphor for communication among employees.

Resources and References

Books and Articles

Fripp, J. (1993). *Learning through simulations.* New York: McGraw-Hill.

Gredler, M. (1994). *Designing and evaluating games and simulations.* Houston, TX: Gulf.

Greenblat, C. S. (1988). *Designing games and simulations.* Thousand Oaks, CA: Sage.

Langdon, D. G. (Series Ed.), & Thiagarajan, S., & Stolovitch, H. (Vol. Author). (1978). *The instructional design library: Vol. 12. Instructional simulation games.* Englewood Cliffs, NJ: Educational Technology.

Simulation & Gaming: An International Journal of Theory, Practice, and Research (published quarterly by Sage Periodicals Press, 2455 Teller Road, Thousand Oaks, CA 91320, phone: 805-499-0721).

Thiagarajan, S. (1994). Games and simulations. In W. R. Tracey (Ed.), *Human resource management and development handbook.* New York: AMACOM.

Thiagarajan, S. (1997). *Simulation games by Thiagi.* Bloomington, IN: Workshops by Thiagi.

Association

North American Simulations and Gaming Association (NASAGA) (1128 East Bluff Drive, Penn Yann, NY 14527, Web site: http://www.nasaga.org).

Founded in the early 1960s, this nonprofit organization has been a common meeting ground for simulation gamers. Membership benefits include a subscription to *Simulation & Gaming*, reduced conference fees, and inclusion in the *NASAGA Membership Directory*. Annual conferences are held in October.

Intervention Author

Sivasailam "Thiagi" Thiagarajan, Ph.D.
President
Workshops by Thiagi, Inc.
4423 East Trailridge Road
Bloomington, IN 47408-9633
Phone: 812-332-1478
E-mail: thiagi@thiagi.com
Web site: http://www.thiagi.com

STRATEGIC PLANNING
■ ■ ■ ı ı ı AND VISIONING

Level of Performance	Business Unit	Process	Work Group	Individual
Establish	●	○	●	○
Performance Change Improve	●	○	●	○
Maintain	●	○	●	○
Extinguish	●	○	●	○

Alternative Names

Mega planning
Macro planning
Micro planning
Ideal visioning
Strategic thinking

Definitions

Strategic planning is the process of identifying the direction in which an organization should head, why it should head there, and how to tell when it has arrived. Strategic planning aligns everything that an organization uses, does, produces, and delivers while also defining value added for external clients.

Visioning is the process of defining in measurable terms the future that the organization is committed to creating. An *ideal vision* is the measurable statement of the kind of world the organization commits to create for tomorrow's child. An ideal vision is used to derive an organization's mission; the mission statement describes which parts of the vision the organization commits to deliver and move toward. When the ideal vision and the mission are established, the strategic plan describes the results that are required to achieve the vision and the mission.

Description

Several essential questions are answered by engaging in strategic planning and visioning:

- Where are we headed?
- Why do we want to go there?
- How we will know when we have arrived?

Strategic planning and visioning are critical in setting an organization's direction and in determining societal, organizational, and individual success criteria. They are also basic to determining what it takes—in terms of resources, interventions, actions, and results—to get from here to there (from the current state to the desired state). The performance technologist may facilitate the development of a strategic plan or may identify the need for one and then work with a consultant who specializes in this intervention.

When using a vision and a mission for performance improvement, the measurable criteria serve to (1) align organizational and human performance objectives with organizational purposes and (2) supply the basis for evaluation and continuous improvement.

Strategic planning and visioning interventions are changing with the times. Today's planning and visioning activities are being required to address not only conventional bottom-line indicators of success (such as quarterly profits or market share), but also another, more basic bottom-line consideration, which is the value added to society (Kaufman, 1998; Kaufman & Watkins, 1996).

The strategic planning process is often best facilitated by an outsider so that participants are free to share goals, objectives, and strategic plans openly. A strategic plan should be no more than ten pages in length and should identify only (1) where the organization is headed, (2) why it is headed there, (3) how all parties will know when they have arrived, and (4) the resources required to get the organization from the current to the desired state. If a strategic plan is loaded with details and analysis, it is usually a blueprint for micromanaging and is likely to be a tactical or operational plan. However, tactical or operational plans should be derived from an accepted strategic plan. Note that the strategic plan should be proactive in defining *what should be* and *what could be* based on adding value to external clients in society. Although the process of creating the plan can take as little as one day to complete, strategic planning should be a continuing process within any organization.

Most people initially prefer an ideal vision that has a positive sound, such as, "All people will live in a healthy, positive, safe, and satisfying environment in which all things both survive and thrive. People may create any type of world they desire as long as they don't violate the basic ideal vision" (Kaufman, 1998, pp. 52–58). Although such a statement can be comfortable and uplifting, it provides little "meat" in terms of what performance technologists require for planning, design, development, implementation, and continuous improvement.

Because performance and results are essential ingredients of performance technology, it is necessary to take the positive ideal vision one step further and state it in the form of results and consequences. Then measurable statements of deviation from the positive can be made. A basic ideal vision is written with the same precision and rigor as any measurable performance objective.

An example of a measurable and useful ideal vision follows (Kaufman, 1998, p. 54):

> There will be no losses of life or elimination or reduction of levels of well-being, survival, self-sufficiency, quality of life, livelihood, or loss of property from any sources including but not limited to the following: war and/or riot; unintended human-caused changes to the environment, including permanent destruction of the environment and/or rendering it nonrenewable; murder, rape, or crimes of violence, robbery, or destruction of property; etc.

From this ideal vision an organization would identify what it is committed to moving toward in its mission objective. An example of an organizational mission objective is this: "We at XYZ Enterprises will reduce the number of incidents of juvenile crime in our community to zero by the year 2050." Subsequent objectives would then include the *benchmarks* that must be met in the years 2010, 2020, and so on, for the organization to accomplish the mission objective.

Strategic planning plus is one responsive, practical, and pragmatic model for strategic planning and visioning initiatives (Kaufman 1992, 1998). It begins with the identification of the measurable societal contributions to be delivered and then identifies the required or desired results to be achieved at the organizational level and subsequently at individual performance levels. Seen in this manner, organizations (and their parts) are the means to both external client and societal ends. In the hypothetical example above, the strategic plan would then identify that an individual might be expected to produce (in cooperation with community groups) "a list of potential strategies approved by community representatives" as a required product leading toward the accomplishment of the organizational mission and ideal vision. This process of cascading down from the highest to the lowest level ensures that everything the organization uses, does, produces, and delivers is aligned with positive societal consequences and payoffs.

The process offers the performance technologist an effective tool with which to test any performance initiative being considered by asking: "Will what is being considered move us closer to or further from our mission and ideal vision?"

This approach of integrating strategic planning and ideal visioning is capable of providing organizations and individuals with justifiable directions and criteria for success. It is by linking what an organization uses, does, produces, and delivers to external clients that the strategic plan becomes an integral part of performance technology. If the performance technologist has no strategic plan or ideal vision with which to test the viability of an intervention, he or she has no rational way to justify decisions on intervention selection and implementation.

Steps of Strategic Planning and Visioning

The four steps of strategic planning and visioning are as follows:

1. Develop or obtain agreement on the ideal vision that states the future results for society and for external clients.
2. Align the organization's mission objective with the ideal vision so that it states what parts and portions of that vision the organization is committed to delivering or moving toward.
3. Identify the functions (products to be successfully completed) that are required to move the organization from the current to the desired state.
4. Identify the costs and consequences of meeting the needs—closing the gaps between current results and consequences and required ones.

Performance Technology Tools Used in Strategic Planning

The strategic plan integrates the following tools of performance technology:

- Needs assessment (to identify the performance gaps between current and required results for society, external clients, and the organization and also to identify the performance gaps for the functions to be delivered)
- Measurable performance objectives (to define current and required results)
- Evaluation and continuous improvement

When to Use

The circumstances under which strategic planning can be used are as follows:

- When top management wants to ensure that everything that is used, done, produced, and delivered adds value to the organization as well as to external clients and society
- When no formal plan exists to ensure that what the organization delivers adds value to external clients and society

If the performance technologist is not involved in developing the new strategic plan or the vision, he or she may use the existing one to identify the extent to which various performance initiatives will add value to associates, the organization, and external clients.

Case Studies

Two case studies illustrate strategic planning, with particular attention to the new issue of the value added to society.

An Organization with an Unused Strategic Plan

An executive was disappointed with her organization's current strategic plan. She observed that it was long, detailed, laborious, and never used when decisions were to be made. She noted that she had prepared a "vision for the organization," as a large consulting firm had suggested. The vision identified the major means by which the organization would achieve success: quality management, customer focus, a market-driven philosophy, and the use of technology. As she somewhat proudly noted, this vision statement was created to be similar to those of many other successful organizations. It included phrases such as "committed to long-term growth," "achieving outstanding value for our clients," and "our most important resource is our people."

Following the procedures of conventional strategic planning, she asked her associates to identify how each would contribute to this vision. She then began to realize that most of her people only used the words of her vision to justify doing the same things as before. Although she had followed what she thought was competent advice, her organization was losing market share, shareholder value, and its good reputation.

By using a planning process focusing on societal value added, she found that she could now justify resources, methods, approaches, products, and deliverables in terms of what they added in value to external clients and society. Her previous strategic planning approach focused on current means for doing business (quality, reengineering, technology, and so on) and tended to lock her and the organization into business as usual. The societal framework and mind-set—strategic thinking—changed how the organization does business, justified many current products, identified many opportunities, and provided the basis for eliminating some activities and products that did not add value to internal and/or external clients. She requested the assistance of a staff performance technologist to shift from a means-and-resources-focused approach to a results-referenced one.

Some of her associates were at first uncomfortable with changing how they thought and planned, but soon they realized that a proactive and continual planning process focused on value added to society was very practical. It even allowed them to be responsive to and prove value for clients and society, adding desired meaning to their jobs. For example, the new organizational vision defined a community in which all individuals are self-sufficient and crime, poverty, and discrimination do not exist. From this vision they derived an organizational mission stating which parts of the vision the organization was committed to delivering. It should be noted that although the organizational vision and mission did not specify long-term growth and profit, the organization pursued its vision knowing that providing useful results to the community would be financially profitable. Profits did improve, as did customer satisfaction and the morale of associates.

A Government Agency

A government agency was under intense pressure to cut costs and reduce the number of employees. Each review by the legislature cited the agency for poor results and high costs. The agency had followed conventional strategic planning approaches, identifying strengths, weaknesses, opportunities, and threats and writing a values-vision-mission statement that said, "Excellence in service to our citizens." Yet the newspapers often reported negative stories about the way in which the agency conducted business and printed examples of how efforts at downsizing were futile. There was eventually talk of firing the agency secretary and bringing in a popular politician as a replacement. Employees were nervous and therefore spent a lot of time documenting their worth and looking for new jobs.

The secretary and his executive staff adopted a societal-referenced planning and decision-making model to get a new perspective. The agency came up with a new mission based on adding value to society: "Put ourselves out of business through success." "Out of business?" asked some associates. The answer came back, "We are not likely accomplish this goal in our time, but if we aren't intending to be so good at what we do that we are no longer needed, then what do we have in mind?" This was a major shift in how they thought about themselves, their current clients, and their responsibilities. With a societal orientation they found that many of their services added no value to citizens. This perspective allowed them to rethink their services; by eliminating those of no value, they became leaner, more efficient, more effective. They had begun to work themselves out of business. Then they reorganized their operations to improve how they worked with and related to their clients. The following year they won an award from a citizens' committee for exemplary service to the state.

Figure 1 offers an introductory *map* (algorithm or flow diagram) that describes several of the primary steps in developing a societal-referenced strategic plan. The clouds represent additional topics and questions that should be addressed during each step of the development process.

Resources and References

Kaufman, R. (1992). *Strategic planning plus: An organizational guide* (Rev. ed.). Thousand Oaks, CA: Sage.

Kaufman, R. (1998). *Strategic thinking: A guide to identifying and solving problems.* Arlington, VA: American Society for Training and Development (ASTD).

Kaufman, R., & Watkins, R. (1996). Mega planning: A framework for integrating strategic planning, needs assessment, quality management, benchmarking, and reengineering. In J. E. Jones & E. Biech (Eds.), *The HR Handbook* (Vol. 1). Amherst, MA: HRD Press.

Mintzberg, H. (1994). *The rise and fall of strategic planning.* New York: Free Press.

Watkins, R., Triner, D., & Kaufman, R. (1996). The death and resurrection of strategic planning [Review of the book *The rise and fall of strategic planning*]. *International Journal of Educational Reform, 5*(3), 390–393.

FIGURE 1. MAP FOR DEVELOPING A STRATEGIC PLAN.

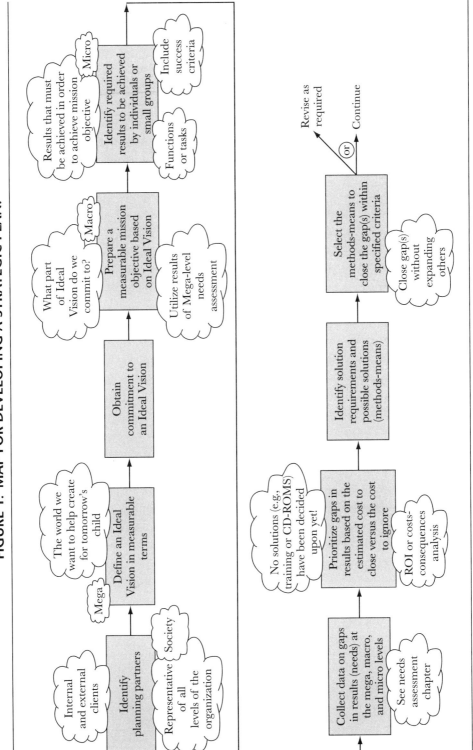

Intervention Authors

Roger Kaufman, Ph.D.
Professor and Director
Office for Needs Assessment and Planning
Florida State University
3500 University Center, Building C
Tallahassee, FL 32306
Phone: 850-644-6435
E-mail: rkaufman@onap.fsu.edu

Ryan Watkins, Ph.D.
Research Associate
Office for Needs Assessment and Planning
Florida State University
3500 University Center, Building C
Tallahassee, FL 32306
Phone: 850-644-6435
E-mail: rwatkins@onap.fsu.edu

▪ ▪ ▪ ▪ ▪ ▪ STRUCTURED WRITING

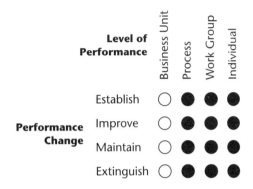

Level of Performance	Business Unit	Process	Work Group	Individual
Performance Change Establish	○	●	●	●
Improve	○	●	●	●
Maintain	○	●	●	●
Extinguish	○	●	●	●

Alternative Name

Information Mapping®

Definition

Structured writing is a synthesis of tools and techniques for the analysis of complex subject matters and jobs. It consists of a group of standards and techniques for the management of large amounts of rapidly changing information and also procedures for planning, organizing, sequencing, and presenting communications, especially training courses and documentation in business.

Description

Structured writing originated with Robert E. Horn in 1965, when he was a research associate at the Institute for Educational Technology at Columbia University. Horn developed structured writing in response to the contemporary need in business, science, and technology to quickly learn and reference growing amounts of complex and rapidly changing information.

Information Blocks

Information blocks are the basic units of subject matter in structured writing analysis. They replace the paragraph as the fundamental unit of analysis and information presentation. The traditional definition of the paragraph is much too vague, especially for use in standardized writing about complex business, scientific, and technical subject matter. Different types are not clearly defined, boundaries are fuzzy, and topic sentences are often overlooked or merely implied. (See Exhibit 1 for an example of the traditional approach.)

Information blocks, on the other hand, are precisely defined and classified. Blocks are composed of one or more sentences and/or diagrams, tables, or other illustrations about a limited topic. They usually have no more than nine sentences. Each block is always identified clearly with a label. Information blocks are normally part of a larger structure called an *information map*. In short, they are a reader-focused unit of basic or core parts of a subject matter.

Information blocks are constrained by the following principles:

- *The chunking principle:* Group all information into small, manageable units.
- *The relevance principle:* In each chunk include information related to one main point only (based on the purpose or function of that information for the reader).
- *The consistency principle:* For similar subject matters, use similar words, labels, formats, sequences, and organization.
- *The labeling principle:* Label each chunk and group of chunks according to specific criteria.

Different types of blocks vary widely in appearance and construction. The example below—the definition block—is one of the most simple-looking types of blocks.

Definition: The Master Payroll File is a group of records containing all of the payroll and employee information used by the weekly payroll program.

For more examples of information blocks, see Exhibit 2. Note how six information blocks are presented, each with a title. One information block is a table that assists the reader with an analysis.

Information Map

The *information map* is a collection of one to nine information blocks. It provides an important intermediate level of document organization. The information map enables systematic sequencing and formatting and helps the reader to understand the

EXHIBIT 1. THE TRADITIONAL APPROACH.

Spills and releases, continued

All PCB releases must be reported immediately to Environmental Compliance in headquarters. PCB releases also include transformer leaks.

The contact number for reporting a spill is 1-800-555-1212. This number is used to report a spill as well as for asking questions about spills or releases.

You must place a second phone call to Environmental Compliance within 12 hours of the spill or release to provide complete details. This is not required if you are otherwise instructed by Environmental Compliance.

Report by telephone any of the chemical substance of concern spills or releases listed below if the release quantity is equal to or larger than the amounts listed.

—any solid chemical substance in any form that weighs one pound or greater. If the spill is immediately and totally cleaned up, it needs to be reported.

—liquid chemicals that are greater than approximately five gallons. If the substance is mercury, then report releases of approximately one pound.

—any hazardous waste, particularly from hazardous waste storage tank that weighs one pound or greater.

—oil of any kind to surface water that creates a sheen upon the water.

—any substance in excess of permit conditions.

—any spill or release from any underground storage tank in any amount.

You must provide the following information when you call to report a spill or release: Your name and return phone number, the type of substance and volume involved in the spill, the State and location of the spill, any other information that is available, and the activation of the site spill prevention control and countermeasures plan.

Continued on next page

Page 132

Source: Information Mapping, Inc. Used with permission.

structure of the subject matter and the document. Exhibit 2 is an example of an information map. Six information blocks are combined with a title to make the map.

Information Types

There are approximately forty different types of information blocks, which cover approximately 80 percent of the domain of relatively stable subject matter. This

EXHIBIT 2. THE STRUCTURED WRITING APPROACH.

Notification of Spills or Releases

Purpose	Follow the guidelines below to determine when to notify Environmental Compliance in headquarters of spills or releases.
PCB releases	Report all PCB releases, including transformer leaks, <u>immediately</u> to Environmental Compliance in headquarters.
Chemical spills And releases	Report spills or releases into the environment of any chemical substance of concern in quantities equal to or larger than those shown in the table below.

Type of Spill/Release	Quantity of Spill/Release
Any solid chemical substance in any form	Weighs one pound or greater <u>Note:</u> If the spill is immediately and totally cleaned up, it must still be reported.
Liquid chemicals	Greater than approximately five gallons <u>Exception:</u> If the substance is mercury, then report releases of approximately one pound.
Any hazardous waste, particularly from a hazardous waste storage tank	Weighs one pound or greater
Oil of any kind to surface water	Creates a sheen upon the water
Any substance	In excess of permit conditions
From any underground storage tank	Any amount

How to report	Report spills or releases by phone. Phones are staffed 24 hours a day. **Phone number:** Call 1-800-555-1212 to report or to ask questions about spills or releases.
Information to report	When calling to report a spill or release, provide the following information: • your name and return phone number • the type of substance and volume involved • the State and location of the spill • any other information that is available, and • activation of the site spill prevention control and countermeasures plan.
Second phone call	You must complete a second telephone call providing complete details <u>within 12 hours</u>, unless otherwise instructed by Environmental Compliance.

7-10

Source: Information Mapping, Inc. Used with permission.

domain includes introductory textbooks, training manuals, process and procedure documentation, and most reference materials. Those forty blocks can be sorted into seven basic classifications called *information types*.

The seven information types are as follows:

- Procedure
- Process
- Concept
- Structure
- Classification
- Principle
- Fact

The information types provide a key set of categories for specifying and describing how human beings think, especially about what have been classified as relatively stable discourse domains. Structured writing guidelines have been developed that permit each information block to be assigned to one or more of these information types and then written according to standards developed specifically for that type.

Domains of Discourse

Other domains of discourse exist, each with its own information types. Domains of discourse are defined as the specification of information block types for a particular class of documents, all of which share the same type of author-reader assumptions and the same stance or point of view toward subject matter. Other domains, such as disputed discourse and business report and memo writing, have also been analyzed.

Other Aspects

Other aspects of the methodology include the following:

- Systematic criteria for labeling information blocks
- Systematic specification of document formats
- Document life cycle methodology
- Systematic criteria for integration of graphics

When to Use

The use of structured writing is appropriate under the following circumstances:

- When performance is primarily based on task and knowledge
- When there are large amounts of information that may be needed by some workers
- When just-in-time learning and reference are needed (structured writing documents are easily used as job aids)
- When computer-stored knowledge bases need to be developed (when modularity and ease of reference are important)
- When a document must be used frequently
- When simplified document updating and maintenance are a priority

When Not to Use

Structured writing is not useful in the following situations:

- When the performance situation involves psychomotor functioning
- When people need to be trained in face-to-face skills, such as interpersonal relations

Case Study

In a software development company, a new version of a software application that handles order entry, inventory, invoicing, and shipping is being developed. Reports describing the new product and the research and development process must be prepared and circulated to hundreds of people in the software company and their users. The technical specifications and details of functionality must be described and approved. The marketing department must sign off on the salability of the product. Customer service, maintenance, and finance must make plans to understand and incorporate the changes. Structured writing is frequently used in the memos and reports that professionals and managers write to explain all of these details, to achieve efficiency and clarity of communication.

The new software is then sold to a high-tech company. As a result, many people's job duties will change. In some departments, several hundred jobs will be affected. Salespeople need information on how to enter orders. Order-entry associates must be trained in the new interfaces and database procedures. Documentation about how to use the new software and how hardware works will be developed in-house. A Web site will be prepared to handle orders over the Internet. Customer service representatives must have information to answer customer questions. Inventory management procedures change, and those managers and their staff must be trained. Financial procedures must be updated to incorporate the new system.

In both of these organizations, the software company and the high-tech company, efficiency and effectiveness of communication are required. The software is complex and may require several thousand pages of documentation and training materials. This presents significant problems for the high-tech company's information services manager. She will probably use some of the documentation provided by the software company and then develop some that is specific to her users in the company.

Structured writing is used in both companies because of its precision and modularity. Modularity of information blocks and standardized labeling allow key information to be identified, distributed, and managed with ease. In the order-entry software example, knowledge bases are created that permit reuse of the same blocks of information in different documents, thus avoiding duplication of effort and inaccuracy. Documents such as system descriptions, desk procedures, process descriptions, and policies and procedures will all benefit from structured writing. The standardized modularity also allows information to be efficiently adapted for display on computer screens; the standardized labeling system makes orientation, context, and maintenance less problematic than usual in on-line documents.

Efficiency in writing is facilitated because of the standardization. Thus teams of writers can contribute to writing the same document with minimal editorial work needed to coordinate styles.

Exhibits 1 and 2 show how clear information can be made, once the text presented in Exhibit 1 has been put in the structured writing format illustrated in Exhibit 2.

Resources and References

Horn, R. E. (1989). *Mapping hypertext: Analysis, linkage, and display of knowledge for the next generation of on-line text and graphics.* Lexington, MA: Lexington Institute (available from Information Mapping, Inc., phone: 800-463-6627).

Horn, R. E. (1992a). Clarifying two controversies about information mapping's method. *Educational and Training Technology International, 2*(29), 109–117.

Horn, R. E. (1992b). *How high can it fly? Examining the evidence on information mapping's method of high performance communication.* Lexington, MA: Lexington Institute (available from Information Mapping, Inc., phone: 800-463-6627). Covers research done by university and business researchers, including summaries of eight doctoral dissertations on the methodology.

Horn, R. E. (1993, February). Structured writing at twenty-five. *Performance and Instruction,* pp. 11–17.

Schaffer, E. (1982, February). The potential benefits of the information mapping technique. *Performance and Instruction,* pp. 34–38.

Intervention Author

Robert E. Horn
President
Macro VU, Inc.
2819 Jackson Street, #101
San Francisco, CA 94115
Phone and fax: 415-775-7377
E-mail: bobhorn@well.com

Note: Information Mapping® is a registered trademark of Information Mapping, Inc., 411 Waverley Oaks Rd., Waltham, MA 02154.

■ ■ ■ ■ ■ ■ TEAM PERFORMANCE

Level of Performance	Business Unit	Process	Work Group	Individual
Performance Change Establish	○	○	●	●
Improve	○	○	●	●
Maintain	○	○	●	●
Extinguish	○	○	●	●

Definition

Team performance is governed by a set of attitudes and actions that help team members to work together cooperatively so that they can efficiently and effectively achieve the team's goals.

Description

High team performance is the result of the way in which the team members work together to achieve a shared objective. It assumes that to achieve that objective every member has his or her own responsibility for particular tasks, but that those tasks are interdependent. If one member is to perform well, all must perform well. The whole point of instituting teams comes from this idea of interdependent success. For teams to thrive and perform well, there must be a supportive, team-oriented culture in place. This requires a management that is willing to provide the time that teams need to become established as well as the feedback and rewards that reinforce teamwork. It also requires that team members receive training in various skills related to teamwork.

There are many obstacles to high performance in teams: poor management support, uncooperative members, poor team leadership, lack of training, insufficient resources, and poorly articulated goals. A group is not a team because management says so. Instead, a successful team evolves through various stages; it can take a team several months to more than a year to progress from the initial stage, during which members get to know one another, to the stage characterized by high performance. During this evolution, management must back the team and provide it with the resources and authority it needs to succeed. This support includes training, time for meetings, and any tools and information that team members need in order to fulfill their individual and group responsibilities.

Another consideration in developing high team performance is team size. The optimal number of members is seven, but a team with five or nine members can also function well. This size facilitates efficient interaction among members. Communication can become cumbersome when a team has more than nine members; teams with fewer than five members may not exhibit enough diversity in viewpoint, skills, experience, and so on, to produce high-quality work.

For a team to perform well, the following roles must be filled:

- *Sponsor:* A manager who has set up or empowered the team to perform its tasks, who provides the team with the resources it needs to do its work, and provides feedback on how well the team is doing. Make sure a sponsor is in place who is committed to the team's success.
- *Facilitator:* A team expert who can help the team get started and who serves as a resource to help members function together effectively as a team. Having a facilitator helps teams prevent problems as well as solve them when they occur.
- *Team leader:* A person who calls and conducts meetings, acts as a liaison with management, serves as an interface with other teams, helps the team to keep its focus, solves problems between team members, deals with disruptive team members, and removes roadblocks to performance. A competent and caring team leader helps the team run smoothly.
- *Team members:* Individuals who are experts in the various tasks and activities that must be carried out for the team to achieve its goals. The team members must know their individual jobs and must also be trained in understanding how to operate in a team situation.

In order to perform at a high level, the team must possess the following skills:

- *Functional/technical skills:* These skills consist of expertise in the various areas required to do the work.

- *Interpersonal and conflict resolution skills:* These skills include the ability of members to get along with one another so that they can effectively and efficiently execute their interdependent tasks. Critically important is the ability to solve small disputes quickly, before they escalate.
- *Problem-solving skills:* These skills include the ability to define and understand problems, the ability to solve them, and the ability to make continuous improvements in how work is done.
- *Decision-making skills:* These skills include an understanding of how to reach consensus on the many large and small decisions the team is required to make.

High team performance requires, in summary, a supportive, team-oriented culture, time for the team members to learn how to work together to achieve a mutually held objective, and training in teamwork roles and skills.

When to Use

An organization should consider establishing teams when the creation of its products or services requires the coordinated interaction of several people. If that is not the case, then teams are probably not a good idea.

An intervention designed to improve team performance is appropriate under the following circumstances.

When Management Does Not Provide Support

If management is not supporting a team or providing the tools and resources that the team needs to perform well, the team leader or facilitator should talk with management about providing the necessary support. Management must be prepared to invest in training and to provide regular feedback and rewards to demonstrate its commitment to the team.

When Teams Are Struggling

When one or more teams are struggling and not achieving their goals, the team leader needs to intervene and discuss possible causes with the members. Sometimes a team does not have a clear objective, and its members are not sure what to do or how to do it; in this case the leader and members should discuss goals, expectations, and strategies for meeting the goals. Lack of skills in various areas can also cause problems in teams; in this case training in interpersonal communication, meeting skills, or team decision making might be appropriate.

When Disruptive Behaviors Are Being Displayed

Disruptions of various sorts may occur, including the following:

- One member who dominates team meetings
- One or more members who do not participate fully
- One member who disparages the ideas of the other members
- Digressing from the subject or task at hand
- Feuding among team members

Each of these situations undermines team performance and calls for an intervention by the team leader, usually in a one-on-one meeting. Such meetings must take advantage of communication and problem-solving skills so that the discussion focuses on the problem rather than the person.

When There Is a Lack of Cooperation Between Teams

Sometimes teams work at cross-purposes, and this lack of cooperation results in mistakes, conflict, and wasted effort. This situation may indicate that management is not fully behind the teams or that the teams are not fully aware of the interdependent nature of their work. The issue usually can be resolved by employing conflict resolution methods.

Case Study

XEL Communications is a small firm with 180 employees that supplies circuit boards to companies like its former parent, GTE, as well as several of the Baby Bell companies. To succeed against large competitors like Northern Telecom and AT&T, owner and CEO Bill Sanko decided that his company needed to have quick turnaround on orders and be more responsive to customers. He expressed the situation in this way: "We needed everybody in the building thinking about and contributing to how we could better satisfy our customers; how we could improve quality; how we could reduce costs."

Sanko developed a vision statement to help bring about the desired state. Part of that statement included the comment "We will be an organization where each of us is a self-manager." From this goal, the vice president of manufacturing, John Puckett, designed the plant for cellular production, with each cell staffed by teams who could manufacture several different circuit boards. That was in 1988.

By 1993 the company had completely rebuilt itself around teams. It was cited as a role model by dozens of other companies and was featured in a video on team-based management produced by the Association for Manufacturing Excellence. Visitors to the plant would see charts on the wall tracking attendance, on-time deliveries, and other measures of team performance. After five years of self-managed teams, the cost of assembly has dropped 25 percent, inventory has been cut by half, and quality has improved by 30 percent. And the all-important cycle time—the amount of time from start of production to delivery of final product—has dropped from eight weeks to four days.

Lessons Learned

Still, XEL has learned that team-based structures also make special demands on a company and its management. Its people have learned several lessons that any company going in this direction should be aware of. These lessons are explained in the following paragraphs.

Team Building Does Not Proceed Neatly from Stage to Stage. Although it is true that teams do evolve through different stages to get to high performance, it is also true that teams sometimes regress. Such regressions can have consequences throughout the company. At XEL, for example, the stockroom team broke down. Puckett received complaints from its customers and other teams and found out that certain members were cheating on their time cards. Puckett had to intervene and actually disbanded teams in this part of the company, bringing in a supervisor to take over. His goal, though, was for the supervisor to work himself out of a job by reestablishing the best practices demonstrated by another successful manufacturing team.

Sponsors Need Skills That MBA Programs Do Not Teach. With self-managing teams, managers must know when to intervene and when to back off, as shown by performance indicators. Three skills that Puckett has discovered are what he calls (1) *diplomacy,* the job of managing relations among teams, which can get difficult sometimes; (2) *monkey managing,* the fine art of not allowing someone else's monkey, or problem, to jump onto your back; and (3) *innovation triage,* which means that managers must encourage and reward innovation but make sure that teams do not go too far and adversely affect other parts of the organization.

Employees Need New Skills. Employees need to learn additional skills, such as statistical process control, so that they can fill in for one another from time to time and make sure there is no breakdown in production. Employees also need an attitude that makes them care about the quality of their work and the motivation to set their own priorities rather than waiting for someone else to do it for them.

Compensation and Performance Reviews Must Be Changed. Pay can no longer be based on individual performance. XEL created a reward program based on the acquisition of skills, the performance of the team, and profit sharing. The company also adopted a peer-review program in which the team members evaluate one another in terms of their contributions to the team's performance.

Conclusion

The move to teams at XEL has affected how all employees and managers think about their jobs. One team member sums it up this way: "Some of the new hires, it blows their minds when they come in. Most people are used to these structured deals, where you do your little piece and you send it on, and you don't care what happens to it after that. Here you're involved in the whole picture. You have the mind-set: OK, this is the flow and this is what we have to do to accomplish that."

Resources and References

Manz, C. C., & Sims, H. P., Jr. (1993). *Business without bosses: How self-managing teams are building high performance companies.* New York: Wiley.

Reddy, W. B., & Kaleel, J. (Eds.). (1988). *Team building: Blueprints for productivity and satisfaction.* Alexandria, VA: NTL Institute for Applied Behavioral Science.

Romig, D. A. (1996). *Breakthrough teamwork: Outstanding results using structured teamwork.* Burr Ridge, IL: Irwin.

Scholtes, P. R., Joiner, B. L., & Streibel, B. J. (1996). *The team handbook* (2nd ed.). Madison, WI: Joiner Associates.

Syer, J., & Connolly, C. (1996). *How teamwork works: The dynamics of effective team development.* New York: McGraw-Hill.

Woods, J. A. (1997). *10-minute guide to teams and teamwork.* New York: Alpha Books.

Intervention Author

John A. Woods
President
CWL Publishing Enterprises
Editor
The Quality Yearbook
3010 Irvington Way
Madison, WI 53713
Phone: 608-273-3710
Fax: 608-274-4554
E-mail: jwoods@execpc.com
Web site: http://www.execpc.com/cwlpubent/

Case Study Author

The case study is based on J. Case, "What the Experts Forgot to Mention," *Inc.*, September 1993, pp. 66–77.

■ ■ ı ı ı ı TEAMING

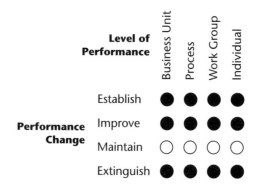

	Level of Performance	Business Unit	Process	Work Group	Individual
	Establish	●	●	●	●
Performance Change	Improve	●	●	●	●
	Maintain	○	○	○	○
	Extinguish	●	●	●	●

Alternative Names

Teamwork
Team building
Participatory management
Self-directed teams

Definition

"A team is a small group of people with complementary skills who are committed to a common purpose, goals, and approach for which they hold themselves mutually accountable" (Katzenbach & Smith, 1993).

Description

Organizations are entering a time of enormous challenge: competition with other organizations for existing resources; customers who will compare delivery of service to the best delivery possible; processes that must be reengineered to effect substantial gains in cycle time, cost of service, and quality; heavier workloads as a result of downsizing and technology that is advancing faster than we can understand. We all want a magic pill to fix our problems—an instantaneous cure-all that is quick, cheap, and painless. But there is no magic pill. And introducing teams is no magic pill either. Teams are a means to an end—a way to achieve something that is greater than the sum of each individual's contribution. This sum is called *synergy*, a synchronized energy that is capable of producing more than is expected, allowing an organization to have an excess of resources available to tackle the challenges it faces.

Teams are not new. In fact, the pre–Industrial Age shop was built on the concept of a team of craftsmen. With the advent of manufacturing and Frederick Taylor's concept of modern management, teams became obsolete. Management believed that people produced best when given small, repetitive tasks with a supervisor nearby to make sure the work was done properly.

In the early 1980s the introduction of Total Quality Management (TQM) in the United States brought renewed interest in the use of three types of teams: (1) multifunctional policymaking teams; (2) cross-functional planning and problem-solving teams; and (3) self-directed teams. Deming and others stressed that the workforce had capability and talent that was not being utilized; these people, whom others thought needed a supervisor, owned homes, paid taxes, raised children, and handled all types of problems on their own. Organizations were not using their human resources to the greatest advantage. With this new realization, the team concept took off. Today 73 percent of organizations have some employees actively involved in teams (*Total Quality Newsletter*, 1994).

When to Use

Using teams is appropriate under the following circumstances.

When Leadership Is Needed Throughout the Organization

Creating teams is an excellent idea when top management recognizes that leadership is needed throughout the organization and that therefore power can be shared. Top management support is crucial to the success of teams. To start a team in the middle of the organizational structure is ultimately to create a cultural collision with the top. However, when top management is eager to hear new and varied opinions, invites thinking that is outside-the-box, and recognizes that the person who does the job is usually the most knowledgeable about the job, then an environment exists in which teams can thrive.

There are two crucial points in the process as the team develops when top management needs to clearly demonstrate support for the change to a team culture:

- At the beginning, top leadership needs to articulate the compelling marketplace reasons why the organization has decided to restructure using teams.
- Later in the process, top leadership needs to confront people who are obstructing and resisting the process.

If management does not take a firm stance in support of teams, others in the organization will see teams as just another "program of the month," to be endured until its time has passed.

When One Person Cannot Have All the Answers

Obviously it is impossible for any one person to have or be expected to have all the answers. This is just one of the many reasons that teams are beneficial to organizations. The world is changing at such a rapid pace that it is no longer possible for us to believe we can have all the answers, no matter how smart we are. Consider these facts: most of Hewlett-Packard's revenues come from products that did not exist a year ago. Ninety percent of Miller revenues come from beers that did not exist two years ago ("Study Finds People as Assets Pays Off. . . ," 1995). Fifteen years ago there were no faxes, answering machines, or cell phones. Rotary phones and typewriters were commonplace; computers were usually dumb terminals. A *learning organization* recognizes how important it is to bring diverse viewpoints and knowledge together in an effort to keep up.

Teams create an environment in which people with diverse knowledge and experiences come together to solve problems or complete tasks and, as a result, see the benefit of seeking out multiple viewpoints and perspectives.

When Processes Cross Functional Areas

As a result of our schooling, most of us tend to be linear thinkers—not moving to the next step until the previous step has been completed. But this linear thinking keeps us from seeing the process flow of our activities. Peter Drucker (1988) has said that organizational success in the future will be based on those who manage the white spaces on the organizational chart. In other words, teams tear down hierarchical structure; they bend the lines on the organizational chart from a vertical model to a flatter, more egalitarian model. The new model is called *molecular* because it creates a very flexible structure that allows for teams to be formed quickly based on marketplace need. Whenever this happens, the gains are immediate and impressive, as work redundancy, miscommunication, and internal competitiveness are eliminated.

When Business As Usual Is a Threat to Success

We have to acknowledge that our competitors are all in the same race we are. If we stand still, they will surpass us without doing much at all. One organizational president put it succinctly when he told his employees, "Lead, follow, or leave." Although it is hard to hear that kind of advice, it is meant as a wake-up call to all those who suffer from entitlement—the belief that they are entitled to their jobs and associated benefits for life regardless of their performance.

The very act of being part of a team breaks the business-as-usual mold, exposing employees to new information and ideas that they have not previously heard. They become more knowledgeable about the business, how it makes money, what customers need and want, who their coworkers are, and how departments interface. They also become intolerant of mediocre performance, performance that supervisors and managers compensated for in the old hierarchical model.

When Skills Are Not Being Used

When talent, skills, and abilities exist in the organization but are not used because of the current structure, teams can remedy the situation. Recently a self-directed team was dealing with a difficult chemical plant problem. The team member who came up with the idea that ultimately fixed the problem was a maintenance worker who owned his own small business on the side. He had never been asked to contribute thinking skills at work before, so he never did. Ask any group of employees if they have talents that are not used at work, and a majority will raise their hands.

With teams, the concept of a job changes, growing much bigger to encompass much more (see Figure 1). As a result, people use many more of the skills they already have, and they are cross-trained in new skills. The result is a far more talented and diversified workforce.

Case Study

The world of banking is becoming more and more chaotic every day. Mergers, acquisitions, takeovers, technology, and a global banking community have changed

FIGURE 1. INDIVIDUAL'S JOB VERSUS TEAM MEMBER'S JOB.

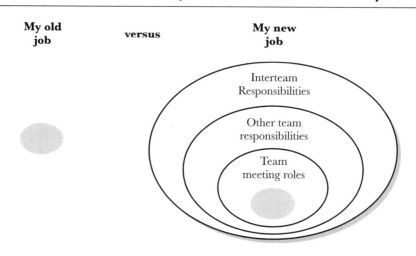

the way we bank and will bank in the future. Soon we will do most of our banking from home and will pay our bills without writing checks. We will be able to bank whenever and wherever we want. Obviously, this scenario poses threats for a small community savings bank.

The dilemma for this bank and many others is how to shift from a paradigm that has five tellers at high-walled stations to personal bankers who are capable of helping the customer do one-stop shopping. In addition, the branch manager would have to shift from performing mostly operational functions to being out in the community making contacts and bringing business into the bank.

The community savings bank saw retail teams as the answer. The bank president was the visionary and had started the team process several years earlier with two pilot teams in the servicing and processing areas. These teams were very successful and were able to operate autonomously, without any day-to-day supervision. Their former supervisors were put on a high-performance operational team to introduce new concepts such as transaction processing and to reengineer existing processes.

With the success of these teams as an inspiration, the president decided to take the big step of moving teams into the retail area. The idea would be to create self-directed teams composed of former tellers, customer service representatives, and personal bankers. This would free the branch manager to spend much more time in marketing and sales, bringing in and talking to the customer.

The president met with his senior leadership team to explore the idea of teams, not only in retail but throughout the organization. As expected, the leaders were apprehensive; in fact, they spent many months struggling with their own inability to be a team. In the meantime, however, the vice president of retail banking took the ball and ran with it. She met with her seven branch managers, talked about the vision, and began a training program for them that introduced the concept of teams and put particular emphasis on their changing role, from manager to coach. The training included the following kinds of skill development:

- A solid grasp of how teams work and why the organization saw teams as an important key to its future success
- Discussion about the number of roles that would be changing—including those of the branch manager and all the staff—and what the change would look like
- Identification of certain tasks that the branch manager was doing that made sense to delegate to the teams (everything from scheduling vacations and doing overdraft letters to shoveling the sidewalk)

Resistance was immediate on the part of two managers. They were not able to believe that their staffs would be able to do the work in their absence. Later it emerged that they also feared the change in their own jobs. The vice president encouraged much discussion and met individually with these managers to restate the vision again and again. At this point the managers were meeting monthly, and not a lot was being accomplished from month to month.

It was time to create a matrix listing the tasks to be done and specific deadlines. The resulting chart (Figure 2) dramatically changed the speed of the process, as each branch could see its progress in relation to that of the other branches.

As the managers began to move ahead, it became clear that it was time to launch a team-training program for all the branch staff. The bank agreed on the following six modules to launch the process:

- How teams work
- Mission, goals, roles, and procedures
- Meeting skills
- Interpersonal skills, including giving and receiving feedback
- Conflict resolution

To reduce the expenses, the bank invited internal staff members to become trainers. To everyone's surprise, fifteen people expressed a desire to be trainers. They each completed an application process and were interviewed by human resources, the vice president of branch banking, and an external consultant. From these fifteen a group of eight was selected and given training in adult-learning theory and presentation skills. The external consultant-trainer provided scripts and

FIGURE 2. TEAM DEVELOPMENT MATRIX.

	Biweekly meetings—9/15	Help/Hinder—11/15	Non-negotiables shared—9/30	Mission—11/30	Manager's role clarification—1/31	Goal setting—1/31	Charter—1/31	Completion of training—12/10	Conflict protocol—3/30	Hand-off plan completed—1/31	Myths about teams/coaches—11/20
Branch A	Y	N	Y	Y	Y	N	N	Y	N	N	Y
Branch B	Y	Y	N	Y	Y	N	N	Y	N	N	Y
Branch C	Y	Y	N	Y	Y	N	N	N-1	N	N	Y
Branch D	Y	Y	Y	N	Y	N	N	Y	N	N	Y
Branch E	Y	N	Y	Y	Y	N	N	Y	N	N	Y
Branch F	Y	Y	Y	N	Y	N	N	Y	Y	N	Y
Branch G	Y	Y	N	Y	Y	N	N	Y	N	N	Y

workbooks for each of the modules and conducted the initial session (on how teams work) for all the retail teams.

Throughout the process the senior leadership continued to meet and finally approved the implementation of the training. Several continued to express their misgivings, stating that the summer vacation schedule would make the training impossible. The vice president of branch banking moved the process ahead by using summer help to free people to attend daytime training.

A second implementation strategy was to use team members from servicing and processing to act as coaches for the retail teams. A coach attended every training module to add firsthand experience to the training, as many of the trainers had little or no experience with teams. In addition, each retail team was assigned a coach who attended meetings and worked with both the team and the manager to help the process and encourage the momentum toward teams.

Around the midpoint of the training process, the branches began to see changes in staff attitude and behavior. Even at this early stage, the following clear gains were emerging:

- Team meetings were scheduled and run by staff members, instead of by management. As a result, participation and idea generation improved dramatically.
- More work was getting done by the same number of people; tasks previously done by management were delegated.
- Team members began volunteering to cover for each other when members had to go to training or branches were understaffed.
- Team members started to challenge the old rules, questioning why certain employees were not expected to perform at the same levels as other employees in the entry-level positions.
- Turnover, which had been a particular problem with tellers, stopped as soon as the move to teams took place.

These results are typical of what can be expected when leadership drives the process and the organization puts resources behind its commitment. And it is only the beginning. As the teams mature, this bank can expect even greater returns from its investment in its people.

Resources and References

Deeprose, D. (1995). *The team coach*. New York: AMACOM.

Drucker, P. F. (1988). The coming of the new organization. *Harvard Business Review, 66*, 45–53.

Harrington-Mackin, D. (1994). *The team building tool kit.* New York: AMACOM.

Harrington-Mackin, D. (1996). *Keeping the team going.* New York: AMACOM.

Katzenbach, J. R., & Smith, D. K. (1993). *The wisdom of teams: Creating the high performance organization.* Boston: Harvard Business School Press.

Study finds people as assets pays off on bottom line. (1995, July). In *Lakewood report: Competitive renewal through workplace innovation: The financial and non-financial returns to innovative workplace practices* (pp. 12–23).

Total Quality Newsletter. (1994, January), p. 2.

Intervention Author

Deborah Mackin
President
New Directions Consulting, Inc.
P.O. Box 788
North Bennington, VT 05257
Phone: 800-730-3631
E-mail: newdirec@sover.net

▪ ▪ ▪ ▪ ▪ ▪ TRAINING

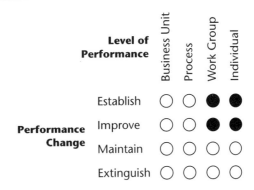

	Level of Performance	Business Unit	Process	Work Group	Individual
	Establish	○	○	●	●
Performance	Improve	○	○	●	●
Change	Maintain	○	○	○	○
	Extinguish	○	○	○	○

Associated Names

There are many specific methods of training, such as the following:

Accelerated learning
Lecture
On-the-job training

Definition

Reynolds (1995, p. 126) offers this definition of *training:* "In HRD instructional experiences provided primarily by employers for employees, designed to develop new skills, knowledge, and attitudes that are expected to be applied immediately upon (or within a short time after) arrival on or return to the job."

Description

There is no question that among the many interventions available and used to change performance, training is the most widely known and used. The following description attempts to define what training is, clarifies what it is not, and tells what it is best suited for in changing performance.

To clarify what training is, we need to start with a definition of *intervention*. An intervention is any means used to bring about a change in an individual, a group, a process, or a business unit. Training, then, is not one intervention; instead, it is better thought of as a series of interventions that match the performance need and the application environment with the learner.

Training consists of four basic interventions: *objectives, content, interaction,* and *feedback.* These interventions are discussed in the following paragraphs.

Objectives

Objectives spell out the expected outcome in terms of what the trainee will be able to know or do after the training. The classic objective contains a performance intent, criteria, and conditions. By giving trainees objectives, we may change their perception of what is to be learned. Usually, the objectives describe new skills or knowledge to be acquired. Nevertheless, their very presence and use represent an intervention.

Content

The content of training is the information presented to help trainees learn what it is they need to learn. The content may be delivered by a trainer, by audiovisual means, by computer, or by other commonly available means of transmitting information. The content is intended to be directly related to the objectives, at the right level for the audience, and sequenced according to skill development needs. The full range of modalities may be employed, from oral to written to visual and even to touching and feeling.

Interaction

This is the opportunity for the trainee to demonstrate that he or she has learned. If the interaction demonstrates that learning has not taken place, a prescriptive path may ensue to allow additional clarifying content and interaction until learning does take place, a process commonly called *remediation.* Interaction can take many forms, ranging from simple questioning to sophisticated simulations of on-the-job experiences.

Feedback

This is the information, or comparative data, provided after interactions so that the trainee (and the instructor, if involved) can compare the interaction to an exemplary model. In a simple sense, feedback is the answer to a question. In the more real interactions, feedback provides a model of performance as it is actually done on the job. For example, a video might demonstrate an on-the-job transaction to which a trainee can compare his or her actions; a simulator might provide visual and auditory feedback of a device's mechanical operation that would approximate the real device.

All training should include these four interventions. Training programs employ various combinations of these four—plus others—for different learning ends, content, and environments. A number of years ago, for example, the author identified almost fifty different training methods. A sample list of these methods will help illustrate the variety available:

- The adjunct study guide
- Algorithms
- The audio tutorial system
- Audio workbook
- Backward chaining
- The construct lesson plan
- Core package
- Computer-assisted (or -aided) instruction
- Direct instruction
- Experiential-learning packages
- Frame games
- Grouprograms
- Guided-design approach
- Incident process
- Individually responsive instruction
- Instructional simulation games
- Learner-controlled instruction
- Lecture method
- On-the-job training
- Peer tutorial instruction
- Programmed instruction
- Project individual learning plans

- Rolemaps
- Session plans
- Student contracts
- Suggestive-accelerative learning
- Teaching-learning unit
- Token economy system
- Tutoraids

Each of these training designs can serve as an intervention itself. Of course, many of the more contemporary training methods use the advantages of the computer to deliver distance education or training, just-in-time training, and so forth.

When to Use

The following criteria will help to identify when and where training is the intervention of choice. It is inappropriate to begin an analysis of a performance need with the assumption that a training intervention will be required; rather, it should be determined after the analysis when and where training is really needed. If, however, one is forced to use training as an intervention, then the designer may well look to other interventions (such as job aids) that can be tied to the training.

When Performance Requires a New Skill

There is little question that training serves its best purpose when the performance need is to establish new skills and knowledge. Training can be offered in a controlled environment to ensure that the transfer of skill and knowledge has occurred; it usually can be done with large numbers of people; and it can focus on the specific environment (the organization) in which the skills are to be applied.

In terms of the classic *performance gap* of current performance technology, the establishment of skill or knowledge means that in the current performance state the performers do not possess the skills and knowledge needed, whereas the desired state requires that these skills and knowledge be in place. Training is, then, one intervention option for filling the performance gap, for establishing performance. Other interventions, with or without training, may also be required.

When Existing Performance Must Be Improved

In some cases the performers possess the necessary performance skill but not at the level desired. They may lack proficiency, some of the necessary understanding, or the ability to apply the skill; or their performance may need to be updated or improved to reach to new or additional requirements. In this case training, as an intervention, is probably appropriate.

Because the performers already have the skill and simply need to improve, the training will probably not need to be as intense or extensive as that required to establish performance in the first place. Recognition of this fact is important, as it must be taken into account in planning, designing, and conducting the training experience so that the training is as efficient as possible. Also, the goal of improving existing performance may suggest that other interventions in addition to training will be helpful, such as the introduction of job aids.

Case Study

Any one example of training would not do justice to the great variety of training methods available. Therefore, the editors have chosen to include in this book three interventions that represent a range of training interventions. They are learner-controlled instruction, on-the-job training, and accelerated learning. The reader is referred to these intervention chapters for case examples. A wide range of case examples may also be found in the sources listed in the following section.

Resources and References

Books

American Society for Training and Development (ASTD). (1998). *ASTD handbook*. Washington, DC: Author.

American Society for Training and Development (ASTD). *Basic training for trainers*. Baltimore, MD: Author (available from ASTD, P.O. Box 4856, Hampden Station, Baltimore, MD 21211). Set of informational booklets on training and training skills.

Bently, T. J. (1990). *The business of training*. New York: McGraw-Hill.

Carnevale, A. P., Gainer, L. J., & Meltzer, A. S. (1990). *Workplace basics: The essential skills employers want*. San Francisco: Jossey-Bass.

Carnevale, A. P., Gainer, L. J., & Meltzer, A. S. (1990). *Workplace basics training manual*. San Francisco: Jossey-Bass.

Langdon, D. G. (Ed.). (1978, 1980). *The instructional design library*. Englewood Cliffs, NJ: Educational Technology. A forty-volume set of books on different training and learning methods.

Mayo, G. D., & DuBois, P. H. (1987). *The complete book of training.* San Francisco: Jossey-Bass/Pfeiffer.

Reynolds, A. (1995). *The trainer's dictionary: HRD terms, acronyms, initials and abbreviations.* Amherst, MA: HRD Press.

Associations

American Society for Training and Development (P.O. Box 1443, 1630 Duke Street, Alexandria, VA 22313, phone: 703-683-8100).

International Society for Performance Improvement (1250 L Street, NW, Suite 1250, Washington, DC 20005, phone: 202-404-7969).

Intervention Author

Danny G. Langdon
Partner
Performance International
1330 Stanford Street, Suite D
Santa Monica, CA 90404
Phone: 310-453-8440
E-mail: PerformI@aol.com

■ ■ ■ ■ ■ ■ USABILITY ASSESSMENTS

		Business Unit	Process	Work Group	Individual
Level of Performance					
Performance Change	Establish	○	●	●	●
	Improve	○	●	●	●
	Maintain	○	●	●	●
	Extinguish	○	●	●	●

Alternative Name

User interface evaluation

Definition

The *user interface* is the part of a computer system that a person interacts with directly, such as data-entry screens, graphic icons, menus, and system messages. *Usability assessment* is a type of needs assessment. Its goal is to identify specific design flaws in the user interface that interfere with performance, so that other interventions—such as job aids, user manuals, and training—can be targeted to compensate for these flaws.

Description

This century has seen explosive growth in the use of automated systems to support work. Since World War II, computers have evolved from gargantuan machines tended by a highly trained few to standard equipment in nearly all businesses. By the year 2000, worldwide spending on hardware and software will exceed $900 billion—a 40 percent increase from 1995 ("Wired World," 1997).

387

What has all this investment in technology accomplished? When organizations install computer systems, there is an expectation that everyone will learn to use them properly and that productivity, profitability, and quality will all improve. Far too often, though, design flaws in the computer system's user interface make these systems difficult to learn and difficult to use. Thus the same systems that were installed to support performance end up interfering with performance.

Every computer system has a user interface. Systems with a well-designed user interface can make it easier for people to do their work. However, a system with a poorly designed user interface can lead to the following performance problems for users and their organizations (Shneiderman, 1992):

- It takes too long for people to learn to use the system.
- It takes too much time and effort for people to complete tasks.
- People make too many errors when they use the system.
- People feel frustrated, angry, or inept when they use the system.

Ideally, every computer system should have a well-designed user interface that is easy to learn, easy to use, and enhances the performance of the people who use it. In reality, though, all systems have at least some design flaws. Few user interfaces are all good or all bad; each interface has elements that work well and other elements that do not. The goal of usability assessment is to pinpoint these design flaws, discovering exactly which elements of the user interface are interfering with performance.

Sorting out the elements of a user interface that interfere with performance requires a precise and structured way to describe the user interface. According to Weiss (1994), a system's user interface consists of four elements, each representing a distinct set of human-to-computer interactions: (1) presentation, (2) conversation, (3) navigation, and (4) explanation.

Presentation

Presentation controls how users are shown information. It includes screen design, graphics, and color. For example, all error messages might be colored red to make them easier to see. Icons representing frequent user actions are displayed in a row across the top of the screen.

Conversation

The conversation element controls how the system and the user "talk" to each other. It includes user-to-system communication, such as typing a command or clicking on an icon, and system-to-user communication, such as the wording of an error message. For example, on a sales order-entry screen, users can either type a product code or select the correct code from a pop-up list. When a clerk completes the screen, the system displays a message indicating that the order is ready to be shipped.

Navigation

The navigation element controls how users make their way from one part of the system to another. It includes methods such as selecting from a menu, clicking on an icon, or typing a command. For example, on the World Wide Web, users can get to one company's Web site by typing http://www.buycoolstuffhere.com. This brings them to the home page, where five icons are displayed. Clicking on these icons lets users move around within the site.

Explanation

The explanation element controls the way in which the system teaches users about itself. It includes error handling and on-line help. For example, when a user makes a mistake, the system might display a brief error message. An experienced user can correct the mistake immediately. A new user can press a special help key to get additional instructions on the nature of the mistake, why it happened, and how to fix it.

When to Use

The checklists presented in Figures 1 through 4 can help you to determine which elements of a system's user interface are causing performance problems for users. Any item checked "sometimes" or "never" should alert you to create job aids, user documentation, or training that will compensate for specific flaws in the system's user interface.

- *Presentation elements:* These elements (Figure 1) constitute a system's public face. As they are the first thing users see when they "meet" a new system, poor design in this area can affect their perceptions of the rest of the system.
- *Conversation elements*: These elements (Figure 2) constitute a system's personality. Systems with laborious system-to-user and user-to-system communications are typically time-consuming to master and difficult to use.
- *Navigation elements*: If presentation elements are a system's public face and conversation elements are its personality, navigation elements (Figure 3) are its

FIGURE 1. PRESENTATION ELEMENTS CHECKLIST.

What to Look For	Always	Sometimes	Never
All data a user needs to complete a system task are on display at all times, from the start of the task until the end.			
System messages are visually distinct and consistently appear where the user is likely to be looking on the screen.			
For GUI (graphical user interface) systems, such as Apple Macintosh or Microsoft Windows, the icons that represent system objects and procedures are concrete, familiar, and conceptually distinct.			
Color is used consistently throughout all parts of the system, and color selection communicates meaningful information to users.			

FIGURE 2. CONVERSATION ELEMENTS CHECKLIST.

What to Look For	Always	Sometimes	Never
System messages are unambiguous, nonthreatening, informative; they use terminology that can be readily understood by users.			
There is system feedback for every user action, and the user is kept informed about all actions the system is taking.			
If users communicate with the system via a command language, these commands are easy to learn and to remember.			
If users communicate with the system via a GUI (graphical user interface), the purpose of each icon or other graphic object is immediately apparent and unambiguous.			

FIGURE 3. NAVIGATION ELEMENTS CHECKLIST.

What to Look For	Always	Sometimes	Never
The method for moving around within a single screen and from screen to screen is simple, obvious, and consistent through the entire system.			
Menus are broad (many items on a menu) rather than deep (many menu levels with only a few items on each).			
Graphical icons, menus, or on-screen maps are used in a consistent way to help inexperienced users move around the system without getting lost.			
Experienced users can bypass these navigational aids and use keyboard shortcuts to jump quickly from one part of the system to another.			

FIGURE 4. EXPLANATION ELEMENTS CHECKLIST.

What to Look For	Always	Sometimes	Never
The system either prevents users from making serious, unrecoverable errors or warns them if they are about to do so.			
When a user makes an error, the system explains the cause of the problem and the action the user must take to correct it.			
The system provides on-line help that is accurate, informative, and complete.			
The presentation, conversation, and navigation elements of on-line help are consistent with the design of these elements in the rest of the system.			

circulatory system. When navigation is cumbersome, users can become frustrated at the effort required to get from one part of the system to another.

- *Explanation elements*: Explanation elements are a system's way of reaching out a helpful hand to users. If these elements are designed well, training time can often be reduced. However, even if a system provides on-line help, do not make the mistake of thinking that training is not necessary. At the very least, users have to be taught how to access and make use of the on-line help system.

Case Study

Commercial Security Bank has three hundred branch offices located in Utah, Idaho, Nevada, and Arizona. Last year the bank replaced its fifteen-year-old Customer Accounts Tracking System (CATS) with a snazzy new system that boasts improved speed, greater storage capacity, and a graphical user interface. The new system, called the Data Operations Graphical System (DOGS), was purchased from an outside vendor. A major factor in the purchasing decision was the vendor's assurance that DOGS was so easy to learn that training time would be reduced from two weeks to four hours.

Unfortunately, although CATS was certainly obsolete, DOGS has not turned out to be an improvement. It is extremely cumbersome to learn and use. Tasks that used to take an hour to complete using CATS are taking twice as long with DOGS. The four-hour training module that the vendor provided is insufficient to get employees up to speed. Clearly, the bank will need to provide additional training as well as job aids and user documentation. You have been assigned the job of designing all of these elements. The bank is willing to increase DOGS training time from four hours to three days. It has also agreed to fund the design of any job aids that would support the performance of bank employees on the job. Finally, it has been suggested that you create a supplement to the vendor-supplied user manuals, which weigh five pounds and are currently gathering dust in every branch manager's office.

Usability Assessment Findings

A usability assessment of DOGS reveals that its user interface has the following strengths and weaknesses in presentation, conversation, navigation, and explanation.

Presentation Strengths and Weaknesses. DOGS is a pretty system that uses color effectively. The predominant color scheme is pale gray and lavender, which is easy on the eyes and allows the plum-colored system messages to stand out. Icons and other graphical elements are visually distinct and appealing.

Conversation Strengths and Weaknesses. DOGS uses a different set of terms than the one to which the bank employees are accustomed. For example, suppose an existing bank customer with a checking account wants to open a savings account. The bank has always called this a "new account setup." In DOGS the menu item for this transaction reads "update customer file."

Navigation Strengths and Weaknesses. The method for moving from one part of DOGS to another is complicated and slow. First, the user must click on a icon representing a major system task. That action brings up a menu of options. Clicking on one of these options brings up a second menu. Eventually, after several levels of menus, the user is brought to the correct data-entry screen. There is no way for experienced users to bypass all these levels of menus, and making just one menu selection error results in the display of the wrong data-entry screen. As there is no way to undo a menu selection, the user must go all the way back to the DOGS main screen and start the process again.

Explanation Strengths and Weaknesses. Although DOGS has an on-line help system, the information it provides is not particularly helpful. For example, there is *balloon help*—when the cursor is moved over an icon, a little plum-colored explanatory message pops up on the screen. Although balloon help is visually appealing and easy to use, the messages themselves leave a lot to be desired. For example, moving the cursor over the icon of a telephone displays the message "terminal emulator device."

The Resolution

How will this information help you as you plan the DOGS training? First, because you have only three days available, you know to devote that time to the conversation and navigation elements of the system. You need not waste time showing students the individual DOGS data-entry screens, as these are well designed. Instead, you design the training to concentrate on the cumbersome steps required to get from one part of the system to another. You do not anticipate that students will achieve complete mastery by the end of training, so you also decide to write a twenty-page supplementary user guide that explains navigation procedures in detail. You contemplate calling the guide either "DOGS Race" or "Going to the DOGS." You also design several job aids to compensate for flaws in the DOGS on-line help system. Finally, instead of requiring employees to master terminology discrepancies between DOGS and their internal bank procedures, you recommend to the operations department that it redesign all internal bank forms to use the DOGS terminology.

Resources and References

Lindgaard, G. (1994). *Usability testing and system evaluation.* London: Chapman & Hall.

Nielsen, J. (1993). *Usability engineering.* Boston: AP Professional.

Shneiderman, B. (1992). *Designing the user interface.* Reading, MA: Addison-Wesley.

Weiss, E. (1994). *Making computers people-literate.* San Francisco: Jossey-Bass.

Wired world. (December 8, 1997). *Computerworld,* p. 7.

Intervention Author

Elaine Weiss, Ed.D.
President
Educational Dimensions
3584 Kings Cove Way
Salt Lake City, Utah 84121
Phone: 801-943-1401
Fax: 801-944-1643
E-mail: eweiss@aol.com

▪ ▪ ▪ ▪ ▪ ▪ WORK GROUP ALIGNMENT

Level of Performance	Business Unit	Process	Work Group	Individual
Establish	○	○	●	○
Improve	○	○	●	○
Maintain	○	○	●	○
Extinguish	○	○	●	○

Performance Change labels the Establish / Improve / Maintain / Extinguish rows.

Alternative Name

Building high-performance teams

Definition

Work group alignment is an intervention in which a given department, work group, or team establishes a systematic process to follow in defining and improving its work. The intended result is to ensure that the group's deliverables are in keeping with the expectations and needs of its business unit, its core processes, its customers, and its colleagues in other departments.

Description

Every organization has at least one work group whose performance is not what it should be. Everyone knows that this group's sales never meet quota, its production always falls below target, and its product or deliverable–whether it is mail or computer chips–fails to meet expectations. Every such group needs work group alignment.

395

In order to become aligned, a work group must go through a multistep process. The six required steps are described in the following paragraphs.

Step 1: Gathering Information

The work group needs to gather all available information about the purpose, goal, and strategic plan of the entire organization, the needs of its own customers–whether internal or external–and the needs of its colleagues and coworkers within the organization. The data must include the opinions and observations of all people associated with the work group.

Step 2: Describing the Current and Desired States

The work group must create two descriptions of itself: (1) the way it is today and (2) the way it should be. The description of the current state should include current inputs, outputs (deliverables, such as marketing materials, training courses, or engineering studies), processes, consequences, conditions, and feedback. The description of the desired state should cover the same dimensions.

Step 3: Analyzing the Gap

After comparing the differences between the current and desired states, the work group should describe the gap or difference between the two.

Step 4: Choosing Interventions to Close the Gap

The work group next should choose interventions that will close the gap between the two states and thereby achieve alignment. For example, the group should consider ground rules, job methods, new input documents, job descriptions, reorganization, and changes in decision authority, to name just a few. The clearer the description of the gap, the easier it is to determine what is needed to close it.

Step 5: Developing an Implementation Plan

The work group should develop an implementation plan for the interventions by establishing the priorities, the timing, the budget, the evaluation measures, and how the changes will be communicated.

Step 6: Implementing and Measuring the Change

The work group should go forward with its plans and then use the chosen evaluation measures to determine its level of progress.

When to Use

This intervention is appropriate under the following circumstances:

- When a work group is clearly not functioning effectively and efficiently (for example, missing deadlines, engaging in turf battles, not supporting strategic objectives)
- When a change has occurred in the organization and the work group is resisting or otherwise not supporting that change
- When a new manager has been appointed for the work group and the group members are reluctant to accept leadership from this person
- When a newly appointed manager wants to get a handle on the group's work
- When a work group is experiencing stress, burnout, or other responses to organizational change

Case Study

A female electronic engineer was appointed to manage the market support engineers at a high-tech company. The work group mission was to support the marketing of new electronic products by publishing the parts list, including prices, and by developing the training and repair strategies for the field. The work group's clients, field engineers around the world, used the group's published documents to determine how to respond to customer calls.

The work group had a terrible reputation. None of its internal customers believed the group did a good job; in fact, the new manager had only a brief honeymoon period before the work group would be examined for potential elimination. The group consisted of seven engineers; each was technically competent, most worked hard. But there were more than 250,000 products that had to be supported. Each engineer felt that he or she was making a contribution but that the job was impossible. In addition, a template for a database had been created fifteen years earlier to help support the work. The template, which was to be filled in for each product, had grown over the years until it was now an onerous thirty-page document that was rarely completed. Finding the information to enter on the template was a daunting process, requiring a great deal of diligence and persistence in obtaining the information from people who were reluctant to provide it.

By using the work group alignment intervention, the manager brought in a process and a facilitation that gave her a neutral opportunity to learn what the work of the department really was. In describing the outputs, the work group realized that although the market support document was the primary output, the more desirable output was advice on complicated repair issues. It became clear that information was needed from customers and partners. In a facilitated meeting, the work group developed and tested a customer questionnaire. By going out to interview and survey customers, the work group learned how out of alignment it was.

Customers told the work group members that there were two times when they needed the data that the group provided:

- Some needed it twelve to eighteen months before the product launched. These customers needed the work group's technical data in order to plan training activities, learning labs, job aids, tool lists, and so on. These internal customers did not need the data to be terribly detailed or accurate; once they knew what to plan for, their sources could give the detailed information they needed. Their need was for an early warning.
- Some needed the data just weeks before the launch. These internal customers needed to order parts to send them to warehouse depots; they needed information just before the new product was launched. However, this information needed to be very complete and accurate to be useful.

In neither case were customers satisfied. The early window was missed by data being published just four months prior to launch; the other group needed much more detail than was available at that time.

By reviewing the customer data in its next meeting, the work group members saw the gap between what was and what should be. They then revised their single process into two separate processes. One process was "long lead" and provided only high-level data. The output was a new report, available to those internal customers who needed the long planning time.

A second process was developed with a different output: a very detailed parts list that could be used to stock warehouses and for certain other specific uses.

The work group was aligned to the needs of the company (to support electronic products) to external customers (that is, the ultimate buyers) and to its own internal customers (who were field engineers and other support departments).

The following side benefits were realized:

- The manager was quickly integrated into the work group. The work group saw the intellectual and political skills of the manager, and all reservations about her appointment and ability to lead them disappeared.
- The skills and knowledge that the work group needed were revealed, as were other obstacles to the performance of the job. An internal performance consultant had data from the alignment activity to use in planning a number of interventions to close that gap.
- The work group developed camaraderie based on mutual respect, which was an unexpected consequence of the open and frank discussion. The camaraderie resulted from the dispassionate discussion of work from the aspect of its outputs, inputs, conditions, consequences, processes, and feedback. The gap between "what is" and "what should be" was seen in a positive light; the work group made the plan to get to the desired state, so its members were very comfortable about moving in that direction.

Resources and References

This intervention is a logical extension of several different common interventions. It is based on the process mapping and reengineering models, and it integrates the best of the teamwork skills and abilities models. It is also based on the needs of clients for methods of aligning work groups. As a stand-alone intervention, however, relatively little has been written about it.

Argyris, C. (1982). *Reasoning, learning and action: Individual and organizational.* San Francisco: Jossey-Bass.

Gilbert, T. (1978). *Engineering worthy performance.* New York: McGraw-Hill.

Kotter, J. P., & Heskett, J. L. (1992). *Corporate culture and performance.* New York: Free Press.

Langdon, D. G. (1995). *The new language of work.* Amherst, MA: HRD Press.

Rummler, G. A., & Brache, A. P. (1990). *Improving performance: How to manage the white space on the organization chart.* San Francisco: Jossey-Bass.

Schein, E. H. (1992). *Organizational culture and leadership* (2nd ed.). San Francisco: Jossey-Bass.

Stolovitch, H. D., & Keeps, E. J. (1992). *Handbook of performance technology: A comprehensive guide for analyzing and solving performance problems in organizations.* San Francisco: Jossey-Bass.

Weisbord, M. R. (1992). *Productive workplaces: Organizing and managing for dignity, meaning and community.* San Francisco: Jossey-Bass.

Intervention Author

Kathleen S. Whiteside
Partner
Performance International
1330 Stanford, Suite D
Santa Monica, CA 90404
Phone: 310-829-7006
Fax: 310-829-3457
E-mail: KatPerform@aol.com

ABOUT THE EDITORS

Danny G. Langdon is a leading expert in work systems, instructional design, and performance improvement systems. He is the author of six books in the field of instructional and performance technology, has written chapters for ten other books, and has published many articles. He is a past international president of the International Society for Performance Improvement (ISPI) and has received three international awards from ISPI for innovative contributions to the field of performance technology.

Among other positions during his career of more than thirty years, Danny has served as the director of corporate training for the Morrison Knudsen Corporation and director of performance improvement for International Technology Corporation. He is a founding partner in Performance International, 1330 Stanford Street, Suite D, Santa Monica, CA 90404, phone: 310-453-8440, e-mail: PerformI@aol.com. Danny is the originator of the Language of Work approach to business improvement through job modeling, process mapping, work group alignment, and reengineering.

Kathleen S. Whiteside has more than twenty-five years of experience in the field of training and performance improvement, including several years as corporate director of human resources for a large service organization. She is a past international president of ISPI and the author of several articles on human performance. She has guest edited an issue of *Performance Improvement* and has written chapters for the *Performance Improvement Handbook* (1987 and 1998) of the American Society for Training and Development (ASTD).

Kathleen is a founding partner in Performance International. She has managed several organization-wide performance improvement efforts, coached many training managers in the transition to performance consulting, and helped to sell performance consulting to executives. She is a master facilitator. She can be reached at Performance International, 1330 Stanford Street, Suite D, Santa Monica, CA 90404, phone: 310-829-7006, e-mail: KatPerform@AOL.com

Monica M. McKenna is a senior consultant with Performance International as well as the principal consultant of her own performance improvement consulting firm. She received her bachelor's degree in communication and a master's degree in instructional design and technology from the University of Iowa, Iowa City.

Monica has been a consultant to business and industry, manager of training and development at Southern California Edison, and a senior training development specialist at Arthur Andersen & Co. She has led a number of large-scale training projects, provided coaching and development to a wide variety of training professionals, and facilitated many change management interventions. She has more than fifteen years of experience in such performance improvement interventions as performance management, career development, team management, strategy development, 360-degree feedback, challenge education, compensation, employee orientation, and leadership development.

Monica is a frequent presenter and committee member with ISPI, serves on the executive board of the Vermont Section of the American Society for Quality, is an examiner for the Vermont State Quality Award, and is a faculty member of the Community College of Vermont.

She can be reached at 647 Andrus Pitch Road, Cornwall, VT 05753, phone: 802-462-2111, fax: 802-462-2115, e-mail: mmckenna@sover.net.